# HAMMOND

# THE COMPARATIVE WORLD ATLAS

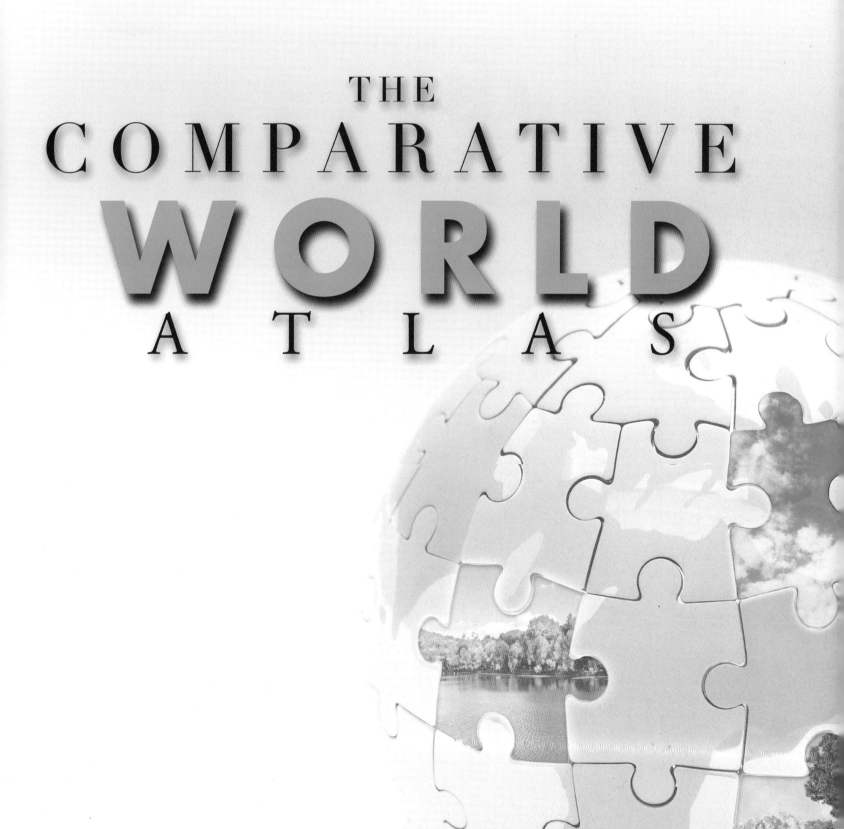

HAMMOND WORLD ATLAS CORPORATION

CORPORATE EXECUTIVES

Andreas Langenscheidt
Chairman

Marc Jennings
President

Vera Lorenz
Director of Cartography

HAMMOND STAFF

Database Resources and Cartography
Theophrastos E. Giouvanos

John A. DiGiorgio
Walter H. Jones, Jr.
Sharon Lightner
Harry E. Morin
James Padykula
Thomas J. Scheffer
Kathleen Schlueter

Cover Design
Marian Purcell

HAMMOND PUBLICATIONS ADVISORY BOARD

John P. Augelli
Professor and Chairman,
Department of Geography-Meteorology,
University of Kansas

Roger S. Boraas
Former Professor of Religion,
Upsala College

Alice C. Hudson
Chief, Map Division,
The New York Public Library

P. P. Karan
Professor, Department of Geography,
University of Kentucky

Vincent H. Malmstrom
Professor, Department of Geography,
Dartmouth College

Tom L. McKnight
Professor, Department of Geography,
University of California, Los Angeles

Christopher L. Salter
Professor and Chairman,
Department of Geography,
University of Missouri

Whitney Smith
Executive Director,
The Flag Research Center,
Winchester, Massachusetts

Norman J. W. Thrower
Professor, Department of Geography,
University of California, Los Angeles

SPECIAL ADVISORS

DATA RESEARCH
Population Research Center
University of Texas
Austin, Texas

OFFICE OF POPULATION RESEARCH
Princeton University
Princeton, New Jersey

Printed in Canada

# INTERPRETING MAPS

Designed to enhance your knowledge and enjoyment of maps, these pages explain map scales and projections, describe how to locate information quickly and show you how to weave together the sections of this atlas to gain a more dynamic world view.

# GLOBAL RELATIONSHIPS

Beginning with general world physical and political maps, subsequent chapters highlight a variety of the earth's natural features, dealing first with its structure and then with its air, water and land components. Next, maps, charts and graphs unveil the complex relationships between people and their environments. Coverage includes: demographic trends, population distribution and growth, and global energy production; the consequences of pollution: acid rain, deforestation, ozone depletion and global warming; comparisons of GNP per capita and literacy and life expectancy around the globe.

# MAPS OF THE WORLD

This new collection of regional maps artfully balances political and physical detail, while proprietary map projections present the most distortion-free views of the continents yet seen. Special thematic maps are included in each continental section. Numbers following each entry indicate map scale (M = million).

Europe and
Northern Asia

Asia

North America

Africa,
Polar Regions

South America

Australia and
Pacific

# INDEX

A Master Index lists places and features appearing in this atlas, complete with page numbers, population of places, and latitude and longitude.

# Contents

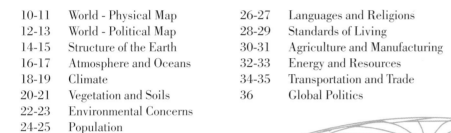

## THE COMPARATIVE WORLD ATLAS

### QUICK REFERENCE GUIDE

The world at your fingertips: a concise, current, alphabetical listing of the world's continents and countries; U.S. and Canadian states, provinces and territories; and the size, population and capital of each. Page numbers and reference keys for each entry are visible at a glance.

### Australia and Pacific

### Africa, Polar Regions

### North America

### South America

Revised 2007 edition
ENTIRE CONTENTS
© COPYRIGHT 2004 BY HAMMOND WORLD ATLAS CORPORATION
All rights reserved. No part of this book may be reproduced or utilized in any form or by any means, electronic or mechanical, including photocopying, recording or by any information storage and retrieval system, without permission in writing from the Publisher.

Printed in Canada

LIBRARY OF CONGRESS
CATALOGING-IN-PUBLICATION DATA

Hammond World Atlas Corporation.
    Hammond comparative world atlas.
    p.  cm.
    Revision of 2002 ed.
    Includes index.

ISBN 0-8437-0853-0 (hc)
ISBN 0-8437-0852-2 (sc)
1. Atlases.
I. Title. Hammond comparative world atlas.
II. Title.
G1021. H2738      2004
912--DC22                    2004052374
                            CIP
                            MAPS

# Using This Atlas

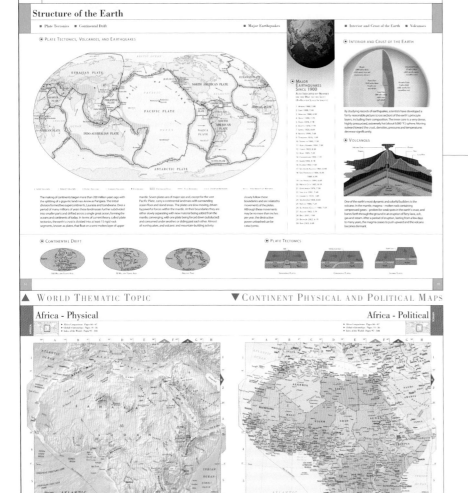

This new Comparative World Atlas has been thoughtfully designed to be easy and enjoyable to use, both as a general reference and as a valuable addition to the classroom. A short time spent familiarizing yourself with its organization will help you to benefit fully from its use.

## How to Locate Information Quickly

For familiar locations such as continents, countries and major political divisions, the Quick Reference Guide helps you quickly pinpoint the map you need. For less familiar places, begin with the Master Index.

### Quick Reference Guide (p.8)

This concise guide lists continents, countries, states, provinces and territories in alphabetical order, complete with the size, population and capital of each. Page numbers and alpha-numeric reference keys are visible at a glance.

### Master Index (p.97)

When you're looking for a specific place or physical feature, your quickest route is the Master Index. This 2,600-entry alphabetical index lists both the page number and latitude-longitude coordinates for major places and features found on the Regional Maps.

## MAP PROJECTIONS

This chapter explores some of the most widely used examples of how mapmakers project the earth's curved surface onto a flat plane. Included is Hammond's new Optimal Conformal Projection which keeps scale distortion over selected areas to the minimum degree possible.

## GLOBAL RELATIONSHIPS

Double spread World Physical and World Political maps are accompanied by Land Elevation/Ocean Depth Profiles and Comparative Land Areas and Population graphics. World thematic maps, charts and diagrams highlight important social, cultural, economic and geographic factors affecting today's world. Here, readers can explore complex relationships among such topics as population growth, environmental problems, climate and agriculture or compare worldwide standards of living, resources and manufacturing.

## CONTINENT COMPARISONS

Eight thematic maps are shown for each continent (except Antarctica) enabling the map reader to visualize a variety of topics for the same region or to compare similar topics for different regions.

## MAP SCALES

A map's scale is the relationship of any length on that map to an identical length on the earth's surface. A scale of 1:7,000,000 means that one inch on the map represents 7,000,000 inches (110 miles, 178 kilometers) on the earth's surface. Thus, a 1:7,000,000 scale is larger than a 1:14,000,000 scale just as 1/7 is larger than 1/14.

Along with these proportional scales, each map is accompanied by a linear (bar) scale, useful in making accurate measurements between places on the maps.

In this atlas, the most densely populated regions are shown at a scale of 1:10,500,000. Other major regions are presented at 1:14,000,000 and smaller scales, allowing you to accurately compare areas and distances of similar regions.

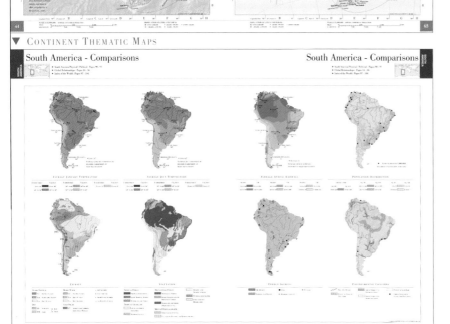

## REGIONAL MAPS

This atlas section is grouped by continent starting with facing-page physical and political maps. Following two pages of thematic topics, in-depth regional maps offer abundant detail including boundaries, cities, transportation networks, rivers and major mountain peaks. Map backgrounds are shown in a pleasing combination of elevation coloration and relief shading, with boundary bands defining the extent of each nation's internal and external limits.

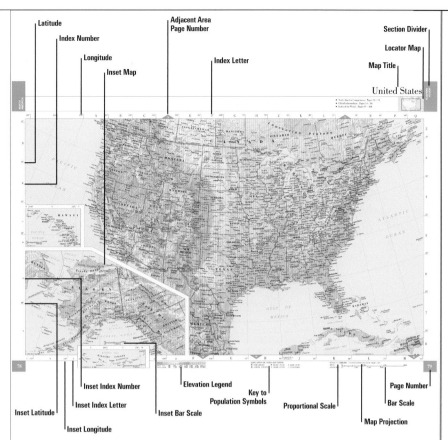

- Latitude
- Index Number
- Longitude
- Inset Map
- Adjacent Area Page Number
- Index Letter
- Section Divider
- Locator Map
- Map Title
- United States
- Inset Index Number
- Inset Index Letter
- Inset Latitude
- Inset Longitude
- Inset Bar Scale
- Elevation Legend
- Key to Population Symbols
- Proportional Scale
- Map Projection
- Page Number
- Bar Scale

## PRINCIPAL MAP ABBREVIATIONS

| | | | | | | | |
|---|---|---|---|---|---|---|---|
| ARCH. | ARCHIPELAGO | FT. | FORT | NAT'L | NATIONAL | PT. | POINT |
| AUT. | AUTONOMOUS | G. | GULF | NO. | NORTHERN | R. | RIVER |
| B. | BAY | GD. | GRAND | NP | NATIONAL PARK | RA. | RANGE |
| C. | CAPE | GT. | GREAT | OBL. | OBLAST | REP. | REPUBLIC |
| CAN. | CANAL | HAR. | HARBOR | OCC. | OCCUPIED | RES. | RESERVOIR, |
| CAP. | CAPITAL | L., IS. | ISLAND(S) | OKR. | OKRUG | | RESERVATION |
| CHAN. | CHANNEL | INT'L | INTERNATIONAL | PASSG. | PASSAGE | SA. | SIERRA |
| CR. | CREEK | L. | LAKE | PEN. | PENINSULA | SD. | SOUND |
| DES. | DESERT | LAG. | LAGOON | PK. | PEAK | SO. | SOUTHERN |
| FD. | FIORD, FJORD | MT. | MOUNT | PLAT. | PLATEAU | STR. | STRAIT |
| FED. | FEDERAL | MTN. | MOUNTAIN | PN | PARK NATIONAL | TERR. | TERRITORY |
| FK. | FORK | MTS. | MOUNTAINS | PRSV. | PRESERVE | VOL. | VOLCANO |

## CITY POPULATIONS

In addition to population symbols locating cities and towns on the regional maps, the Master Index provides at a glance the population of all major cities as well as the country's capital.

## WORLD STATISTICS

These statistical tables list the dimensions of the earth's principal mountains, islands, rivers and lakes, along with other useful geographic information.

## MASTER INDEX

This provides an A to Z listing of names found on the world, continent and regional maps. Each entry is accompanied by a page location and population of places, as well as latitude and longitude coordinates.

### Boundary Policies
This atlas observes the boundary policies of the U.S. Department of State. Boundary disputes are customarily handled with a special symbol treatment, but de facto boundaries are favored if they seem to have any degree of permanence, in the belief that boundaries should reflect current geographic and political realities. The portrayal of independent nations in the atlas follows their recognition by the United Nations and/or the United States government.

### A Word About Names
Our source for all foreign names and physical names in the United States is the decision lists of the U.S. Board of Geographic Names, which contain hundreds of thousands of place names. If a place is not listed, the Atlas follows the name form appearing on official foreign maps or in official gazetteers of the country concerned. For rendering domestic city, town and village names, this atlas follows the forms and spelling of the U.S. Postal Service.

### Hammond Also Uses
accepted conventional names for certain major foreign places. Usually, space permits the inclusion of the local form in parentheses. To make the maps more readily understandable to English-speaking readers, many foreign physical features are translated into more recognizable English forms.

## LEGEND TO REGIONAL MAPS

- ━▪━▪━ First Order (National) Boundary
- ─▪─▪─ First Order Water Boundary
- ━▪━▪━ First Order Disputed Boundary
- ━◦━◦━ Second Order (Internal) Boundary
- ▬▬▬ Third Order (Internal) Boundary
- ⋯⋯⋯ Undefined Boundary
- ───── International Date Line
- ───── Shoreline, River
- ─ ─ ─ Intermittent River
- ⋯⋯⋯ Canal/Aqueduct
- ───── Highway/Roads
- ───── Railroads
- ▢ Lake, Reservoir
- ▢ Intermittent Lake
- ▢ Dry Lake
- ▦ Salt Pan
- ▦ Desert/Sand Area
- Swamp
- Lava Flow
- Glacier
- _Stockholm_ First Order (National) Capital
- _Lausanne_ Second Order (Internal) Capital

| | | | | | |
|---|---|---|---|---|---|
| ⪢ | Pass | ✳ | Rapids | ⚑ | Park |
| ⁖ | Ruins | ● | Dam | ■ | Point of Interest |
| ● | Falls | ▲ | Point Elevation | ⌣ | Well |

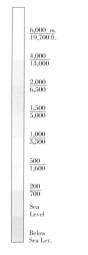

| | |
|---|---|
| 6,000 m. | 19,700 ft. |
| 4,000 | 13,000 |
| 2,000 | 6,500 |
| 1,500 | 5,000 |
| 1,000 | 3,300 |
| 500 | 1,600 |
| 200 | 700 |
| Sea Level | |
| Below Sea Lev. | |

The colors in this bar represent elevation ranges of land areas above or below sea level. Boundaries between colors are leveled both in feet and meters. Selective shading highlights those regions with significant relief variations.

# Map Projections

■ **Basic Principles and Terms**  ■ **Examples of Popular Map Projections**

There is only one way to represent a sphere with absolute precision: on a globe. All attempts to project our planet's surface onto a plane unevenly "stretch or tear" the sphere as it is flattened, inevitably distorting shapes, areas, distances and/or directions.

To make a flat map cartographers place an imaginary grid pattern on the globe. Points and lines on this pattern are then transferred, or "projected," to a corresponding flat surface pattern, which has been previously constructed, from one of a wide variety of mathematical formulas devised for this purpose. To understand some of the most widely used map projections, it is necessary to briefly describe this imaginary grid pattern that has been imposed on the Earth to locate features, and places and to measure their special relationship to each other.

The Earth rotates around its axis once a day. Its end points are the North and South poles; the line circling the Earth midway between the poles is the Equator. The arc from the Equator to each pole is divided into 90 degrees of latitude. The Equator itself represents 0° latitude and is divided into 360 degrees of longitude. Lines circling the globe from pole to pole, which intersect with the Equator at 90-degree angles, are called meridians, or

great circles. The meridian passing through the Greenwich Observatory near London was chosen by international agreement as the prime meridian, or 0° longitude, in 1884. Meridians and lines of latitude (parallels) form the global coordinate grid, or graticule. The distance from the prime meridian to a given point to the west or east, expressed in degrees is its geographic longitude. Similarly, distances north or south of the Equator represent geographic latitude. Although all meridians are equal in length, parallels become shorter as they approach the poles. Thus, while the distance between two parallels (one degree of latitude) is approximately 112 km everywhere on Earth, the distance between two meridians (one degree of longitude) varies between 112 km at the Equator and zero at the poles where the meridians converge. Each degree of longitude and latitude is divided into 60 minutes. One minute of latitude equals one nautical mile (1.85 km).

On a flat surface, any regular set of parallels and meridians upon which a map can be drawn makes a map projection. However, since representing a sphere on a flat plane always creates distortion, only the parallels or the meridians or some other set of lines can be true (i.e. the same length as on a globe at corresponding scale).

The larger the area covered by the map the larger the amount of distortion; thus, distortion is greatest on world maps. Many maps seek to preserve either true area relationships (equal-area projections) or true angles and shapes (conformal projections). Other maps are more concerned with achieving true distance and directional accuracy. Instead of trying to preserve any single true relationship, some maps achieve an overall balance by compromise.

## ▶ WORLD MAP PROJECTIONS

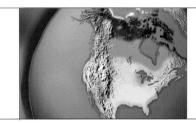

A globe's surface can be transformed to fit within any outline on a flat surface. In fact, such shapes as diamonds, hearts, stars and even stylistic butterflies have enclosed a map of the earth. However, three traditional shapes - rectangles, circles and ovals - are used to portray most maps of the world.

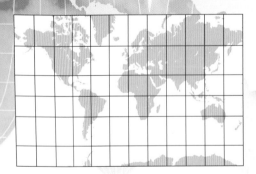

**Mercator Projection**
A rectangular- shaped map with vertical meridians and horizontal parallels, it is the only map on which a straight line, drawn anywhere on the map, indicates true direction along its entire length. The map has reasonably true shapes and distances within 15 degrees of the equator, but distortion increases dramatically into the higher latitudes.

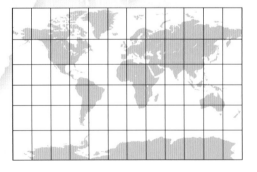

**Miller Cylindrical Projection**
Similar in appearance to the Mercator Projection, the Miller Cylindrical lessens distortions in the higher latitudes by closing up the spacing between parallels. Although this destroys the unique navigational property of the Mercator, it does present a more realistic view of land areas in the northern parts of Europe, Asia and North America.

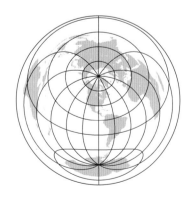

**Azimuthal Equidistant Projection**
A circular-shaped projection whose oblique view is the only projection in which directions and distances are depicted accurately from the projection's center point to any other place on the globe. Any straight line passing through the center is a great circle route. Distortion of areas and shapes increases away from the center.

# OTHER MAP PROJECTIONS

Since continents and smaller regions occupy only a part of the entire earth's surface, other projections can be employed to minimize distortion and, where possible, preserve true shapes, areas, distances or directions. But, although smaller in size, the areas being mapped are still parts of a sphere and the flattening process will still result in distortions in the maps.

**Albers Equal-Area Projection**

**Lambert Conformal Conic Projection**

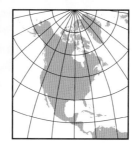

**Optimal Conformal Projection**

## Conic Projections

These maps are created by mathematically projecting points and lines from a globe onto a cone which caps the globe. The cone can be placed either tangent to the globe at a preselected parallel or it can intersect the globe at two preselected parallels. The use of two standard parallels, one near the top of the map, the other near the bottom of the map, reduces the scale error. In one type of conic projection, Albers, the parallels are spaced evenly to make the projection equal-area. In the Lambert Conformal Conic Projection the parallels are spaced so that any small quadrangle of the grid will have the same shape as on the globe.

**Polyconic Projection**

### Polyconic Projection

Best suited for maps with a long north-south orientation, this projection is mathematically based upon an infinite number of cones tangent to an infinite number of points (parallels) on the globe. All meridians are curved lines except for the central meridian, which shows true distance and direction.

### Gnomonic Projection

Viewing the surface of the globe from its center point creates this projection with very bad distortions away from the map's center. However, this projection has a unique quality - all great circles (shortest lines between points on a sphere) are shown as straight lines. Therefore, the path of the shortest distance between any two points on the map is a straight line.

### Lambert Azimuthal Equal-Area Projection

Mathematically projected on a plane surface tangent to any point on a globe, this is the most common projection (also known as Zenithal Equal-Area) used for maps of the Eastern and Western hemispheres. It is also a good projection for continents, as it shows correct areas with little distortion of shape.

**Lambert Azimuthal Equal-Area Projection**

### Hammond's Optimal Conformal Projection

As its name implies, this new conformal projection presents the optimal view of an area by reducing shifts in scale over an entire region to the minimum degree possible. While conformal maps generally preserve all small shapes, large shapes can become very distorted because of varying scales, causing considerable inaccuracy in distance measurements. Consequently, unlike other projections, the Optimal Comformal does not use one standard formula to construct a map. Each map is a unique projection - the optimal projection for that particular area. The result is the most distortion-free conformal map possible.

**Gnomonic Projection**

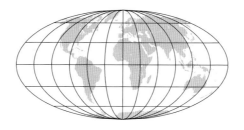

**Orthographic Projection**

This projection looks like a picture of a globe. It is neither conformal nor equal-area. Although the distortion on the peripheries is extreme, we see it correctly, because the eye perceives it not as a map but as a picture of a three-dimensional globe. Obviously, only a hemisphere (half globe) can be shown.

**Mollweide Projection**

An early example of an oval-shaped (also called pseudocylindrical) projection is this equal-area map of the earth within an ellipse. Shapes are elongated in the lower latitudes. Since its presentation in 1805 it has been an inspiration for similar oval-shaped maps and has even been "interrupted" to minimize distortion of continental or ocean areas.

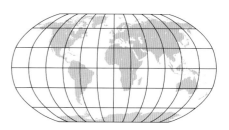

**Robinson Projection**

This modern, oval-shaped projection uses tabular coordinates rather than mathematical formulas to make the world "look right." Although not true with respect to shapes, sizes, distances or directions, its compromising features show a better balance of size and shape in high latitude lands and very low distortion near the equator.

■ Countries and Other Areas ■ Statistics

This concise alphabetical reference lists continents, countries, states, territories, possessions and other major geographical areas, complete with the size, population and capital or chief town of each. Page numbers and alpha-numeric reference keys (which refer to the grid squares of latitude and longitude on each map) are visible at a glance. The population figures are the latest and most reliable figures obtainable.

| Place | Square Miles | Square Kilometers | Population | Capital or Chief Town | Page/Index Ref. |
|---|---|---|---|---|---|
| Afghanistan* | 250,000 | 647,500 | 31,056,997 | Kabul | 49/F 6 |
| Africa | 11,701,147 | 30,306,000 | 910,849,725 | ................ | 65 |
| Alabama, U.S. | 52,237 | 135,293 | 4,447,100 | Montgomery | 87/G 3 |
| Alaska, U.S. | 615,230 | 1,593,444 | 626,932 | Juneau | 78/W12 |
| Albania* | 11,100 | 28,749 | 3,581,655 | Tiranë | 44/C 3 |
| Alberta, Canada | 255,285 | 661,185 | 2,974,810 | Edmonton | 76/E 3 |
| Algeria* | 919,591 | 2,381,740 | 32,930,091 | Algiers | 68/F 2 |
| Andorra* | 181 | 468 | 71,201 | Andorra la Vella | 42/E 5 |
| Angola* | 481,351 | 1,246,700 | 12,127,071 | Luanda | 70/C 3 |
| Antarctica | 5,500,000 | 14,245,000 | ................ | ................ | 71 |
| Antigua and Barbuda* | 170 | 440 | 69,108 | St. John's | 89/J 4 |
| Argentina* | 1,068,296 | 2,766,890 | 39,921,833 | Buenos Aires | 96/C 4 |
| Arizona, U.S. | 114,006 | 295,276 | 5,130,632 | Phoenix | 82/D 4 |
| Arkansas, U.S. | 53,182 | 137,742 | 2,673,400 | Little Rock | 83/J 4 |
| Armenia* | 11,506 | 29,800 | 2,976,372 | Yerevan | 45/C 4 |
| Asia | 17,159,867 | 44,444,100 | 3,958,768,088 | ................ | 49 |
| Australia* | 2,967,893 | 7,686,850 | 20,264,082 | Canberra | 59 |
| Austria* | 32,375 | 83,851 | 8,192,880 | Vienna | 42/G 4 |
| Azerbaijan* | 33,436 | 86,600 | 7,961,619 | Baku | 45/D 4 |
| Bahamas, The* | 5,382 | 13,939 | 303,770 | Nassau | 89/F 2 |
| Bahrain* | 257 | 665 | 698,585 | Manama | 52/F 3 |
| Bangladesh* | 55,598 | 144,000 | 147,365,352 | Dhaka | 53/E 4 |
| Barbados* | 166 | 430 | 279,912 | Bridgetown | 89/J 5 |
| Belarus* | 80,154 | 207,600 | 10,293,011 | Minsk | 43/G 5 |
| Belgium* | 11,780 | 30,513 | 10,379,067 | Brussels | 42/E 3 |
| Belize* | 8,865 | 22,960 | 287,730 | Belmopan | 88/D 4 |
| Benin* | 43,483 | 112,620 | 7,862,944 | Porto-Novo | 68/F 5 |
| Bhutan* | 18,147 | 47,000 | 2,279,723 | Thimphu | 53/E 3 |
| Bolivia* | 424,163 | 1,098,582 | 8,989,046 | La Paz; Sucre | 94/F 7 |
| Bosnia & Herzegovina* | 19,741 | 51,129 | 4,498,976 | Sarajevo | 44/C 3 |
| Botswana* | 231,803 | 600,370 | 1,639,833 | Gaborone | 70/D 5 |
| Brazil* | 3,286,470 | 8,511,965 | 188,078,227 | Brasília | 91/D 3 |
| British Columbia, Canada | 365,946 | 947,800 | 3,907,735 | Victoria | 76/D 3 |
| Brunei* | 2,228 | 5,770 | 379,444 | Bandar Seri Begawan | 56/E 4 |
| Bulgaria* | 42,823 | 110,912 | 7,385,367 | Sofia | 44/D 3 |
| Burkina Faso* | 105,869 | 274,200 | 13,902,972 | Ouagadougou | 68/E 5 |
| Burundi* | 10,745 | 27,830 | 8,090,068 | Bujumbura | 70/E 1 |
| California, U.S. | 158,869 | 411,470 | 33,871,648 | Sacramento | 82/B 3 |
| Cambodia* | 69,900 | 181,040 | 13,881,427 | Phnom Penh | 56/C 3 |
| Cameroon* | 183,568 | 475,441 | 17,340,702 | Yaoundé | 68/H 7 |
| Canada* | 3,855,101 | 9,984,670 | 33,098,932 | Ottawa | 76 |
| Cape Verde* | 1,556 | 4,030 | 420,979 | Praia | 12/H 5 |
| Central African Republic* | 240,533 | 622,980 | 4,303,356 | Bangui | 69/J 6 |
| Chad* | 495,752 | 1,283,998 | 9,944,201 | N'Djamena | 69/J 4 |
| Chile* | 292,258 | 756,950 | 16,134,219 | Santiago | 91/B 6 |
| China, People's Rep. of* | 3,705,386 | 9,596,960 | 1,313,973,713 | Beijing | 54/G 4 |
| China, Republic of (Taiwan) | 13,892 | 35,980 | 23,036,087 | T'aipei | 55/M 7 |
| Colombia* | 439,733 | 1,138,910 | 43,593,035 | Bogotá | 94/D 3 |
| Colorado, U.S. | 104,100 | 269,618 | 4,301,261 | Denver | 82/F 3 |
| Comoros* | 838 | 2,170 | 690,948 | Moroni | 65/G 6 |
| Congo, Democratic Republic of the* | 905,563 | 2,345,410 | 62,660,551 | Kinshasa | 65/E 5 |
| Congo, Republic of the* | 132,046 | 342,000 | 3,702,314 | Brazzaville | 65/D 4 |
| Connecticut, U.S. | 5,544 | 14,358 | 3,405,565 | Hartford | 85/F 3 |
| Costa Rica* | 19,730 | 51,100 | 4,075,261 | San José | 88/E 5 |
| Côte d'Ivoire* | 124,502 | 322,460 | 17,654,843 | Yamoussoukro | 68/D 5 |
| Croatia* | 22,050 | 56,538 | 4,494,749 | Zagreb | 44/C 2 |
| Cuba* | 42,803 | 110,860 | 11,382,820 | Havana | 89/F 3 |
| Cyprus* | 3,571 | 9,250 | 784,301 | Nicosia | 52/B 1 |
| Czech Republic* | 30,450 | 78,866 | 10,235,455 | Prague | 44/B 2 |
| Delaware, U.S. | 2,396 | 6,206 | 783,600 | Dover | 84/F 4 |
| Denmark* | 16,629 | 43,069 | 5,450,661 | Copenhagen | 43/C 4 |
| District of Columbia, U.S. | 68 | 177 | 572,059 | Washington | 84/E 4 |
| Djibouti* | 8,880 | 23,000 | 486,530 | Djibouti | 69/P 5 |
| Dominica* | 290 | 751 | 68,910 | Roseau | 89/J 4 |
| Dominican Republic* | 18,815 | 48,730 | 9,185,984 | Santo Domingo | 89/H 4 |
| East Timor* | 5,743 | 14,874 | 1,062,777 | Dili | 57/H 7 |
| Ecuador* | 109,483 | 283,561 | 13,547,510 | Quito | 94/C 4 |
| Egypt* | 386,659 | 1,001,447 | 78,887,007 | Cairo | 69/L 2 |

| Place | Square Miles | Square Kilometers | Population | Capital or Chief Town | Page/Index Ref. |
|---|---|---|---|---|---|
| El Salvador* | 8,124 | 21,040 | 6,822,378 | San Salvador | 88/C 5 |
| England, U.K. | 50,356 | 130,423 | 49,138,831 | London | 42/D 3 |
| Equatorial Guinea* | 10,831 | 28,052 | 540,109 | Malabo | 68/G 7 |
| Eritrea* | 46,842 | 121,320 | 4,786,994 | Asmara | 69/N 5 |
| Estonia* | 17,462 | 45,226 | 1,324,333 | Tallinn | 43/G 4 |
| Ethiopia* | 435,184 | 1,127,127 | 74,777,981 | Addis Ababa | 69/N 5 |
| Europe | 4,066,019 | 10,531,000 | 729,239,896 | ................ | 39 |
| Fiji* | 7,055 | 18,272 | 905,949 | Suva | 62/G 6 |
| Finland* | 130,128 | 337,032 | 5,231,372 | Helsinki | 43/G 3 |
| Florida, U.S. | 59,928 | 155,214 | 15,982,378 | Tallahassee | 87/H 4 |
| France* | 211,208 | 547,030 | 60,876,136 | Paris | 42/E 4 |
| French Guiana | 35,135 | 91,000 | 195,506 | Cayenne | 95/H 3 |
| French Polynesia | 1,608 | 4,167 | 270,485 | Papeete | 63/L 6 |
| Gabon* | 103,347 | 267,670 | 1,424,906 | Libreville | 68/H 7 |
| Gambia, The* | 4,363 | 11,300 | 1,641,564 | Banjul | 68/B 5 |
| Gaza Strip | 139 | 360 | 1,376,289 | Gaza | 52/B 2 |
| Georgia* | 26,911 | 69,700 | 4,661,473 | T'bilisi | 45/C 4 |
| Georgia, U.S. | 58,977 | 152,750 | 8,186,453 | Atlanta | 87/G 3 |
| Germany* | 137,847 | 357,021 | 82,422,299 | Berlin | 42/F 3 |
| Ghana* | 92,456 | 239,460 | 22,409,572 | Accra | 68/E 6 |
| Greece* | 50,942 | 131,940 | 10,688,058 | Athens | 44/D 4 |
| Greenland, Denmark | 840,000 | 2,175,600 | 56,361 | Nuuk (Godthåb) | 73/N 2 |
| Grenada* | 131 | 340 | 89,703 | St. George's | 89/J 5 |
| Guadeloupe, France | 687 | 1,779 | 448,713 | Basse-Terre | 89/J 4 |
| Guam, U.S. | 209 | 541 | 154,805 | Hagåtña | 62/D 3 |
| Guatemala* | 42,042 | 108,889 | 12,293,545 | Guatemala | 88/C 4 |
| Guinea* | 94,927 | 245,860 | 9,690,222 | Conakry | 68/C 5 |
| Guinea-Bissau* | 13,946 | 36,120 | 1,442,029 | Bissau | 68/B 5 |
| Guyana* | 83,000 | 214,970 | 767,245 | Georgetown | 94/G 3 |
| Haiti* | 10,714 | 27,750 | 8,308,504 | Port-au-Prince | 89/G 4 |
| Hawaii, U.S. | 6,459 | 16,729 | 1,211,537 | Honolulu | 78/S 9 |
| Honduras* | 43,277 | 112,087 | 7,326,496 | Tegucigalpa | 88/D 4 |
| Hong Kong, China | 422 | 1,092 | 6,940,432 | Victoria | 55/K 7 |
| Hungary* | 35,919 | 93,030 | 9,981,334 | Budapest | 44/C 2 |
| Iceland* | 39,768 | 103,000 | 299,388 | Reykjavík | 39/B 2 |
| Idaho, U.S. | 83,574 | 216,456 | 1,293,953 | Boise | 80/E 5 |
| Illinois, U.S. | 57,918 | 150,007 | 12,419,293 | Springfield | 84/B 4 |
| India* | 1,269,339 | 3,287,588 | 1,095,351,995 | New Delhi | 53/C 4 |
| Indiana, U.S. | 36,420 | 94,328 | 6,080,485 | Indianapolis | 84/C 3 |
| Indonesia* | 741,096 | 1,919,440 | 245,452,739 | Jakarta | 56/E 6 |
| Iowa, U.S. | 56,275 | 145,752 | 2,926,324 | Des Moines | 81/K 5 |
| Iran* | 636,293 | 1,648,000 | 68,688,433 | Tehran | 52/F 2 |
| Iraq* | 168,753 | 437,072 | 26,783,383 | Baghdad | 52/D 2 |
| Ireland* | 27,136 | 70,282 | 4,062,235 | Dublin | 42/C 3 |
| Ireland, Northern, U.K. | 5,459 | 14,138 | 1,685,267 | Belfast | 42/C 3 |
| Israel* | 8,019 | 20,770 | 6,352,117 | Jerusalem | 52/B 2 |
| Italy* | 116,305 | 301,230 | 58,133,509 | Rome | 39/F 4 |
| Jamaica* | 4,243 | 10,990 | 2,758,124 | Kingston | 89/F 4 |
| Japan* | 145,882 | 377,835 | 127,463,611 | Tokyo | 55/Q 4 |
| Jordan* | 35,637 | 92,300 | 5,906,760 | Amman | 52/C 2 |
| Kansas, U.S. | 82,282 | 213,110 | 2,688,418 | Topeka | 83/H 3 |
| Kazakhstan* | 1,049,150 | 2,717,300 | 15,233,244 | Astana | 46/G 5 |
| Kentucky, U.S. | 40,411 | 104,665 | 4,041,769 | Frankfort | 87/G 2 |
| Kenya* | 224,960 | 582,646 | 34,707,817 | Nairobi | 69/N 7 |
| Kiribati* | 313 | 811 | 105,432 | Tarawa | 62/H 5 |
| Korea, North* | 46,540 | 120,539 | 23,113,019 | P'yŏngyang | 55/N 3 |
| Korea, South* | 38,023 | 98,480 | 48,846,823 | Seoul | 55/N 4 |
| Kuwait* | 6,880 | 17,820 | 2,418,393 | Kuwait | 52/E 3 |
| Kyrgyzstan* | 76,641 | 198,500 | 5,213,898 | Bishkek | 46/H 5 |
| Laos* | 91,428 | 236,800 | 6,368,481 | Vientiane | 49/K 8 |
| Latvia* | 24,938 | 64,589 | 2,274,735 | Riga | 43/G 4 |
| Lebanon* | 4,015 | 10,399 | 3,874,050 | Beirut | 52/B 2 |
| Lesotho* | 11,718 | 30,350 | 2,022,331 | Maseru | 70/E 6 |
| Liberia* | 43,000 | 111,370 | 3,042,004 | Monrovia | 68/D 6 |
| Libya* | 679,358 | 1,759,537 | 5,900,754 | Tripoli | 69/J 2 |
| Liechtenstein* | 62 | 160 | 33,987 | Vaduz | 42/F 4 |
| Lithuania* | 25,174 | 65,200 | 3,585,906 | Vilnius | 43/F 4 |
| Louisiana, U.S. | 49,651 | 128,595 | 4,468,976 | Baton Rouge | 86/E 4 |
| Luxembourg* | 999 | 2,587 | 474,413 | Luxembourg | 42/F 4 |

| Place | Square Miles | Square Kilometers | Population | Capital or Chief Town | Page/Index Ref. |
|---|---|---|---|---|---|
| **M** Macedonia, Former Yugoslav | | | | | |
| Republic of * | 9,781 | 25,333 | 2,050,554 | Skopje | 44/D 3 |
| Madagascar* | 226,657 | 587,041 | 18,595,469 | Antananarivo | 70/K10 |
| Maine, U.S. | 33,741 | 87,388 | 1,274,923 | Augusta | 85/G 2 |
| Malawi* | 45,745 | 118,480 | 13,013,926 | Lilongwe | 70/F 3 |
| Malaysia* | 127,316 | 329,750 | 24,385,858 | Kuala Lumpur | 56/D 4 |
| Maldives* | 116 | 300 | 359,008 | Male | 49/G 9 |
| Mali* | 478,764 | 1,240,000 | 11,716,829 | Bamako | 68/E 4 |
| Malta* | 124 | 320 | 400,214 | Valletta | 44/B 4 |
| Manitoba, Canada | 250,946 | 649,951 | 1,119,585 | Winnipeg | 76/G 3 |
| Marshall Islands* | 70 | 181 | 60,422 | Majuro | 62/G 3 |
| Maryland, U.S. | 12,297 | 31,849 | 5,296,486 | Annapolis | 84/E 4 |
| Massachusetts, U.S. | 9,241 | 23,934 | 6,349,097 | Boston | 85/F 3 |
| Mauritania* | 397,953 | 1,030,700 | 3,177,388 | Nouakchott | 68/C 4 |
| Mauritius * | 788 | 2,040 | 1,240,827 | Port Louis | 13/M 7 |
| Mexico * | 761,601 | 1,972,546 | 107,449,525 | Mexico | 88/A 3 |
| Michigan, U.S. | 96,705 | 250,465 | 9,938,444 | Lansing | 84/C 2 |
| Micronesia, Federated | | | | | |
| States of* | 271 | 702 | 108,004 | Palikir | 62/D 4 |
| Minnesota, U.S. | 86,943 | 225,182 | 4,919,479 | St. Paul | 81/K 4 |
| Mississippi, U.S. | 48,286 | 125,060 | 2,844,658 | Jackson | 87/F 3 |
| Missouri, U.S. | 69,709 | 180,546 | 5,595,211 | Jefferson City | 83/J 3 |
| Moldova* | 13,067 | 33,843 | 4,466,706 | Chişinău | 44/E 2 |
| Monaco* | 0.7 | 1.9 | 32,543 | ............ | 42/F 5 |
| Mongolia* | 606,163 | 1,569,962 | 2,832,224 | Ulaanbaatar | 54/G 2 |
| Montana, U.S. | 147,046 | 380,849 | 902,195 | Helena | 80/F 4 |
| Montenegro* | 5,333 | 13,812 | 620,150 | Podgorica | 44/C 3 |
| Morocco* | 172,414 | 446,550 | 33,241,259 | Rabat | 68/C 1 |
| Mozambique* | 309,494 | 801,590 | 19,686,505 | Maputo | 70/G 4 |
| Myanmar (Burma)* | 261,969 | 678,500 | 47,382,633 | Yangon | 49/J 7 |
| **N** Namibia* | 318,694 | 825,418 | 2,044,147 | Windhoek | 70/C 5 |
| Nauru* | 8 | 21 | 13,287 | Yaren (district) | 62/F 5 |
| Nebraska, U.S. | 77,358 | 200,358 | 1,711,263 | Lincoln | 83/G 2 |
| Nepal* | 54,363 | 140,800 | 28,287,147 | Kathmandu | 53/D 3 |
| Netherlands* | 16,033 | 41,526 | 16,491,461 | The Hague; Amsterdam | 42/F 3 |
| Nevada, U.S. | 110,567 | 286,367 | 1,998,257 | Carson City | 82/C 3 |
| New Brunswick, Canada | 28,355 | 73,440 | 729,500 | Fredericton | 85/H 2 |
| Newfoundland and | | | | | |
| Labrador, Canada | 156,649 | 405,721 | 512,930 | St. John's | 77/K 3 |
| New Hampshire, U.S. | 9,283 | 24,044 | 1,235,786 | Concord | 85/G 3 |
| New Jersey, U.S. | 8,215 | 21,277 | 8,414,350 | Trenton | 84/F 3 |
| New Mexico, U.S. | 121,598 | 314,939 | 1,819,046 | Santa Fe | 82/F 4 |
| New York, U.S. | 53,989 | 139,833 | 18,976,457 | Albany | 84/F 3 |
| New Zealand* | 103,736 | 268,676 | 4,076,140 | Wellington | 59/H 6 |
| Nicaragua* | 49,998 | 129,494 | 5,570,129 | Managua | 88/D 5 |
| Niger* | 489,189 | 1,267,000 | 12,525,094 | Niamey | 68/G 4 |
| Nigeria* | 356,668 | 923,770 | 131,859,731 | Abuja | 68/G 6 |
| North America | 9,355,975 | 24,232,000 | 517,855,731 | ............ | 73 |
| North Carolina, U.S. | 52,672 | 136,421 | 8,049,313 | Raleigh | 87/H 3 |
| North Dakota, U.S. | 70,704 | 183,123 | 642,200 | Bismarck | 81/H 4 |
| Northern Ireland, U.K. | 5,459 | 14,138 | 1,685,267 | Belfast | 42/C 3 |
| Northwest Terrs., Canada | 1,322,905 | 3,426,328 | 37,360 | Yellowknife | 76/D 2 |
| Norway* | 125,181 | 324,220 | 4,610,820 | Oslo | 43/C 3 |
| Nova Scotia, Canada | 21,425 | 55,491 | 908,005 | Halifax | 85/H 2 |
| Nunavut, Canada | 733,590 | 1,900,000 | 26,745 | Iqaluit | 76/G 2 |
| **O** Ohio, U.S. | 44,828 | 116,103 | 11,353,140 | Columbus | 84/D 3 |
| Oklahoma, U.S. | 69,903 | 181,048 | 3,450,654 | Oklahoma City | 86/D 3 |
| Oman* | 82,031 | 212,460 | 3,102,229 | Muscat | 52/G 4 |
| Ontario, Canada | 412,580 | 1,068,582 | 11,410,045 | Toronto | 76/H 3 |
| Oregon, U.S. | 97,132 | 251,571 | 3,421,399 | Salem | 80/C 4 |
| **P** Pakistan* | 310,403 | 803,944 | 165,803,560 | Islamabad | 49/F 7 |
| Palau* | 177 | 458 | 20,579 | Koror | 62/C 4 |
| Panama* | 30,193 | 78,200 | 3,191,319 | Panamá | 88/E 6 |
| Papua New Guinea* | 178,703 | 462,840 | 5,670,544 | Port Moresby | 62/D 5 |
| Paraguay* | 157,047 | 406,752 | 6,506,464 | Asunción | 91/C 5 |
| Pennsylvania, U.S. | 46,058 | 119,291 | 12,281,054 | Harrisburg | 84/E 3 |
| Peru* | 496,223 | 1,285,220 | 28,302,603 | Lima | 94/C 5 |
| Philippines* | 115,830 | 300,000 | 89,468,677 | Manila | 57/H 3 |
| Poland* | 120,725 | 312,678 | 38,536,869 | Warsaw | 39/F 3 |
| Portugal* | 35,672 | 92,391 | 10,605,870 | Lisbon | 42/C 6 |
| Prince Edward Island, Canada | 2,184 | 5,657 | 135,290 | Charlottetown | 85/J 2 |
| Puerto Rico, U.S. | 3,508 | 9,085 | 3,808,610 | San Juan | 89/H 4 |
| **Q** Qatar | 4,416 | 11,107 | 885,359 | Doha | 52/F 3 |
| Québec, Canada | 594,857 | 1,540,680 | 7,237,480 | Québec | 77/J 3 |
| **R** Réunion, France | 972 | 2,517 | 776,948 | St-Denis | 13/M 7 |
| Rhode Island, U.S. | 1,231 | 3,189 | 1,048,319 | Providence | 85/G 3 |
| Romania* | 91,699 | 237,500 | 22,303,552 | Bucharest | 44/D 2 |
| Russia* | 6,592,735 | 17,075,200 | 142,893,540 | Moscow | 46/H 3 |
| Rwanda* | 10,169 | 26,337 | 8,648,248 | Kigali | 70/E 1 |
| **S** Saint Kitts and Nevis* | 101 | 261 | 39,129 | Basseterre | 89/J 4 |
| Saint Lucia* | 239 | 620 | 168,458 | Castries | 89/J 5 |
| Saint Vincent & the Grenadines* | 150 | 389 | 117,848 | Kingstown | 89/J 5 |
| Samoa* | 1,137 | 2,944 | 176,908 | Apia | 63/H 6 |
| San Marino* | 23.4 | 60.6 | 29,251 | San Marino | 42/G 5 |
| São Tomé and Príncipe* | 386 | 1001 | 193,413 | São Tomé | 68/F 7 |
| Saskatchewan, Canada | 251,865 | 652,330 | 978,935 | Regina | 76/F 3 |
| Saudi Arabia* | 756,981 | 1,960,582 | 27,019,731 | Riyadh | 52/D 4 |
| Scotland, U.K. | 30,414 | 78,772 | 5,062,011 | Edinburgh | 42/C 2 |
| Senegal* | 75,749 | 196,190 | 11,987,121 | Dakar | 68/B 5 |
| Serbia* | 34,185 | 88,538 | 10,212,395 | Belgrade | 44/C 3 |
| Seychelles* | 176 | 455 | 81,541 | Victoria | 13/M 6 |
| Sierra Leone* | 27,699 | 71,740 | 6,005,250 | Freetown | 68/C 6 |
| Singapore* | 267.4 | 692.7 | 4,492,150 | Singapore | 56/C 5 |
| Slovakia* | 18,859 | 48,845 | 5,439,448 | Bratislava | 44/C 2 |
| Slovenia* | 7,836 | 20,296 | 2,010,347 | Ljubljana | 44/B 2 |
| Solomon Islands* | 10,985 | 28,450 | 552,438 | Honiara | 62/E 6 |
| Somalia* | 246,200 | 637,658 | 8,863,338 | Mogadishu | 69/Q 6 |
| South Africa* | 471,008 | 1,219,912 | 44,187,637 | Cape Town; Pretoria; Bloemfontein | 70/D 6 |
| South America | 6,879,916 | 17,819,000 | 375,641,175 | ............ | 91 |
| South Carolina, U.S. | 31,189 | 80,779 | 4,012,012 | Columbia | 87/H 3 |
| South Dakota, U.S. | 77,121 | 199,744 | 754,844 | Pierre | 81/H 4 |
| Spain* | 194,884 | 504,750 | 40,397,842 | Madrid | 42/D 5 |
| Sri Lanka* | 25,332 | 65,610 | 20,222,240 | Colombo; Sri Jayeward-enepura Kotte | 53/D 7 |
| Sudan* | 967,494 | 2,505,809 | 41,236,378 | Khartoum | 69/L 5 |
| Suriname* | 63,039 | 163,270 | 439,117 | Paramaribo | 95/G 3 |
| Swaziland* | 6,703 | 17,360 | 1,136,334 | Mbabane | 70/F 6 |
| Sweden* | 173,731 | 449,964 | 9,016,596 | Stockholm | 43/D 3 |
| Switzerland* | 15,943 | 41,292 | 7,523,934 | Bern | 42/F 4 |
| Syria* | 71,498 | 185,180 | 18,881,361 | Damascus | 52/C 1 |
| **T** Taiwan | 13,892 | 35,980 | 23,036,087 | T'aipei | 55/M 7 |
| Tajikistan* | 55,251 | 143,100 | 7,320,815 | Dushanbe | 46/H 6 |
| Tanzania* | 364,805 | 945,090 | 37,445,392 | Dar es Salaam | 70/F 2 |
| Tennessee, U.S. | 42,146 | 109,158 | 5,689,283 | Nashville | 87/G 3 |
| Texas, U.S. | 267,277 | 692,248 | 20,851,820 | Austin | 86/C 4 |
| Thailand* | 198,455 | 513,998 | 64,631,595 | Bangkok | 56/C 2 |
| Togo* | 21,927 | 56,790 | 5,548,702 | Lomé | 68/F 6 |
| Tonga* | 289 | 748 | 114,689 | Nuku'alofa | 63/H 7 |
| Trinidad and Tobago* | 1,980 | 5,128 | 1,065,842 | Port-of-Spain | 89/J 5 |
| Tunisia* | 63,170 | 163,610 | 10,175,014 | Tunis | 68/G 1 |
| Turkey* | 301,382 | 780,580 | 70,413,958 | Ankara | 44/F 4 |
| Turkmenistan* | 188,455 | 488,100 | 5,042,920 | Ashkhabad | 46/F 6 |
| Tuvalu* | 10 | 26 | 11,810 | Funafuti | 62/G 5 |
| **U** Uganda* | 91,135 | 236,040 | 28,195,754 | Kampala | 69/M 7 |
| Ukraine* | 233,089 | 603,700 | 46,710,816 | Kiev | 44/E 2 |
| United Arab Emirates* | 32,000 | 82,880 | 2,602,713 | Abu Dhabi | 52/F 4 |
| United Kingdom* | 94,525 | 244,820 | 60,609,153 | London | 42/D 2 |
| United States* | 3,794,083 | 9,826,630 | 298,444,215 | Washington, D.C. | 78 |
| Uruguay* | 68,039 | 176,220 | 3,431,932 | Montevideo | 96/E 3 |
| Utah, U.S. | 84,904 | 219,902 | 2,233,169 | Salt Lake City | 82/E 3 |
| Uzbekistan* | 172,741 | 447,400 | 27,307,134 | Tashkent | 46/G 5 |
| **V** Vanuatu* | 4,710 | 12,200 | 208,869 | Port-Vila | 62/F 6 |
| Vatican City | 0.17 | 0.44 | 921 | ............ | 42/G 5 |
| Venezuela* | 352,143 | 912,050 | 25,730,435 | Caracas | 94/E 2 |
| Vermont, U.S. | 9,614 | 24,900 | 608,827 | Montpelier | 85/F 2 |
| Vietnam* | 127,243 | 329,560 | 84,402,966 | Hanoi | 49/K 8 |
| Virginia, U.S. | 42,326 | 109,625 | 7,078,515 | Richmond | 87/J 2 |
| Virgin Islands, British | 59 | 153 | 22,643 | Road Town | 89/J 4 |
| Virgin Islands, U.S. | 136 | 352 | 108,612 | Charlotte Amalie | 89/H 4 |
| **W** Wales, U.K. | 8,017 | 20,764 | 2,903,085 | Cardiff | 42/D 3 |
| Washington, U.S. | 70,637 | 182,949 | 5,894,121 | Olympia | 80/C 4 |
| West Bank | 2,263 | 5,860 | 2,385,615 | ............ | 52/C 2 |
| Western Sahara | 102,703 | 266,000 | 273,008 | ............ | 68/B 3 |
| West Virginia, U.S. | 24,231 | 62,758 | 1,808,344 | Charleston | 84/D 4 |
| Wisconsin, U.S. | 65,499 | 169,643 | 5,363,675 | Madison | 84/B 2 |
| World | (land) 57,505,734 | 148,940,000 | 6,525,486,603 | | 12 |
| Wyoming, U.S. | 97,818 | 253,349 | 493,782 | Cheyenne | 80/F 5 |
| **Y** Yemen* | 203,849 | 527,970 | 21,456,188 | Sanaa | 52/E 6 |
| Yukon Territory, Canada | 186,660 | 483,450 | 28,675 | Whitehorse | 76/D 2 |
| **Z** Zambia* | 290,583 | 752,610 | 11,502,010 | Lusaka | 70/E 3 |
| Zimbabwe* | 150,803 | 390,580 | 12,236,805 | Harare | 70/E 4 |

* United Nations Member

# World – Physical

■ World Physical Map    ■ Land Elevation and Ocean Depth Profiles

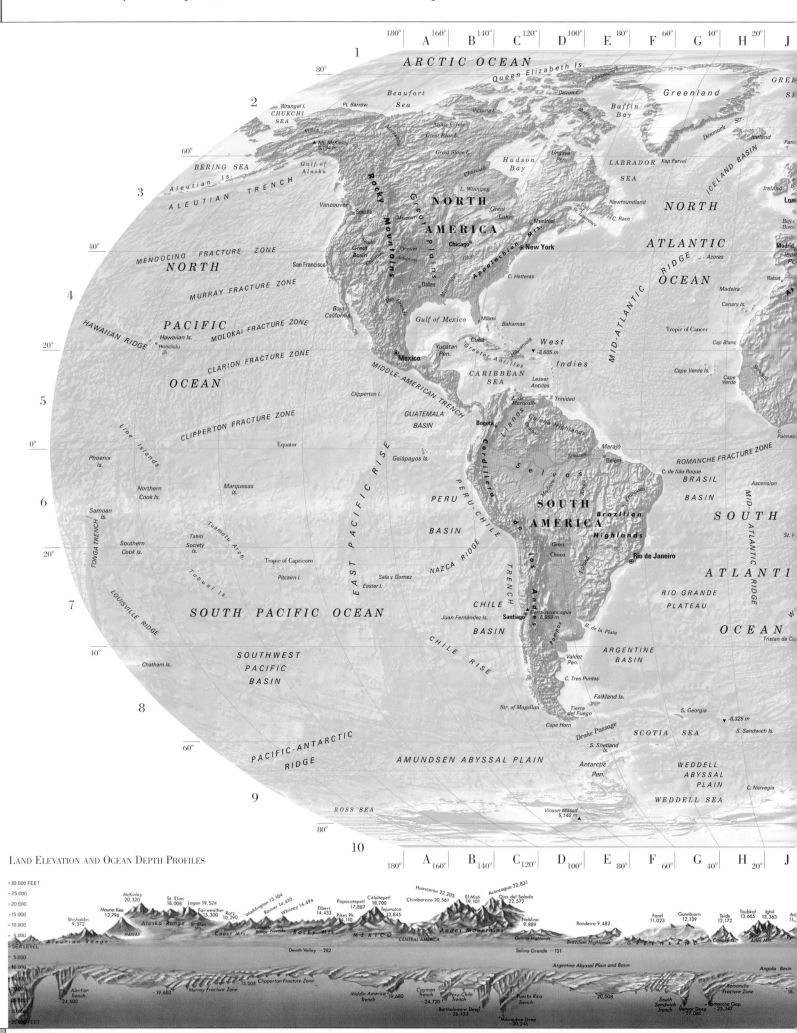

LAND ELEVATION AND OCEAN DEPTH PROFILES

■ World Political Map  ■ Comparative Populations  ■ Comparative Land Areas

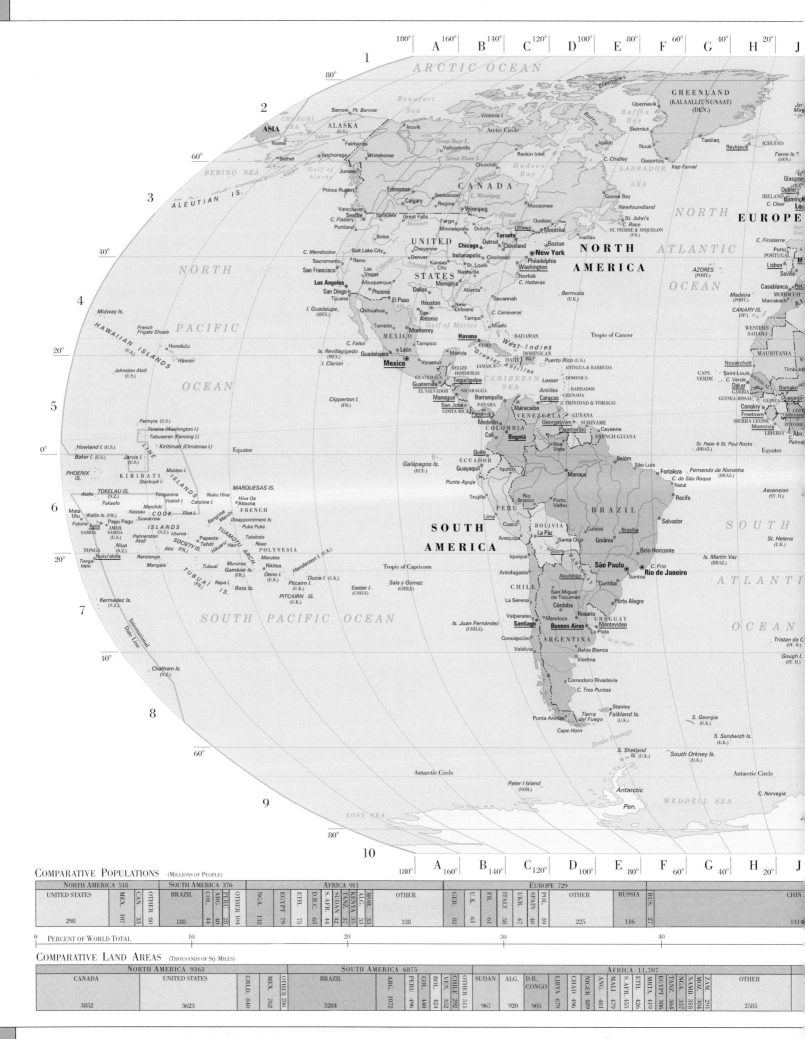

COMPARATIVE POPULATIONS (MILLIONS OF PEOPLE)

| NORTH AMERICA 518 | | | | SOUTH AMERICA 376 | | | | | AFRICA 911 | | | | | | | | | EUROPE 729 | | | | | | | | | RUSSIA | RUS. | CHIN |
|---|---|---|---|---|---|---|---|---|---|---|---|---|---|---|---|---|---|---|---|---|---|---|---|---|---|---|---|---|
| UNITED STATES | MEX. | CAN. | OTHER | BRAZIL | COL. | ARG. | PERU | OTHER | NGA. | EGYPT | ETH. | D.R.C. | S. AFR. | TANZ. | KENYA | MOR. | OTHER | GER. | U.K. | FR. | ITALY | UKR. | SPAIN | POL. | OTHER | | | |
| 298 | 107 | 33 | 80 | 188 | 44 | 40 | 28 | 104 | 132 | 79 | 75 | 63 | 44 | 37 | 35 | 33 | 338 | 82 | 61 | 61 | 58 | 47 | 40 | 39 | 225 | 116 | 27 | 1314 |

0 ────────── PERCENT OF WORLD TOTAL ────────── 10 ────────── 20 ────────── 30 ────────── 40

COMPARATIVE LAND AREAS (THOUSANDS OF SQ. MILES)

| NORTH AMERICA 9363 | | | | | SOUTH AMERICA 6875 | | | | | | | | AFRICA 11,707 | | | | | | | | | | | | | | | | | |
|---|---|---|---|---|---|---|---|---|---|---|---|---|---|---|---|---|---|---|---|---|---|---|---|---|---|---|---|---|---|---|
| CANADA | UNITED STATES | GRLD. | MEX. | OTHER | BRAZIL | ARG. | PERU | COL. | BOL. | VEN. | CHILE | OTHER | SUDAN | ALG. | D.R. CONGO | LIBYA | CHAD | NIGER | ANG. | MALI | S. AFR. | ETH. | MRTA. | EGYPT | TANZ. | NGA. | NAMB. | MOZ. | ZAM. | OTHER |
| 3852 | 3623 | 840 | 762 | 286 | 3284 | 1072 | 496 | 440 | 424 | 352 | 292 | 515 | 967 | 920 | 905 | 679 | 496 | 489 | 481 | 479 | 455 | 426 | 419 | 386 | 364 | 357 | 318 | 304 | 291 | 2585 |

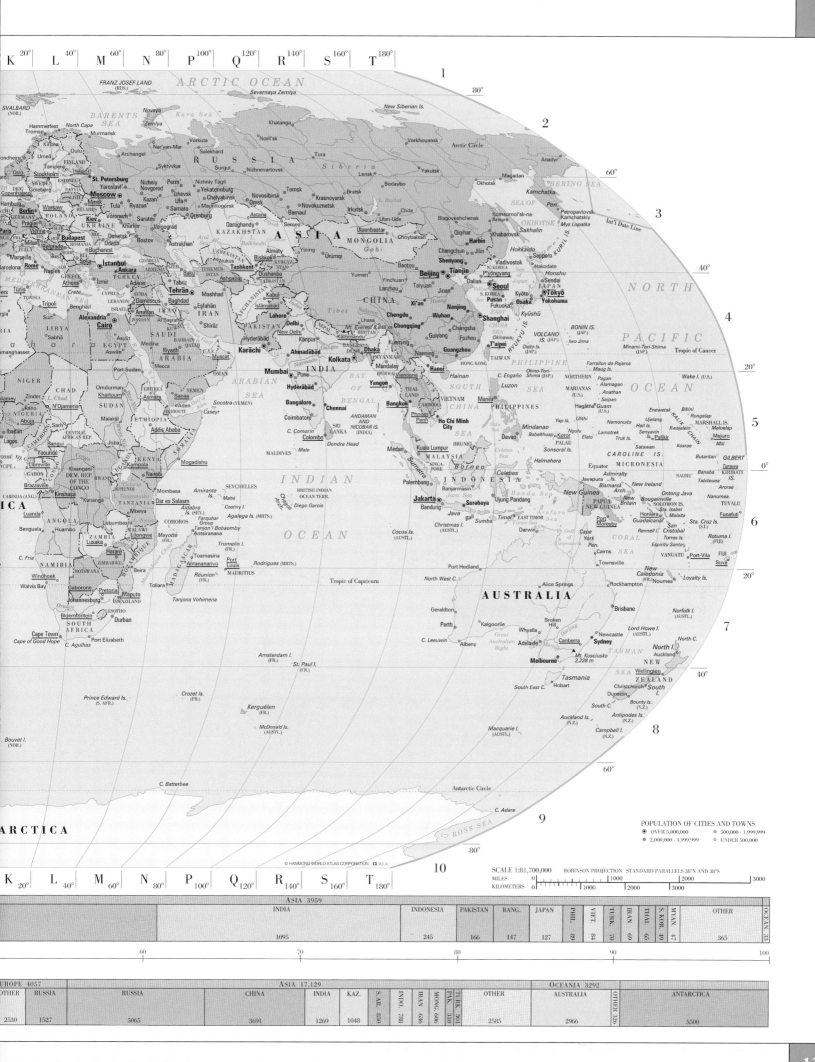

POPULATION OF CITIES AND TOWNS
- ⊛ OVER 5,000,000
- ⊚ 2,000,000 - 4,999,999
- ⊙ 500,000 - 1,999,999
- ○ UNDER 500,000

SCALE 1:81,700,000    ROBINSON PROJECTION    STANDARD PARALLELS 38°N AND 38°S
MILES 0 ___ 1000 ___ 2000 ___ 3000
KILOMETERS 0 ___ 1000 ___ 2000 ___ 3000

© HAMMOND WORLD ATLAS CORPORATION

| ASIA 3959 | | | | | | | | | | | | | |
|---|---|---|---|---|---|---|---|---|---|---|---|---|---|
| INDIA | | INDONESIA | PAKISTAN | BANG. | JAPAN | PHIL. | VIET. | TURK. | IRAN | THAIL. | S. KOR. | MYAN. | OTHER | OCEAN. 33 |
| 1095 | | 245 | 166 | 147 | 127 | 89 | 84 | 70 | 69 | 66 | 49 | 47 | 365 | |

60    70    80    90    100

| EUROPE 4057 | | ASIA 17,129 | | | | | | | | | | OCEANIA 3292 | | |
|---|---|---|---|---|---|---|---|---|---|---|---|---|---|---|
| OTHER | RUSSIA | RUSSIA | CHINA | INDIA | KAZ. | S. AR. | INDO. | IRAN | MONG. | PAK. | TURK. | OTHER | AUSTRALIA | OTHER 326 | ANTARCTICA |
| 2530 | 1527 | 5065 | 3691 | 1269 | 1048 | 850 | 783 | 636 | 606 | 310 | 301 | 2585 | 2966 | | 5500 |

# Structure of the Earth

## ➡ PLATE TECTONICS, VOLCANOES, AND EARTHQUAKES

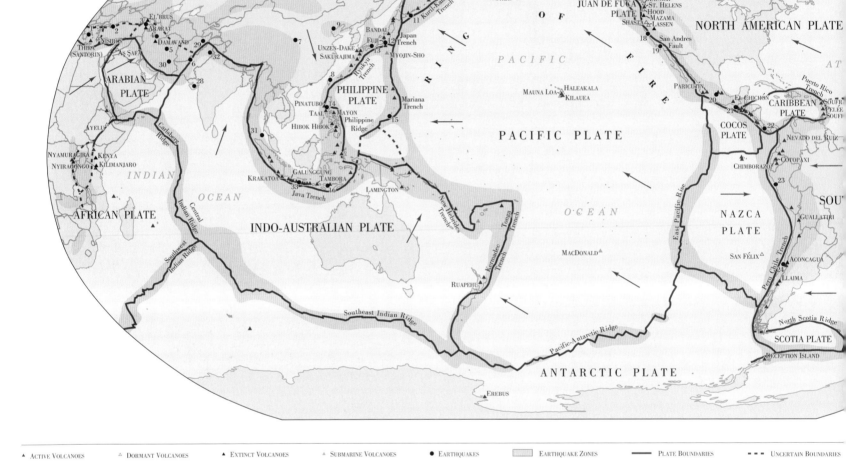

| ▲ ACTIVE VOLCANOES | △ DORMANT VOLCANOES | ▲ EXTINCT VOLCANOES | ▲ SUBMARINE VOLCANOES | ● EARTHQUAKES | ▭ EARTHQUAKE ZONES | ── PLATE BOUNDARIES | - - - UNCERTAIN BOUNDARIES |

The making of continents began more than 200 million years ago with the splitting of a gigantic landmass know as Pangaea. The initial division formed two supercontinents, Laurasia and Gondwana. Over a period of many millions of years these landmasses further subdivided into smaller parts and drifted across a single great ocean, forming the oceans and continents of today. In terms of current theory, called plate tectonics, the earth's crust is divided into at least 15 rigid rock segments, known as plates, that float on a semi-molten layer of upper mantle. Seven plates are of major size and, except for the vast Pacific Plate, carry a continental landmass with surrounding ocean floor and island areas. The plates are slow-moving, driven by powerful forces within the mantle. At their boundaries they are either slowly separating with new material being added from the mantle, converging, with one plate being forced down (subducted) and consumed under another; or sliding past each other. Almost all earthquakes, and volcanic and mountain-building activity

## ➡ CONTINENTAL DRIFT

180 MILLION YEARS AGO

70 MILLION YEARS AGO

PRESENT TIME

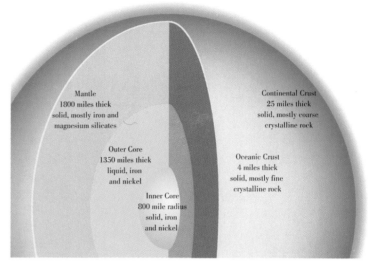

## (➔) INTERIOR AND CRUST OF THE EARTH

Mantle
1800 miles thick
solid, mostly iron and
magnesium silicates

Continental Crust
25 miles thick
solid, mostly coarse
crystalline rock

Outer Core
1350 miles thick
liquid, iron
and nickel

Oceanic Crust
4 miles thick
solid, mostly fine
crystalline rock

Inner Core
800 mile radius
solid, iron
and nickel

By studying records of earthquakes, scientists have developed a fairly reasonable picture (cross section) of the earth's principle layers, including their composition. The inner core is a very dense, highly pressurized, extremely hot (about 9,000 °F.) sphere. Moving outward toward the crust, densities, pressures and temperatures decrease significantly.

## (➔) VOLCANOES

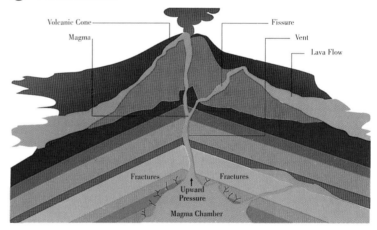

Volcanic Cone
Magma
Fissure
Vent
Lava Flow
Fractures
Fractures
Upward Pressure
Magma Chamber

One of the earth's most dynamic and colorful builders is the volcano. In the mantle, magma – molten rock containing compressed gases – probes for weak spots in the earth's crust, and bursts forth through the ground in an eruption of fiery lava, ash, gas and steam. After a period of eruption, lasting from a few days to many years, the magma ceases to push upward and the volcano becomes dormant.

EURASIAN PLATE
PUY-DE-DÔME
VESUVIUS
25
STROMBOLI
ETNA
26
27
TIMANFAYA
EMI KOUSSI
FOGO
AFRICAN PLATE
CAMEROON
Mid-Atlantic Ridge
ST. PAUL'S ROCKS
ASCENSION
MERICAN TE
OCEAN
Mid-Atlantic Ridge
TRISTAN DA CUNHA

⟵ DIRECTION OF PLATE MOVEMENT

## (➔) MAJOR EARTHQUAKES SINCE 1900
ALSO INDICATED BY NUMBER ON THE MAP TO THE LEFT (R=RICHTER SCALE INTENSITY)

1 ATHENS 1999, 5.9R
2 IZMIT 1999, 7.4R
3 ARMENIA 1988, 6.9R
4 RASHT 1990, 7.7R
5 TABAS 1978, 7.7R
6 QUETTA 1978, 7.7R
7 GANSU 1920, 8.6R
8 NANTAU 1999, 7.6R
9 TANGSHAN 1976, 7.8R
10 SAKHALIN 1995, 7.5R
11 KURIL ISLANDS 1994, 7.9R
12 TOKYO 1923, 8.3R
13 KOBE 1995, 7.2R
14 CABANATUAN 1990, 7.7R
15 GUAM 1993, 8.1R
16 FLORES 1992, 7.5R
17 SOUTHERN ALASKA 1964, 8.4R
18 SAN FRANCISCO 1906, 8.3R; 1989, 6.9R
19 LOS ANGELES 1994, 6.6R
20 MEXICO CITY 1985, 8.1R
21 GUATEMALA 1976, 7.5R
22 SAN JOSÉ 1991, 7.4R
23 CHIMBOTE 1970, 7.8R
24 VALPARAÍSO 1906, 8.6R
25 NAPLES 1980, 7.2R
26 EL ASNAM (CHLEF) 1980, 7.5R
27 AGADIR 1960, 5.7R
28 BHUJ 2001, 7.9R
29 BAGHLĀN 2002, 6.1R
30 BAM 2003, 6.6R
31 SUMATRA 2004, 9.0R
32 KASHMIR 2005, 7.6R
33 YOGYAKARTA 2006, 6.3R

closely follow these boundaries and are related to movements of the plates. Although these movements may be no more than inches per year, the destructive power unleashed can be cataclysmic.

## (➔) PLATE TECTONICS

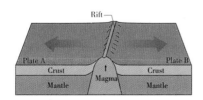

Rift
Plate A
Plate B
Crust
Crust
Magma
Mantle
Mantle

SEPARATING PLATES

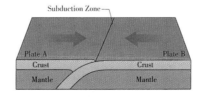

Subduction Zone
Plate A
Plate B
Crust
Crust
Mantle
Mantle

CONVERGING PLATES

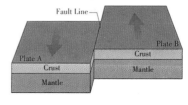

Fault Line
Plate B
Plate A
Crust
Crust
Mantle
Mantle

SLIDING PLATES

# Atmosphere and Oceans

■ Ocean Currents   ■ Hurricanes

## ⊕ OCEAN CURRENTS

WARM CURRENTS ∼∼   COLD CURRENTS ∼∼   DIRECTION OF FLOW ⟶

## ⊕ HURRICANES

Hurricanes are great whirling storms accompanied by violent destructive winds, torrential rains and high waves and tides. They originate over the oceans, and usually move from lower to higher latitudes with increasing speed, size and intensity. Movement over land quickly reduces their force. Hurricane winds cause severe property damage, but drowning is the greatest cause of hurricane deaths. Floods can be the hurricane's most serious threat.

Hurricane or Typhoon

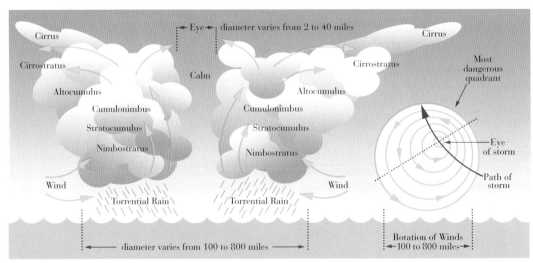

Illustrations not to scale

## ⊙ AIR PRESSURE AND WINDS

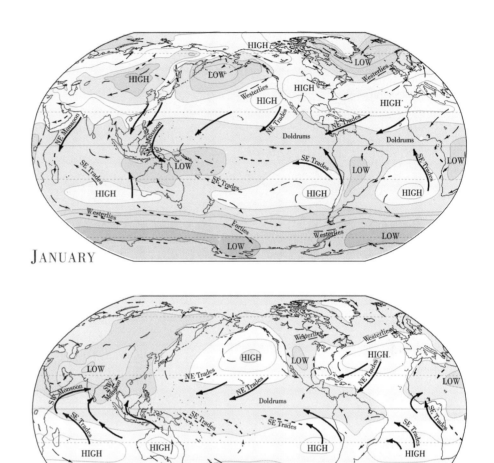

JANUARY

JULY

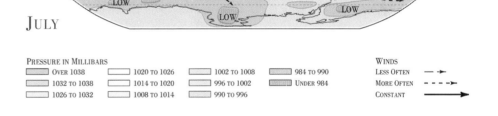

| PRESSURE IN MILLIBARS | | | | WINDS | |
|---|---|---|---|---|---|
| OVER 1038 | 1020 TO 1026 | 1002 TO 1008 | 984 TO 990 | LESS OFTEN | → |
| 1032 TO 1038 | 1014 TO 1020 | 996 TO 1002 | UNDER 984 | MORE OFTEN | --‣ |
| 1026 TO 1032 | 1008 TO 1014 | 990 TO 996 | | CONSTANT | ⟶ |

## ⊙ WARM AND COLD FRONTS

A front is the boundary surface between two air masses which have different characteristics, primarily different temperatures. Depending upon the amount of moisture in the warm air, warm fronts usually produce steady, moderate precipitation over a broad area ahead of the front on the ground. Cold fronts tend to move faster than warm fronts. They are generally confined to a narrower frontal zone but may contain dense thunderheads and severe storms.

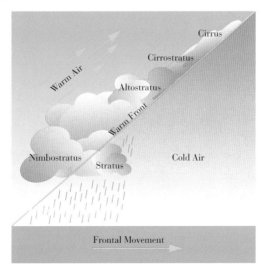

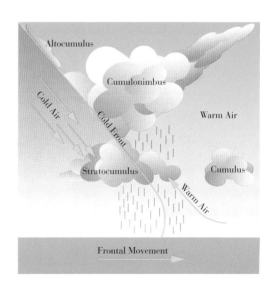

Right: Warm Front.   Left: Cold Front.

# Climate

■ **Climate Regions** ■ **Average Temperatures**

## ◉ CLIMATE REGIONS

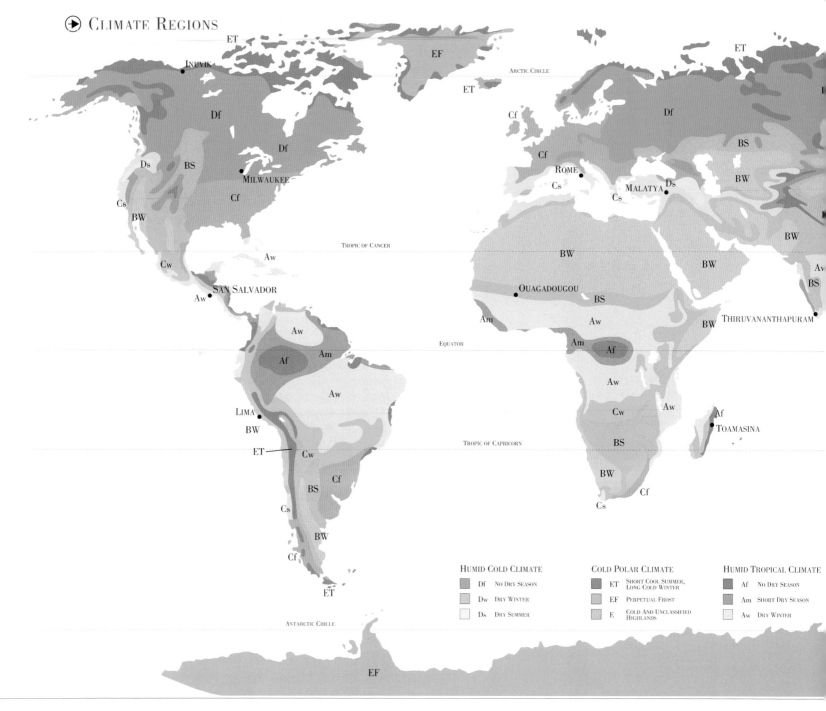

ET

EF

ARCTIC CIRCLE

INUVIK

ET

Df

Cf

Df

ET

Df

Cf

BS

Df

Cf

ROME

BS

Ds

MALATYA

BW

BS

Ds

Cs

Cw

Cs

BW

Cs

TROPIC OF CANCER

Aw

BW

BW

Aw

San Salvador

OUAGADOUGOU

BS

BW

THIRUVANANTHAPURAM

Aw

Aw

Am

Aw

BS

Aw

Af

Am

EQUATOR

Am

Af

Af

Aw

Aw

Af

TOAMASINA

Cw

Aw

LIMA

BW

Aw

BS

ET

Cw

BW

TROPIC OF CAPRICORN

Cf

Cf

BS

Cs

Cs

BW

Cf

Cs

BW

Cf

ET

ANTARCTIC CIRCLE

EF

### HUMID COLD CLIMATE

| | | |
|---|---|---|
| Df | No Dry Season |
| Dw | Dry Winter |
| Ds | Dry Summer |

### COLD POLAR CLIMATE

| | | |
|---|---|---|
| ET | Short Cool Summer, Long Cold Winter |
| EF | Perpetual Frost |
| E | Cold And Unclassified Highlands |

### HUMID TROPICAL CLIMATE

| | | |
|---|---|---|
| Af | No Dry Season |
| Am | Short Dry Season |
| Aw | Dry Winter |

## ◉ AVERAGE TEMPERATURES

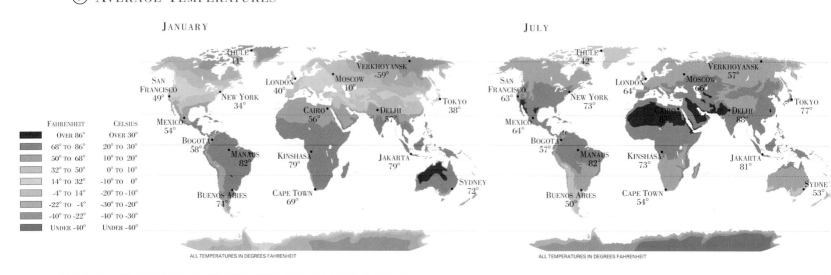

JANUARY

| FAHRENHEIT | CELSIUS |
|---|---|
| OVER 86° | OVER 30° |
| 68° TO 86° | 20° TO 30° |
| 50° TO 68° | 10° TO 20° |
| 32° TO 50° | 0° TO 10° |
| 14° TO 32° | -10° TO 0° |
| -4° TO 14° | -20° TO -10° |
| -22° TO -4° | -30° TO -20° |
| -40° TO -22° | -40° TO -30° |
| UNDER -40° | UNDER -40° |

THULE 11°

VERKHOYANSK -59°

SAN FRANCISCO 49°

LONDON 40°

MOSCOW 10°

NEW YORK 34°

TOKYO 38°

MEXICO 54°

CAIRO 56°

DELHI 57°

BOGOTA 58°

MANAUS 82°

KINSHASA 79°

JAKARTA 79°

BUENOS AIRES 74°

CAPE TOWN 69°

SYDNEY 72°

ALL TEMPERATURES IN DEGREES FAHRENHEIT

JULY

THULE 42°

VERKHOYANSK 57°

SAN FRANCISCO 63°

LONDON 64°

MOSCOW 66°

NEW YORK 73°

TOKYO 77°

MEXICO 64°

CAIRO 88°

DELHI 88°

BOGOTA 57°

MANAUS 82°

KINSHASA 73°

JAKARTA 81°

BUENOS AIRES 50°

CAPE TOWN 54°

SYDNEY 53°

ALL TEMPERATURES IN DEGREES FAHRENHEIT

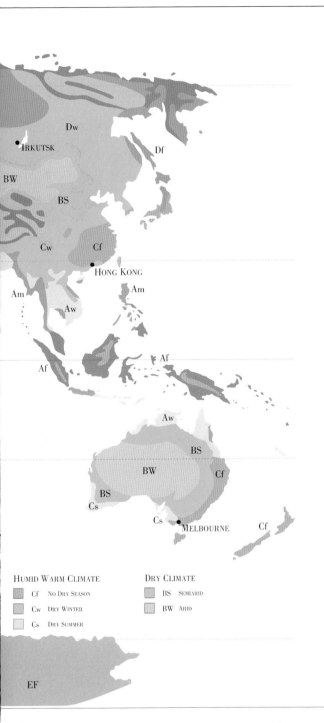

Dw

• IRKUTSK

Df

BW

BS

Cw

Cf

• HONG KONG

Am

Am

Aw

Af

Af

Aw

BS

BW

Cf

BS

Cs

Cs

• MELBOURNE

Cf

EF

**HUMID WARM CLIMATE**
- Cf  NO DRY SEASON
- Cw  DRY WINTER
- Cs  DRY SUMMER

**DRY CLIMATE**
- BS  SEMIARID
- BW  ARID

## ⊕ AVERAGE ANNUAL RAINFALL

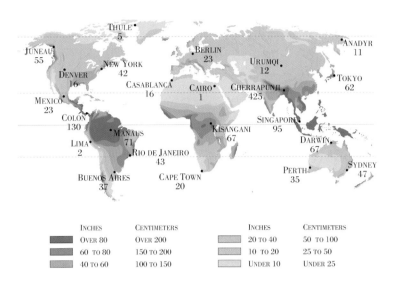

THULE
5

JUNEAU
55

DENVER
16

NEW YORK
42

BERLIN
23

URUMQI
12

ANADYR
11

TOKYO
62

CASABLANCA
16

CAIRO
1

CHERRAPUNJI
425

MEXICO
23

COLON
130

MANAUS
71

KISANGANI
67

SINGAPORE
95

DARWIN
67

LIMA
2

RIO DE JANEIRO
43

PERTH
35

SYDNEY
47

BUENOS AIRES
37

CAPE TOWN
20

| INCHES | CENTIMETERS | | INCHES | CENTIMETERS |
|---|---|---|---|---|
| OVER 80 | OVER 200 | | 20 TO 40 | 50 TO 100 |
| 60 TO 80 | 150 TO 200 | | 10 TO 20 | 25 TO 50 |
| 40 TO 60 | 100 TO 150 | | UNDER 10 | UNDER 25 |

## ⊕ ANNUAL TEMPERATURE RANGE

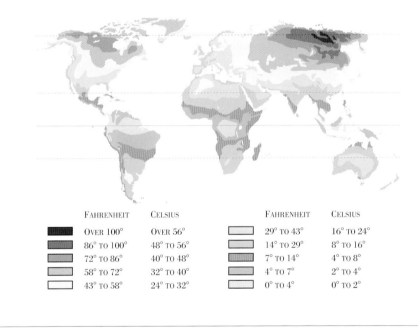

| FAHRENHEIT | CELSIUS | | FAHRENHEIT | CELSIUS |
|---|---|---|---|---|
| OVER 100° | OVER 56° | | 29° TO 43° | 16° TO 24° |
| 86° TO 100° | 48° TO 56° | | 14° TO 29° | 8° TO 16° |
| 72° TO 86° | 40° TO 48° | | 7° TO 14° | 4° TO 8° |
| 58° TO 72° | 32° TO 40° | | 4° TO 7° | 2° TO 4° |
| 43° TO 58° | 24° TO 32° | | 0° TO 4° | 0° TO 2° |

## ⊕ SELECTED CLIMATE STATIONS - TEMPERATURES AND RAINFALL

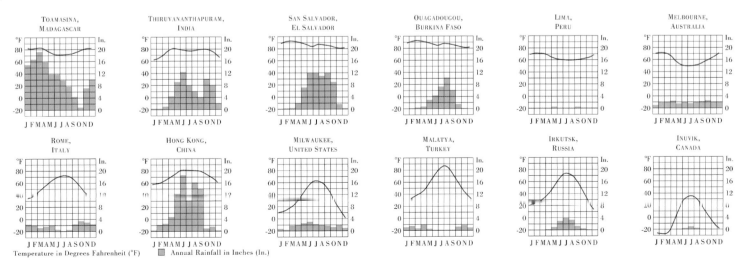

TOAMASINA, MADAGASCAR

THIRUVANANTHAPURAM, INDIA

SAN SALVADOR, EL SALVADOR

OUAGADOUGOU, BURKINA FASO

LIMA, PERU

MELBOURNE, AUSTRALIA

ROME, ITALY

HONG KONG, CHINA

MILWAUKEE, UNITED STATES

MALATYA, TURKEY

IRKUTSK, RUSSIA

INUVIK, CANADA

Temperature in Degrees Fahrenheit (°F)    ■ Annual Rainfall in Inches (In.)

# Vegetation and Soils

■ **Natural Vegetation**

## ⊙ NATURAL VEGETATION

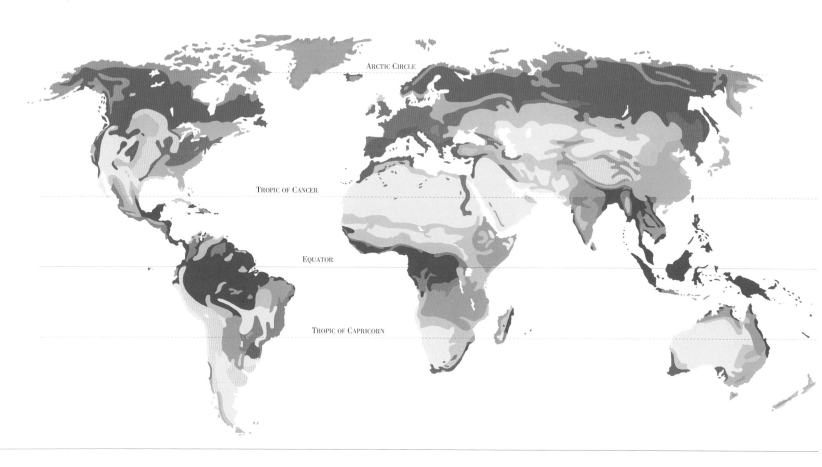

**NEEDLELEAF FOREST**
Found in higher latitudes with shorter growing seasons, and dominated by pure stands of softwood, evergreen conifers (cone-bearing trees) such as pine, fir and spruce. The light undergrowth consists of small shrubs, mosses, lichens and pine needles.

**BROADLEAF FOREST**
Found in the middle latitudes, this forest of deciduous (seasonal leaf-shedding) trees includes the hardwoods maple, hickory and oak. The forest floor is relatively barren, except for thick leaf cover during colder months.

**MIXED NEEDLELEAF AND BROADLEAF FOREST**
A transitional zone between northern softwoods and temperate hardwoods.

**WOODLAND AND SHRUB (MEDITERRANEAN)**
A mid-latitude area of broadleaf evergreens, dense growths of woody shrubs and open grassy woodland, characterized by pronounced dry summers and wet winters.

**SHORT GRASS (STEPPE)**
A mid-latitude, semi-arid area usually found on the fringe of desert regions, with continuous short-grass cover up to 8" (20 cm.) tall, used chiefly to graze livestock.

**TALL GRASS (PRAIRIE)**
Mid-latitude, semi-moist areas with continuous tall-grass cover up to 24" (61 cm.) in height, used for agricultural purposes. Rainfall is insufficient to support larger plants.

**TROPICAL RAIN FOREST (SELVA)**
A dense, evergreen forest of tall, varied hardwood trees with a thick broadleaf canopy and a dark, moist interior with minimal undergrowth.

**LIGHT TROPICAL FOREST (TROPICAL SEMIDECIDUOUS OR MONSOON FOREST)**
As above, with more widely spaced trees, heavier undergrowth, larger concentrations of single species. Dry season prevents most trees from remaining evergreen. Found in monsoon areas.

**TROPICAL WOODLAND AND SHRUB (THORN FOREST)**
Longer dry season results in low trees with thick bark and smaller leaves. Dense undergrowth of thorny plants, brambles and grasses. Transition belt between denser forests and grasslands.

**TROPICAL GRASSLAND AND SHRUB (SAVANNA)**
Stiff, sharp-edged grasses, from 2' to 12' (0.6 m. to 3.7 m.) high, with large areas of bare ground. Scattered shrubs and low trees in some areas.

**WOODED SAVANNA**
A transitional area where savanna joins a tropical or shrub forest, with low trees and shrubs dotting the grasslands.

**DESERT AND DESERT SHRUB**
Barren stretches of soft brown, yellow or red sand and rock wastes with isolated patches of short grass and stunted bushes, turning bright green when fed by infrequent precipitation.

**RIVER VALLEY AND OASIS**
River valleys are lush, fertile lands, with varied vegetation. An oasis is a fertile or verdant spot found in a desert near a natural spring or pool.

**HEATH AND MOOR**
A heath is open, uncultivated land covered with low, flowering evergreen shrubs such as heather. Moors are often high and poorly drained lands, with patches of heath and peat bogs.

**TUNDRA AND ALPINE**
An area of scarce moisture and short, cool summers where trees cannot survive. A permanently frozen subsoil supports low-growing lichens, mosses and stunted shrubs.

**UNCLASSIFIED HIGHLANDS**
Sequential bands or vertical zones of all vegetation types, which generally follow the warm-to-cold upward patterns found in corresponding areas of vegetation. (Map scale does not permit delineation of these areas.)

**PERMANENT ICE COVER**
Permanently ice and snow-covered terrain found in polar regions and atop high mountains.

# ⊙ Types of Soils

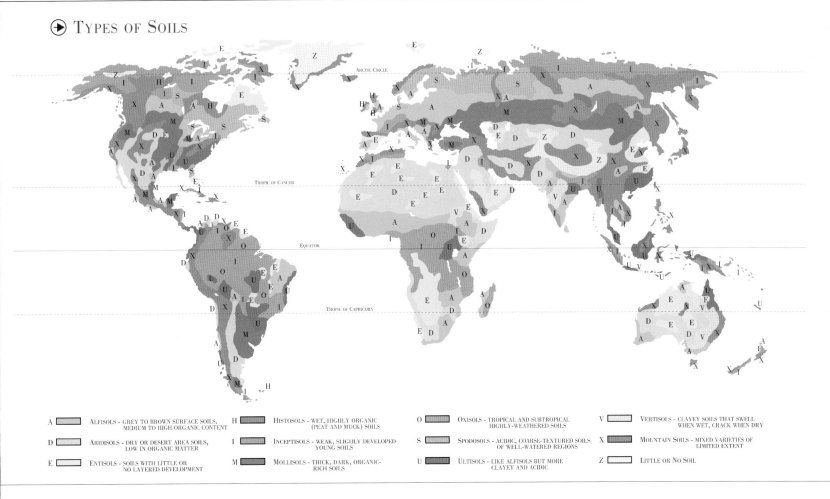

| | | | | |
|---|---|---|---|---|
| A ▭ | ALFISOLS - GREY TO BROWN SURFACE SOILS, MEDIUM TO HIGH ORGANIC CONTENT | H ▭ HISTOSOLS - WET, HIGHLY ORGANIC (PEAT AND MUCK) SOILS | O ▭ OXISOLS - TROPICAL AND SUBTROPICAL HIGHLY-WEATHERED SOILS | V ▭ VERTISOLS - CLAYEY SOILS THAT SWELL WHEN WET, CRACK WHEN DRY |
| D ▭ | ARIDISOLS - DRY OR DESERT AREA SOILS, LOW IN ORGANIC MATTER | I ▭ INCEPTISOLS - WEAK, SLIGHTLY DEVELOPED YOUNG SOILS | S ▭ SPODOSOLS - ACIDIC, COARSE-TEXTURED SOILS OF WELL-WATERED REGIONS | X ▭ MOUNTAIN SOILS - MIXED VARIETIES OF LIMITED EXTENT |
| E ▭ | ENTISOLS - SOILS WITH LITTLE OR NO LAYERED DEVELOPMENT | M ▭ MOLLISOLS - THICK, DARK, ORGANIC-RICH SOILS | U ▭ ULTISOLS - LIKE ALFISOLS BUT MORE CLAYEY AND ACIDIC | Z ▭ LITTLE OR NO SOIL |

# ⊙ Types of Vegetation

**Needleleaf Forest**

These typically coniferous soft-wood forests of Europe, Asia and North America cover about 9 percent of the earth's land.

**Broadleaf Forest**

Located in the most pleasant habitable climatic regions, temperate broadleaf forests have suffered the greatest destruction by people.

**Mixed Forest**

These hardwood and softwood forests, when added to the broadleaf forest area, are home to over half the world's population.

**Prairie**

Unique to the Americas, tall grass prairie lands have been successfully cultivated to become great grain fields of the world

**Steppe**

Slightly more moist than desert, steppe areas are sometimes cultivated but more often used for livestock ranching and herding.

**Tropical Rain Forest**

Teak, mahogany, balsawood, quinine, cocoa and rubber are some of the major products found in the world's tropical rain forest regions.

**Savanna**

A place of winter droughts and summer rainfall, these tropical grass and shrub areas are home to a wide variety of big-game animals.

**Mediterranean**

In addition to southern Europe and northern Africa, this vegetation also can be found in California, Chile, South Africa and Western Australia.

**Desert Shrub**

One-fifth of the world's land is desert and desert shrub, too dry for farming and ranching, and populated largely by nomads and oases-dwellers.

**Tundra**

Found along the Arctic fringe of North America and Eurasia, tundra is of little economic significance except for mineral exploitation.

# Environmental Concerns

■ Desertification and Acid Rain Damage   ■ Green House Effect   ■ Main Tanker Routes and Major Oil Spills

## ⊙ DESERTIFICATION AND ACID RAIN DAMAGE

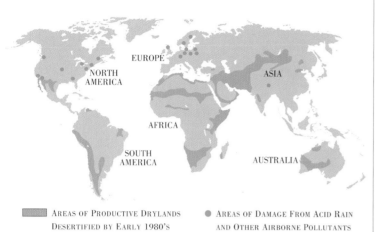

EUROPE
NORTH AMERICA
ASIA
AFRICA
SOUTH AMERICA
AUSTRALIA

▨ AREAS OF PRODUCTIVE DRYLANDS DESERTIFIED BY EARLY 1980'S
● AREAS OF DAMAGE FROM ACID RAIN AND OTHER AIRBORNE POLLUTANTS

## ⊙ GREENHOUSE EFFECT

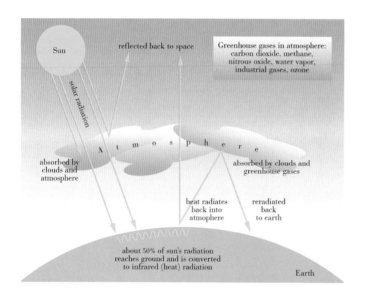

Sun

reflected back to space

Greenhouse gases in atmosphere: carbon dioxide, methane, nitrous oxide, water vapor, industrial gases, ozone

solar radiation

Atmosphere

absorbed by clouds and atmosphere

absorbed by clouds and greenhouse gases

heat radiates back into atmosphere

reradiated back to earth

about 50% of sun's radiation reaches ground and is converted to infrared (heat) radiation

Earth

## ⊙ MAIN TANKER ROUTES AND MAJOR OIL SPILLS

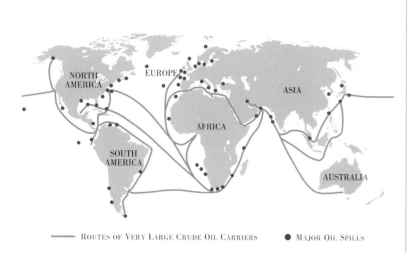

NORTH AMERICA
EUROPE
ASIA
AFRICA
SOUTH AMERICA
AUSTRALIA

— ROUTES OF VERY LARGE CRUDE OIL CARRIERS   ● MAJOR OIL SPILLS

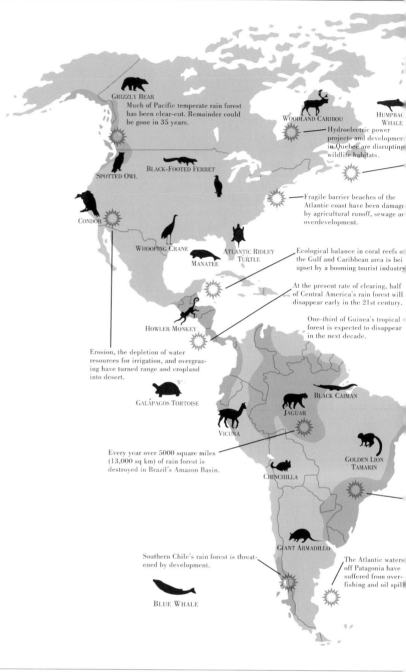

GRIZZLY BEAR
Much of Pacific temperate rain forest has been clear-cut. Remainder could be gone in 35 years.

WOODLAND CARIBOU

HUMPBACK WHALE

Hydroelectric power projects and development in Quebec are disrupting wildlife habitats.

SPOTTED OWL

BLACK-FOOTED FERRET

Fragile barrier beaches of the Atlantic coast have been damaged by agricultural runoff, sewage and overdevelopment.

CONDOR

WHOOPING CRANE

ATLANTIC RIDLEY TURTLE

MANATEE

Ecological balance in coral reefs of the Gulf and Caribbean area is being upset by a booming tourist industry.

At the present rate of clearing, half of Central America's rain forest will disappear early in the 21st century.

One-third of Guinea's tropical forest is expected to disappear in the next decade.

HOWLER MONKEY

Erosion, the depletion of water resources for irrigation, and overgrazing have turned range and cropland into desert.

GALÁPAGOS TORTOISE

BLACK CAIMAN

JAGUAR

VICUNA

GOLDEN LION TAMARIN

Every year over 5000 square miles (13,000 sq km) of rain forest is destroyed in Brazil's Amazon Basin.

CHINCHILLA

GIANT ARMADILLO

Southern Chile's rain forest is threatened by development.

The Atlantic waters off Patagonia have suffered from overfishing and oil spills.

BLUE WHALE

**Acid Rain**

Acid rain of nitric and sulfuric acids has killed all life in thousands of lakes, and over 15 million acres (6 million hectares) of virgin forest in Europe and North America are dead or dying.

**Deforestation**

Each year, 50 million acres (20 million hectares) of tropical rainforests are being felled by loggers. Trees remove carbon dioxide from the atmosphere and are vital to the prevention of soil erosion.

# Vanishing Wilderness and Endangered Species

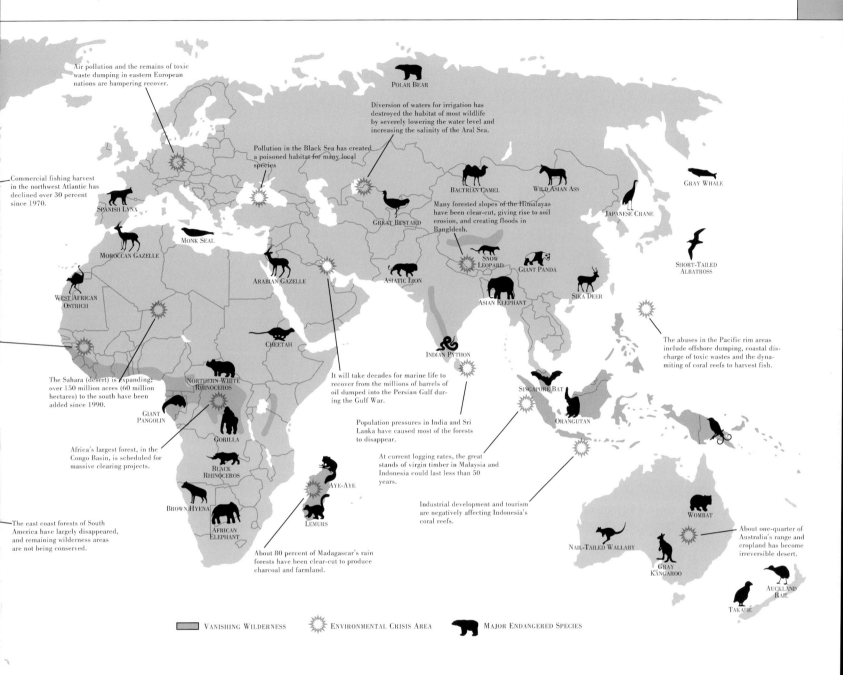

Air pollution and the remains of toxic waste dumping in eastern European nations are hampering recover.

Diversion of waters for irrigation has destroyed the habitat of most wildlife by severely lowering the water level and increasing the salinity of the Aral Sea.

Pollution in the Black Sea has created a poisoned habitat for many local species

Commercial fishing harvest in the northwest Atlantic has declined over 30 percent since 1970.

Many forested slopes of the Himalayas have been clear-cut, giving rise to soil erosion, and creating floods in Bangldesh.

The abuses in the Pacific rim areas include offshore dumping, coastal discharge of toxic wastes and the dynamiting of coral reefs to harvest fish.

The Sahara (desert) is expanding; over 150 million acres (60 million hectares) to the south have been added since 1990.

It will take decades for marine life to recover from the millions of barrels of oil dumped into the Persian Gulf during the Gulf War.

Population pressures in India and Sri Lanka have caused most of the forests to disappear.

Africa's largest forest, in the Congo Basin, is scheduled for massive clearing projects.

At current logging rates, the great stands of virgin timber in Malaysia and Indonesia could last less than 50 years.

Industrial development and tourism are negatively affecting Indonesia's coral reefs.

The east coast forests of South America have largely disappeared, and remaining wilderness areas are not being conserved.

About 80 percent of Madagascar's rain forests have been clear-cut to produce charcoal and farmland.

About one-quarter of Australia's range and cropland has become irreversible desert.

POLAR BEAR
GRAY WHALE
BACTRIAN CAMEL
WILD ASIAN ASS
JAPANESE CRANE
SPANISH LYNX
GREAT BUSTARD
MONK SEAL
MOROCCAN GAZELLE
SNOW LEOPARD
GIANT PANDA
SHORT-TAILED ALBATROSS
ARABIAN GAZELLE
ASIATIC LION
SIKA DEER
WEST AFRICAN OSTRICH
ASIAN ELEPHANT
CHEETAH
INDIAN PYTHON
SINGAPORE BAT
NORTHERN WHITE RHINOCEROS
GIANT PANGOLIN
ORANGUTAN
GORILLA
BLACK RHINOCEROS
AYE-AYE
BROWN HYENA
LEMURS
AFRICAN ELEPHANT
WOMBAT
NAIL-TAILED WALLABY
GRAY KANGAROO
AUCKLAND RAIL
TAKAHE

VANISHING WILDERNESS    ENVIRONMENTAL CRISIS AREA    MAJOR ENDANGERED SPECIES

**Extinction**

Biologists estimate that over 50,000 plant and animal species inhabiting the world's rain forests are disappearing each year due to pollution, unchecked hunting and the destruction of natural habitats.

**Air Pollution**

Billions of tons of industrial emissions and toxic pollutants are released into the air each year, depleting our ozone layer, killing our forests and lakes with acid rain and threatening our health.

**Water Pollution**

Only 3 percent of the earth's water is fresh. Pollution from cities, farms and factories has made much of it unfit to drink. In the developing world, most sewage flows untreated into lakes and rivers.

**Ozone Depletion**

The layer of ozone in the stratosphere shields earth from harmful ultraviolet radiation. But man-made gases are destroying this vital barrier, increasing the risk of skin cancer and eye disease.

# Population

- ■ Population Distribution
- ■ Population Density

## ⊕ POPULATION DISTRIBUTION

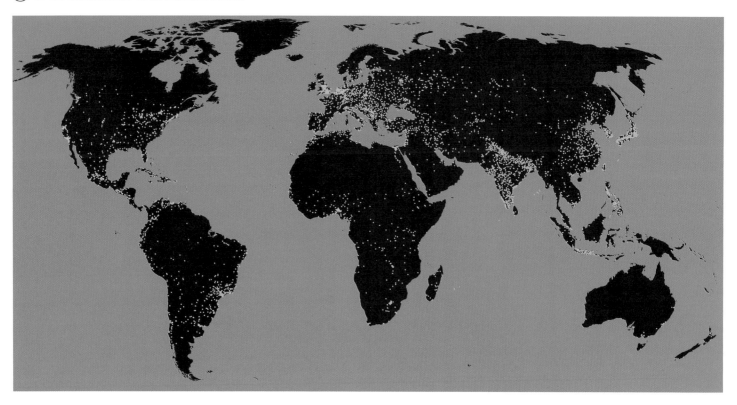

This map provides a dramatic perspective by illuminating populated areas with one point of light for each city over 50,000 residents. Over 675 million people live in cities with populations in excess of 500,000. According to the latest census data, there are 11,650 people per square mile (4,500 per sq km) in London. In New York, there are 32,250 (12,450). Hong Kong has over 18,000 people per square mile (7,000 per sq km), and the Tokyo-Yokohama agglomeration includes over 14,250 (5,500). During the last decade, the movement to the cities has accelerated dramatically, particularly in developing nations. In Lagos, Nigeria, where there are over 28,500 people per square mile (11,000 per sq km), most live in shantytowns. In São Paulo, Brazil, 2,000 buses arrive each day, bringing field hands, farm workers and their families in search of a better life. Tokyo, Mexico and Mumbai are the world's largest urban agglomerations. By 2015, the United Nations predicts that 30 of the 40 largest urban agglomerations will be located in less-industrialized nations.

## ⊕ POPULATION DENSITY PER SQUARE MILE (SQ. KM.)

Legend:
- 1,000 - 5,000 (390 - 2,000)
- 500 - 1,000 (195 - 390)
- 100 - 500 (39 - 195)
- 30 - 100 (12 - 39)
- Under 30 (Under 12)

Source: U.S. Bureau of the Census, International Database

## ⊕ AGE DISTRIBUTION

### BOTSWANA

| AGE | MALE | | FEMALE |
|---|---|---|---|
| 85+ | | | |
| 80-84 | | | |
| 75-79 | | | |
| 70-74 | | | |
| 65-69 | | | |
| 60-64 | | | |
| 55-59 | | | |
| 50-54 | | | |
| 45-49 | | | |
| 40-44 | | | |
| 35-39 | | | |
| 30-34 | | | |
| 25-29 | | | |
| 20-24 | | | |
| 15-19 | | | |
| 10-14 | | | |
| 5-9 | | | |
| 0-4 | | | |

% 8  6  4  2  0  2  4  6  8
(Percent of Total Population Male or Female)

### UNITED STATES

| AGE | MALE | | FEMALE |
|---|---|---|---|
| 85+ | | | |
| 80-84 | | | |
| 75-79 | | | |
| 70-74 | | | |
| 65-69 | | | |
| 60-64 | | | |
| 55-59 | | | |
| 50-54 | | | |
| 45-49 | | | |
| 40-44 | | | |
| 35-39 | | | |
| 30-34 | | | |
| 25-29 | | | |
| 20-24 | | | |
| 15-19 | | | |
| 10-14 | | | |
| 5-9 | | | |
| 0-4 | | | |

% 8  6  4  2  0  2  4  6  8
(Percent of Total Population Male or Female)

### SWEDEN

| AGE | MALE | | FEMALE |
|---|---|---|---|
| 85+ | | | |
| 80-84 | | | |
| 75-79 | | | |
| 70-74 | | | |
| 65-69 | | | |
| 60-64 | | | |
| 55-59 | | | |
| 50-54 | | | |
| 45-49 | | | |
| 40-44 | | | |
| 35-39 | | | |
| 30-34 | | | |
| 25-29 | | | |
| 20-24 | | | |
| 15-19 | | | |
| 10-14 | | | |
| 5-9 | | | |
| 0-4 | | | |

% 8  6  4  2  0  2  4  6  8
(Percent of Total Population Male or Female)

Source: U.S. Bureau of the Census, International Database

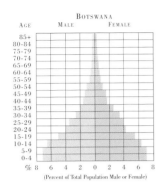
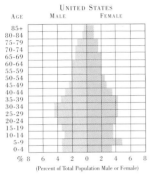
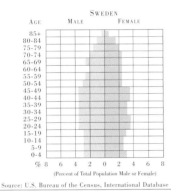

## ⊕ URBAN & RURAL POPULATION COMPONENTS

### WORLD'S LARGEST URBAN AREAS

MILLIONS OF INHABITANTS

Tokyo, Japan 26.5

Mexico, Mexico 18.1

Mumbai (Bombay), India 18.1

São Paulo, Brazil 17.7

New York, U.S. 16.6

Lagos, Nigeria 13.4

Los Angeles, U.S. 13.1

Kolkata, India 12.9

Shanghai, China 12.9

Buenos Aires, Argentina 12.5

Dhaka, Bangladesh 12.3

Jakarta, Indonesia 11.0

Osaka, Japan 11

Beijing, China 10.8

Rio de Janeiro, Brazil 10.5

### URBAN & RURAL POPULATION COMPONENTS

SELECTED COUNTRIES

▨ URBAN   ▨ RURAL

Uruguay 87% / 13%

Australia 85% / 15%

Japan 77% / 23%

United States 74% / 26%

Russia 73% / 27%

Hungary 62% / 38%

Iran 54% / 46%

Egypt 44% / 56%

Philippines 37% / 63%

Portugal 30% / 70%

China 26% / 74%

Maldives 20% / 80%

Bangladesh 15% / 85%

Nepal 6% / 94%

## ⊕ ANNUAL RATE OF POPULATION (NATURAL) INCREASE

3.5 PERCENT OR MORE
2.6 TO 3.4 PERCENT
1.8 TO 2.5 PERCENT
.09 TO 1.7 PERCENT
.01 TO .08 PERCENT
0.0 OR DECREASE

Source: U.S. Bureau of the Census, International Database

# Languages and Religions

■ Religions   ■ Language Families

## ⊕ RELIGIONS

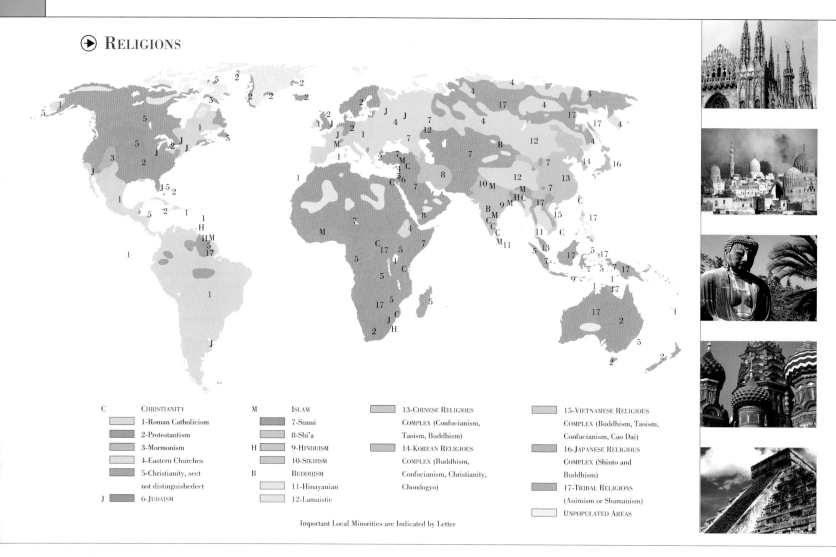

| C | CHRISTIANITY | M | ISLAM | | 13-CHINESE RELIGIOUS COMPLEX (Confucianism, Taoism, Buddhism) | | 15-VIETNAMESE RELIGIOUS COMPLEX (Buddhism, Taoism, Confucianism, Cao Dai) |
|---|---|---|---|---|---|---|---|
| | 1-Roman Catholicism | | 7-Sunni | | | | |
| | 2-Protestantism | | 8-Shi'a | | | | |
| | 3-Mormonism | H | 9-HINDUISM | | 14-KOREAN RELIGIOUS COMPLEX (Buddhism, Confucianism, Christianity, Chondogyo) | | 16-JAPANESE RELIGIOUS COMPLEX (Shinto and Buddhism) |
| | 4-Eastern Churches | | 10-SIKHISM | | | | |
| | 5-Christianity, sect not distinguishedect | B | BUDDHISM | | | | 17-TRIBAL RELIGIONS (Animism or Shamanism) |
| J | 6-JUDAISM | | 11-Hinayanian | | | | |
| | | | 12-Lamaistic | | | | UNPOPULATED AREAS |

Important Local Minorities are Indicated by Letter

## ⊕ LANGUAGE FAMILIES

## ⊙ THE INDO-EUROPEAN LANGUAGE TREE

The most well-established family tree is Indo-European. Spoken by more than 2.5 billion people, it contains dozens of languages. Some linguists theorize that all people – and all languages – are descended from a tiny population that lived in Africa some 200,000 years ago.

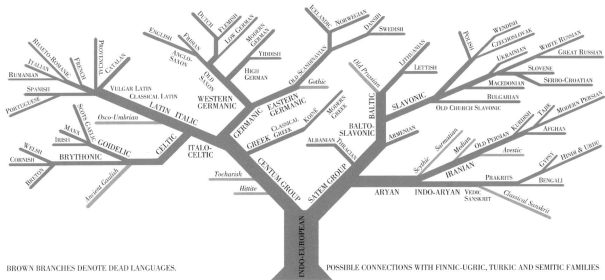

BROWN BRANCHES DENOTE DEAD LANGUAGES.

POSSIBLE CONNECTIONS WITH FINNIC-UGRIC, TURKIC AND SEMITIC FAMILIES

1-INDO-EUROPEAN
1A-GERMANIC
1B-ROMANCE
1C-SLAVIC
1D-BALTIC
1E-CELTIC
1F-ALBANIAN
1G-GREEK
1H-ARMENIAN
1J-IRANIAN
1K-INDO-ARYAN
2-BASQUE
3-CAUCASIAN FAMILIES
4-BURUSHASKI
5-AFRO-ASIATIC
(HAMITO-SEMITIC)
6-NILO-SAHARAN
7-NIGER-CONGO
8-KHOISAN

9-URALIC
10-ALTAIC
11-PALEO-SIBERIAN
FAMILIES
12-SINO-TIBETAN
13-THAI-KADAI
14-KOREAN
15-JAPANESE
16-DRAVIDIAN
17-VIETNAMESE
18-AUSTRO-ASIATIC
19-AUSTRONESIAN
20-PAPUAN
21-AUSTRALIAN
22-ESKIMO-ALEUT
23-AMERICAN INDIAN
FAMILIES
UNPOPULATED AREAS

NOTE: Names may vary, depending on source.

## ⊙ LANGUAGES OF EUROPE

INDO-EUROPEAN FAMILY
GERMANIC SUBFAMILY
ROMANCE SUBFAMILY
CELTIC SUBFAMILY
SLAVIC SUBFAMILY
BALTIC SUBFAMILY
GREEK
ALBANIAN

URALIC FAMILY
FINNIC SUBFAMILY
UGRIC SUBFAMILY
SAMOYED

ALTAIC FAMILY
TURKIC SUBFAMILY

AFRO-ASIATIC FAMILY
MALTESE

BASQUE

# Standards of Living

■ Literacy ■ Life Expectancy ■ Infant Deaths ■ Gross Domestic Product

## ⊕ LITERATE PERCENT OF POPULATION

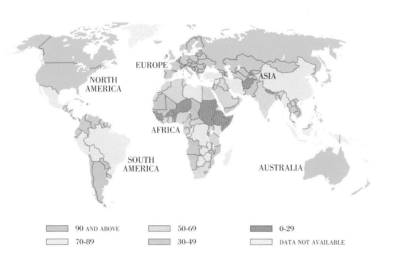

| | | |
|---|---|---|
| 90 AND ABOVE | 50-69 | 0-29 |
| 70-89 | 30-49 | DATA NOT AVAILABLE |

## ⊕ YEARS OF LIFE EXPECTANCY (MEN AND WOMEN)

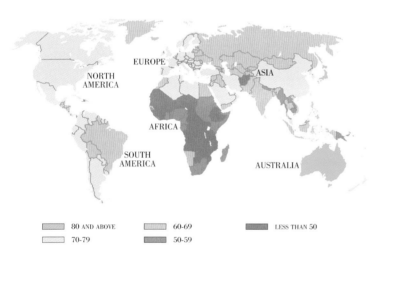

| | | |
|---|---|---|
| 80 AND ABOVE | 60-69 | LESS THAN 50 |
| 70-79 | 50-59 | |

## ⊕ INFANT DEATHS PER 1,000 LIVE BIRTH

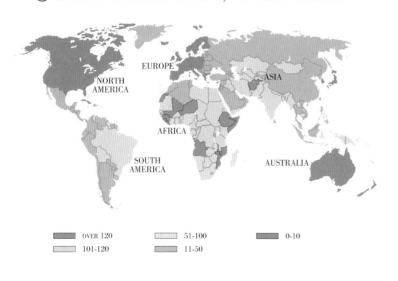

| | | |
|---|---|---|
| OVER 120 | 51-100 | 0-10 |
| 101-120 | 11-50 | |

**UNITED STATES**
The United States and other developed countries have committed greater resources to both public and private education. This has helped their populations develop the skills that are necessary in more complex, technical and competitive societies.

**LATIN AMERICA**
The gulf between rich and poor continues to widen, despite efforts to reform oppressive governments, increase literacy and relieve overburdened cities.

**SOUTH AMERICA**
Political unrest, rising inflation and slow economic growth continue to thwart efforts to bring unity and prosperity to the nations of South America.

## ⊕ GROSS DOMESTIC PRODUCT GROWTH RATES

| BEST GROWTH RATES | | WORST GROWTH RATES | |
|---|---|---|---|
| CHAD | 38 | ZIMBABWE | -12.1 |
| LIBERIA | 21.8 | HAITI | -3.5 |
| EQUATORIAL GUINEA | 20 | SAINT KITTS AND NEVIS | -1.9 |
| VENEZUELA | 16.8 | MYANMAR (BURMA) | -1.3 |
| UKRAINE | 12 | CÔTE D'IVOIRE | -1 |
| ANGOLA | 11.7 | DOMINICA | -1 |
| ETHIOPIA | 11.6 | CENTRAL AFRICAN REP. | 0.5 |
| LIECHTENSTEIN | 11 | ST. VINCENT/GRENADINES | 0.7 |
| URUGUAY | 10.2 | PAPUA NEW GUINEA | 0.9 |
| AZERBAIJAN | 9.8 | RWANDA | 0.9 |
| GEORGIA | 9.5 | EAST TIMOR | 1 |
| CHINA | 9.1 | GUINEA | 1 |
| KAZAKHSTAN | 9.1 | MALTA | 1 |
| ARMENIA | 9 | MARSHALL ISLANDS | 1 |
| QATAR | 8.7 | MICRONESIA | 1 |
| ARGENTINA | 8.3 | NORTH KOREA | 1 |
| MOZAMBIQUE | 8.2 | PALAU | 1 |
| TURKEY | 8.2 | VANUATU | 1.1 |
| ROMANIA | 8.1 | F.Y.R.O. MACEDONIA | 1.3 |
| VIETNAM | 7.7 | KIRIBATI | 1.5 |

Source: CIA World Factbook

■ Gross National Product    ■ Number of Television Sets

# ⊕ GROSS NATIONAL PRODUCT PER CAPITA IN DOLLARS

EUROPE
The healthy, high-tech economies of many western European nations stand in sharp relief to the obsolete factories, high unemployment and ethnic rivalries of Eastern Europe.

EASTERN EUROPE AND RUSSIA
In the former Soviet republics falling birthrates and increased mortality are resulting in shrinking populations even though, in a reversal of recent trends, life expectancy is rising.

CHINA
The limited relaxation of Communist dogma has encouraged growing industrialization and exports, creating new wealth in parts of China.

EAST ASIA
In recent years most of the economies of this region have experienced exceptional growth with relatively low inequality in incomes. This rare combination has been known to achieve dramatic reductions in poverty.

MIDDLE EAST
Water has emerged as a significant factor in Middle East politics. Projected water shortages could lead to economic hardship and regional conflicts.

AFRICA
Disastrous droughts, discriminatory government policies and ancient tribal rivalries, particularly in South Africa and the Sudan, have resulted in political instability and economic hardship.

AUSTRALIA
An influx of Japanese tourists and investors is generating new capital and development, escalating coastal real estate prices and regional tensions.

10,000 AND MORE    5,000-9,999    2,500-4,999    1,000-2,499    700-999
UNDER 700    DATA NOT AVAILABLE

Source: CIA World Factbook

# ⊕ TOTAL GROSS DOMESTIC PRODUCT
BILLIONS OF DOLLARS

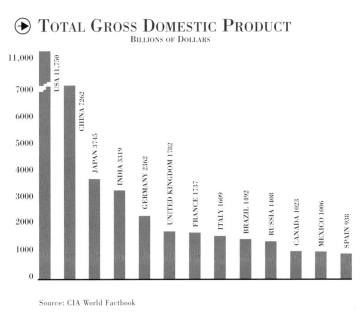

USA 11,750 · CHINA 7262 · JAPAN 3745 · INDIA 3319 · GERMANY 2362 · UNITED KINGDOM 1782 · FRANCE 1737 · ITALY 1609 · BRAZIL 1492 · RUSSIA 1408 · CANADA 1023 · MEXICO 1006 · SPAIN 938

Source: CIA World Factbook

# ⊕ TELEVISION SETS PER 1,000 PEOPLE

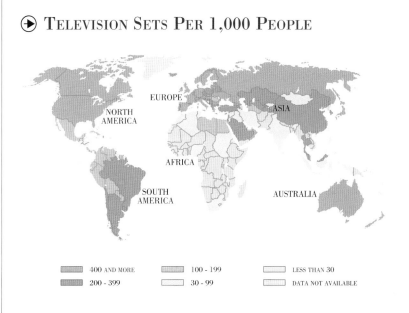

400 AND MORE    100 - 199    LESS THAN 30
200 - 399    30 - 99    DATA NOT AVAILABLE

# Agriculture and Manufacturing

■ Top Producers of Agricultural Commodities   ■ Employment in Agriculture

## ➔ TOP FIVE WORLD PRODUCERS OF SELECTED AGRICULTURAL COMMODITIES

| | 1 | 2 | 3 | 4 | 5 |
|---|---|---|---|---|---|
| WHEAT | CHINA | INDIA | UNITED STATES | RUSSIA | FRANCE |
| RICE | CHINA | INDIA | INDONESIA | BANGLADESH | VIETNAM |
| OATS | RUSSIA | CANADA | UNITED STATES | POLAND | FINLAND |
| CORN (MAIZE) | UNITED STATES | CHINA | BRAZIL | MEXICO | ARGENTINA |
| SOYBEANS | UNITED STATES | BRAZIL | ARGENTINA | CHINA | INDIA |
| POTATOES | CHINA | RUSSIA | INDIA | UKRAINE | UNITED STATES |
| COFFEE | BRAZIL | VIETNAM | INDONESIA | COLOMBIA | MEXICO |
| TEA | CHINA | INDIA | SRI LANKA | KENYA | TURKEY |
| TOBACCO | CHINA | BRAZIL | INDIA | UNITED STATES | INDONESIA |
| COTTON | CHINA | UNITED STATES | INDIA | PAKISTAN | BRAZIL |
| SUGAR | BRAZIL | INDIA | CHINA | THAILAND | PAKISTAN |
| CATTLE (STOCK) | BRAZIL | INDIA | CHINA | UNITED STATES | ARGENTINA |
| SHEEP (STOCK) | CHINA | AUSTRALIA | INDIA | IRAN | SUDAN |
| HOGS (STOCK) | CHINA | UNITED STATES | BRAZIL | GERMANY | SPAIN |
| COW'S MILK | UNITED STATES | INDIA | RUSSIA | GERMANY | FRANCE |
| HEN'S EGGS | CHINA | UNITED STATES | INDIA | JAPAN | RUSSIA |
| WOOL | AUSTRALIA | CHINA | NEW ZEALAND | IRAN | UNITED KINGDOM |
| ROUNDWOOD | UNITED STATES | CANADA | CHINA | BRAZIL | RUSSIA |
| NATURAL RUBBER | THAILAND | INDONESIA | MALAYSIA | INDIA | CHINA |
| FISH CATCHES | CHINA | PERU | JAPAN | INDIA | CHILE |

Names in Black Indicate More Than 10% of Total World Production

Source: United Nations, Food and Agriculture Organization

## ➔ PERCENT OF TOTAL EMPLOYMENT IN AGRICULTURE, MANUFACTURING AND OTHER INDUSTRIES

AGRICULTURE (INCLUDES FORESTRY AND FISHING)   CONSTRUCTION   FINANCE, INSURANCE REAL ESTATE   OTHER (INCLUDES MINING, UTILITIES, TRANSPORTATION)

MANUFACTURING   TRADE AND COMMERCE   SERVICES

0   20   40   60   80   100

India

China

Indonesia

Pakistan

Mexico

Brazil

Spain

Argentina

Italy

Japan

France

Canada

Australia

Germany

United States

United Kingdom

Finance, Insurance, Real Estate Data Included in "Other" for India, China, Indonesia and Pakistan

HERDING

SHIFTING CROPS

LIVESTOCK RANCHING

LIGHT SUBSISTENCE CROPS

RICE & INTENSIVE SUBSISTENCE CROPS

INTENSIVE SUBSISTENCE CROPS

PLANTATION CROPS

LIVESTOCK, GRAINS & FRUIT

HIGH-YIELD CROPS & LIVESTOCK

LIVESTOCK & SUBSISTENCE CROPS

HIGH-YIELD GRAIN CROPS

SPECIALIZED CROPS

DAIRY FARMING

NON-AGRICULTURAL LAND

▲ AIRCRAFT

△ MOTOR VEHICLES

▽ SHIPBUILDING

▼ TRANSPORTATION EQUIPMENT

■ IRON AND STEEL

▣ MACHINERY

□ METALS AND METAL PRODUCTS

◪ ELECTRICAL PRODUCTS

⊡ OPTICAL INSTRUMENTS

● OIL REFINING

○ CHEMICALS

△ TEXTILES

▲ CLOTHING

▼ RUBBER GOODS

▽ GLASS PRODUCTS

■ WOOD AND WOOD PRODUCTS

□ PRINTING AND PUBLISHING

# ⊙ AGRICULTURAL REGIONS

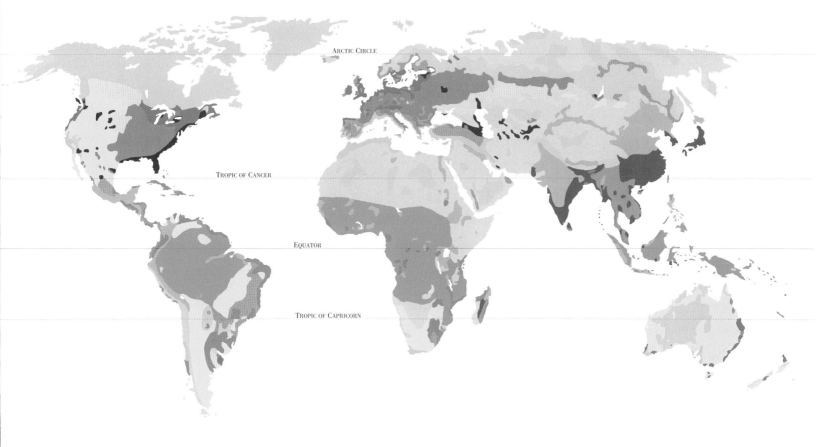

# ⊙ MANUFACTURING REGIONS

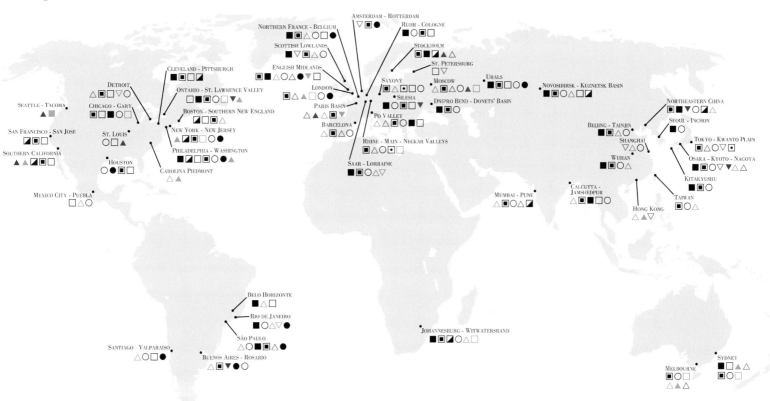

# Energy and Resources

■ Mineral Fuels     ■ Metals and Nonmetals     ■ Top Producers of Selectd Mineral Commodities

## ⊙ MINERAL FUELS

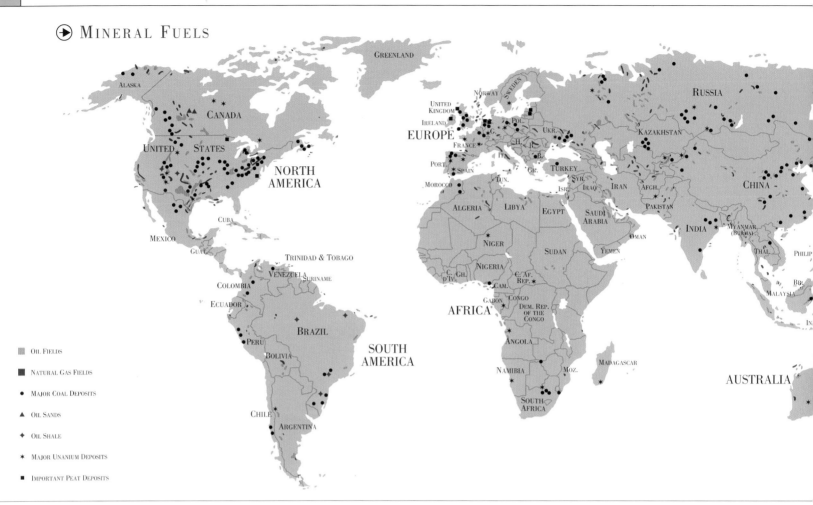

□ OIL FIELDS

■ NATURAL GAS FIELDS

● MAJOR COAL DEPOSITS

▲ OIL SANDS

◆ OIL SHALE

✶ MAJOR URANIUM DEPOSITS

■ IMPORTANT PEAT DEPOSITS

## ⊙ METALS AND NONMETALS

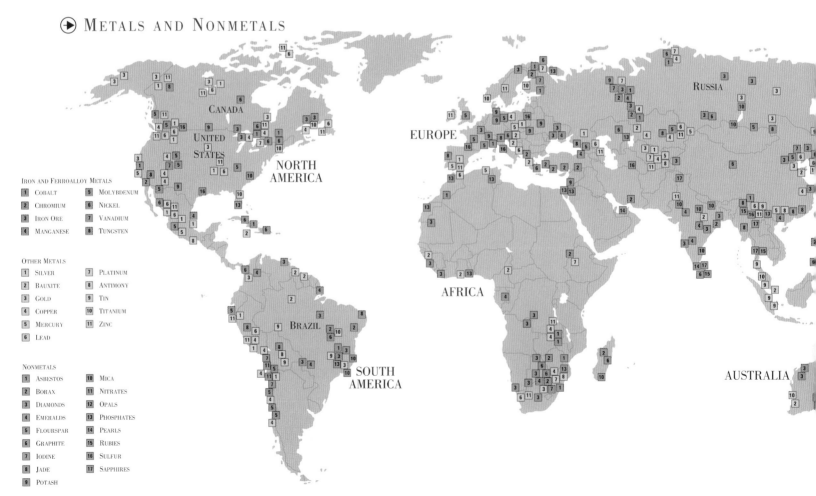

IRON AND FERROALLOY METALS

| 1 | COBALT | 5 | MOLYBDENUM |
| 2 | CHROMIUM | 6 | NICKEL |
| 3 | IRON ORE | 7 | VANADIUM |
| 4 | MANGANESE | 8 | TUNGSTEN |

OTHER METALS

| 1 | SILVER | 7 | PLATINUM |
| 2 | BAUXITE | 8 | ANTIMONY |
| 3 | GOLD | 9 | TIN |
| 4 | COPPER | 10 | TITANIUM |
| 5 | MERCURY | 11 | ZINC |
| 6 | LEAD | | |

NONMETALS

| 1 | ASBESTOS | 10 | MICA |
| 2 | BORAX | 11 | NITRATES |
| 3 | DIAMONDS | 12 | OPALS |
| 4 | EMERALDS | 13 | PHOSPHATES |
| 5 | FLOURSPAR | 14 | PEARLS |
| 6 | GRAPHITE | 15 | RUBIES |
| 7 | IODINE | 16 | SULFUR |
| 8 | JADE | 17 | SAPPHIRES |
| 9 | POTASH | | |

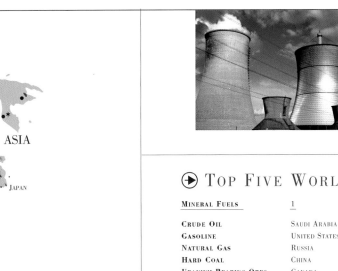

## ⊕ TOP FIVE WORLD PRODUCERS OF SELECTED MINERAL COMMODITIES

| MINERAL FUELS | 1 | 2 | 3 | 4 | 5 |
|---|---|---|---|---|---|
| CRUDE OIL | SAUDI ARABIA | RUSSIA | UNITED STATES | IRAN | CHINA |
| GASOLINE | UNITED STATES | JAPAN | CHINA | CANADA | RUSSIA |
| NATURAL GAS | RUSSIA | UNITED STATES | CANADA | UNITED KINGDOM | NETHERLANDS |
| HARD COAL | CHINA | UNITED STATES | INDIA | AUSTRALIA | SOUTH AFRICA |
| URANIUM-BEARING ORES | CANADA | AUSTRALIA | NIGER | RUSSIA | KAZAKHSTAN |

| METALS | | | | | |
|---|---|---|---|---|---|
| CHROMITE | SOUTH AFRICA | KAZAKHSTAN | INDIA | ZIMBABWE | TURKEY |
| IRON ORE | CHINA | BRAZIL | AUSTRALIA | RUSSIA | INDIA |
| MANGANESE ORE | SOUTH AFRICA | GABON | AUSTRALIA | BRAZIL | CHINA |
| MINE NICKEL | RUSSIA | AUSTRALIA | CANADA | INDONESIA | NEW CALEDONIA |
| MINE SILVER | MEXICO | PERU | CHINA | AUSTRALIA | UNITED STATES |
| BAUXITE | AUSTRALIA | GUINEA | BRAZIL | JAMAICA | CHINA |
| ALUMINUM | CHINA | RUSSIA | CANADA | UNITED STATES | AUSTRALIA |
| MINE GOLD | SOUTH AFRICA | AUSTRALIA | UNITED STATES | CHINA | RUSSIA |
| MINE COPPER | CHILE | INDONESIA | UNITED STATES | AUSTRALIA | RUSSIA |
| MINE LEAD | AUSTRALIA | CHINA | UNITED STATES | PERU | MEXICO |
| MINE TIN | CHINA | PERU | INDONESIA | BRAZIL | BOLIVIA |
| MINE ZINC | CHINA | AUSTRALIA | PERU | CANADA | UNITED STATES |

| NONMETALS | | | | | |
|---|---|---|---|---|---|
| NATURAL DIAMOND | AUSTRALIA | DEM. REP. OF THE CONGO | RUSSIA | BOTSWANA | SOUTH AFRICA |
| POTASH | CANADA | RUSSIA | BELARUS | GERMANY | ISRAEL |
| PHOSPHATE ROCK | UNITED STATES | CHINA | MOROCCO | RUSSIA | TUNISIA |
| SULFUR (ALL FORMS) | UNITED STATES | CANADA | RUSSIA | CHINA | JAPAN |

Names in Black Indicate More Than 10% of Total World Production

Source: U.S. Geological Survey, Mineral Commodity Summary; Handbook of International Economic Statistics

## ⊕ COMMERCIAL ENERGY PRODUCTION/CONSUMPTION

PERCENTAGE OF WORLD TOTAL
▨ PRODUCTION   ▨ CONSUMPTION

United States 15.9% / 22.5%

China 12.6% / 13.3%

Russia 11.7% / 6.7%

Saudi Arabia 5.5% / 1.4%

Canada 4.2% / 3.0%

Iran 2.7% / 1.4%

India 2.5% / 3.5%

Australia 2.4% / 1.2%

Norway 2.4% / 0.4%

Mexico 2.3% / 1.5%

United Kingdom 2.1% / 2.2%

Indonesia 2.0% / 1.0%

Venezuela 1.8% / 0.6%

Germany 1.4% / 3.3%

Source: U.S. Energy Information Administration

## ⊕ NATIONS WITH HIGHEST PERCENTAGE OF NUCLEAR POWER PRODUCTION

▨ NUCLEAR   ▨ THERMAL   ▨ HYDROELECTRIC

Belgium 98% / 1% / 1%

France 75% / 11% / 14%

South Korea 71% / 21% / 8%

Japan 65% / 9% / 26%

Finland 58% / 42%

Sweden 43% / 57%

Spain 41% / 40% / 19%

Switzerland 39% / 61%

Germany 26% / 71% / 3%

Hungary 22% / 78%

Ukraine 21% / 77% / 2%

Bulgaria 17% / 80% / 3%

United Kingdom 11% / 88% / 1%

United States 10% / 86% / 4%

ASIA

JAPAN

PAPUA NEW GUINEA

NEW ZEALAND

ASIA

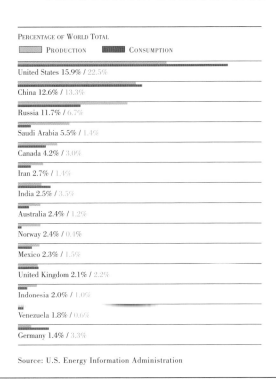

# Transportation and Trade

- World Exports by Region
- Trade Balances of Leading Export Nations

## ➤ WORLD EXPORTS BY REGION

PERCENT (BY VALUE) OF TOTAL EXPORTS

- ▢ To European Community
- ▢ To United States
- ▢ To Asia (excluding Japan)
- ▢ To Japan
- ▢ To European Free Trade Assn.
- ▢ To Canada
- ▢ To Latin America
- ▢ To Africa
- ▢ To Others

**EUROPEAN COMMUNITY**
| 25 | 20 | 17 | 8 | 5 | 5 | 20 |

**UNITED STATES**
| 24 | 20 | 20 | 15 | 12 | 9 |

**ASIA (EXCLUDING JAPAN)**
| 33 | 25 | 22 | 20 |

**JAPAN**
| 37 | 29 | 19 | 4 | 11 |

**EUROPEAN FREE TRADE ASSN.**
| 68 | 9 | 7 | 16 |

**CANADA**
| 76 | 8 | 6 | 5 | 5 |

**LATIN AMERICA**
| 43 | 30 | 8 | 7 | 12 |

**AFRICA**
| 62 | 20 | 6 | 12 |

**AUSTRALIA AND NEW ZEALAND**
| 35 | 28 | 13 | 11 | 13 |

## ➤ TRADE BALANCES OF LEADING EXPORT NATIONS

Source: CIA World Factbook

VALUE IN BILLIONS OF DOLLARS

▢ ANNUAL EXPORTS  ▢ ANNUAL IMPORTS  (DATA BASED ON AVERAGE OVER A 3-YEAR PERIOD)

Germany 869 / 701
United States 812 / 1488
China 590 / 527
Japan 512 / 400
France 403 / 411
United Kingdom 341 / 429
Italy 329 / 323
Canada 320 / 271
South Korea 247 / 215
Belgium 236 / 224
Mexico 187 / 194
Russia 181 / 98
Spain 175 / 230
Taiwan 165 / 156

Malaysia 123 / 97
Saudi Arabia 122 / 37
Sweden 117 / 95
Austria 103 / 101
Brazil 94 / 62
Australia 86/100
Thailand 83 / 69
Poland 75 / 80
Indonesia 72 / 49
India 68 / 92
Turkey 64 / 86
South Africa 43 / 42
Iran 41 / 33
Venezuela 38 / 17

## ⊙ HIGHWAYS AND AIRPORTS

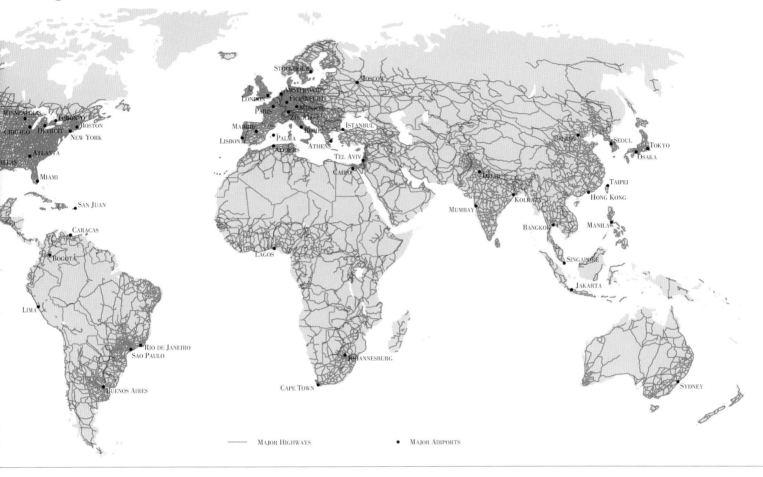

——— MAJOR HIGHWAYS          ● MAJOR AIRPORTS

## ⊙ RAILROADS, WATERWAYS, SEAPORT, AND SHIPPING ROUTES

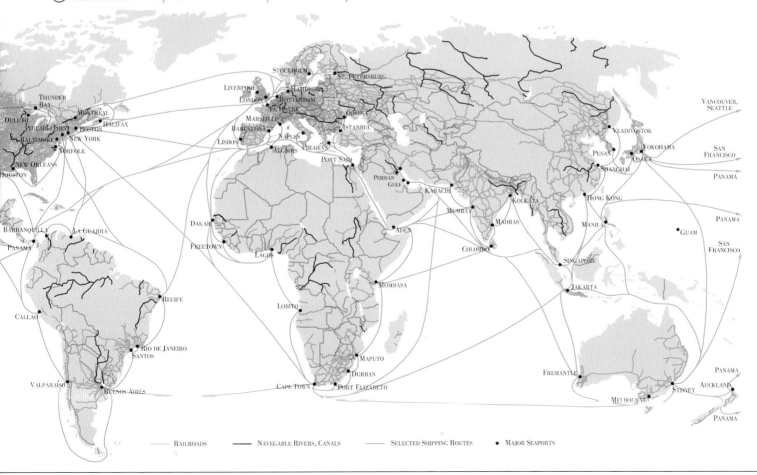

——— RAILROADS          ——— NAVEGABLE RIVERS, CANALS          ——— SELECTED SHIPPING ROUTES          ● MAJOR SEAPORTS

⊙ INTERNATIONAL RELATIONSHIPS

NEW ZEALAND
New Caledonia (FR.)
AUSTRALIA ■
PAPUA NEW GUINEA
EAST TIMOR
VANUATU
SOLOMON IS.
Lombok Strait
FIJI
PALAU
Makassar Strait
Jakarta
Sunda Strait
TUVALU
NAURU
BRUNEI
SING.
Strait of Malacca
PHILIPPINES ■ Manila ★
SOUTH CHINA SEA
VIETNAM
CAMBODIA
INDIAN
Wake I. (U.S.)
TAIWAN
Hong Kong ○
THAI-LAND ■
OCEAN
JAPAN $ ■
Korea Strait
MYANMAR (BURMA)
BAY OF BENGAL
SRI LANKA
Tōkyō
S. KOREA ■
LAOS
Midway Is. (U.S.)
La Pérouse Strait
Sea of Japan
N. KOREA ⊠
Beijing ★
CHINA ⊠
BANGLADESH
MALDIVES
OCEAN
Kuril Is.
Sea of Okhotsk
BHUTAN
INDIA ⊠
Mumbai (Bombay) ○
Hawaii (U.S.)
Bering Sea
Siberia
MONGOLIA
NEPAL
ARABIAN SEA
MAURITIUS
Aleutian Is.
KYR.
PAKISTAN ⊠
TAJ. ⚡
ALASKA (U.S.)
RUSSIA
KAZAKHSTAN ★
AFGHAN.
OMAN
ARCTIC OCEAN
⊠ ★ $
UZB.
Strait of Hormuz
U.A.E. ⊡
TURK.
IRAN ⊠
Persian Gulf
Ras Asér
+ NORTH POLE
AZER. ⚡
QATAR ⊡
BAH.
YEMEN
SOMALIA
MADAGASCAR
Moscow ★
ARM.
GEO. ⚡
IRAQ ⚡
KUWAIT ⊡
SAUDI ARABIA ⊡
Bab el Mandeb
COMOROS
CANADA $
Greenland (DEN.)
SYRIA
DJIBOUTI
Mozambique Channel
FINLAND
UKRAINE
TURKEY ⚡
JORDAN
Red Sea
ERI. ⚡
SWEDEN
BEL.
MOL.
ISR. ⚡
Suez Canal
ETHIOPIA
KENYA
NORWAY ▲
POLAND
ROM.
Black Sea
EGYPT
UNITED STATES $ ⊠
Danish Straits
DEN.
SLVK.
BUL.
GREECE
Dardanelles/Bosporus
SUDAN ⚡
UGANDA
TANZANIA
MOZAMBIQUE
MEXICO
ICELAND ▲
NORTH SEA
GER.
HUN.
MEDITERRANEAN SEA
MALAWI
Gulf of Mexico
UNITED KINGDOM
CZ.
M.
B. ALB.
ITALY
LIBYA ⊡
RWA.
BUR.
ZIMBABWE
Washington ★
IRE.
$⊠
FRANCE $
M.
TUNISIA
CHAD
CENT. AFR. REP.
DEM. REP. OF THE CONGO
ZAMBIA
SWAZ.
C. Race
English Channel
⊠
SPAIN
CAMEROON
CONGO
ANGOLA
LES.
Azores (PORT.)
PORTUGAL ★
ALGERIA ⊡
NIGER
SOUTH AFRICA
GUATEMALA
BEL.
Strait of Gibraltar
MOROCCO
MALI
BURKINA FASO
BENIN
NIGERIA ⊡
E. G.
GABON
NAMIBIA
BOTSWANA
EL SAL.
HON.
CUBA
Bermuda (U.K.)
W. SAHARA (Occ. by Morocco)
TOGO
SÃO TOMÉ & PRÍNCIPE
Cape of Good Hope
NIC.
JAM.
BAHAMAS
MAURITANIA
GHANA
Cape Town ★
COSTA RICA
HAITI
DOMINICAN REP.
Mona Passage
SENEGAL
GUINEA
CÔTE D'IVOIRE
PANAMA
Caribbean Sea
Windward Passage
G.-B.
CAPE VERDE
Panama Canal
WEST INDIES
St. Lucia Channel
SIERRA LEONE
LIBERIA
ECUADOR
COLOMBIA
VENEZUELA ⊡
St. Vincent & Grenada-Tobago Passages
GUYANA
PERU
SURINAME
FRENCH GUIANA

PACIFIC OCEAN
ATLANTIC OCEAN
KIRIBATI
CAPE VERDE

BOLIVIA
BRAZIL
C. de São Roque
CHILE
PARAGUAY
ARGENTINA
Rio de Janeiro ★
Buenos Aires ★
URUGUAY

INTERNATIONAL RELATIONSHIPS

|  | NORTH ATLANTIC TREATY ORGANIZATION (NATO) |
| --- | --- |
|  | ORGANIZATION OF AMERICAN STATES (OAS)-INCLUDES U.S. & CANADA |
|  | FORMER WARSAW PACT NATIONS NOW UNDERGOING DEMOCRATIC REFORMS |
|  | ASSOCIATION OF SOUTHEAST ASIAN NATIONS (ASEAN) - INCLUDES CAMBODIA, LAOS, VIETNAM |
|  | COMMUNIST GOVERNMENTS |
|  | COMMONWEALTH OF INDEPENDENT STATES (CIS) |
|  | LEAGUE OF ARAB STATES |

■ COUNTRIES HAVING DEFENSE TREATIES WITH THE U.S. (EXCLUDING NATO AND OAS)
⊡ ORGANIZATION OF PETROLEUM EXPORTING COUNTRIES (OPEC)
● EUROPEAN UNION (EU)
▲ EUROPEAN FREE TRADE ASSOCIATION
⚡ UNITED NATIONS PEACEKEEPING AREAS
⊠ NUCLEAR WEAPON STATES
⊠ SUSPECTED NUCLEAR WEAPONS STATES
⁓ SELECTED STRATEGIC WATERWAYS
$ GROUP OF SEVEN (G-7)
★ FORMER U.S.S.R.

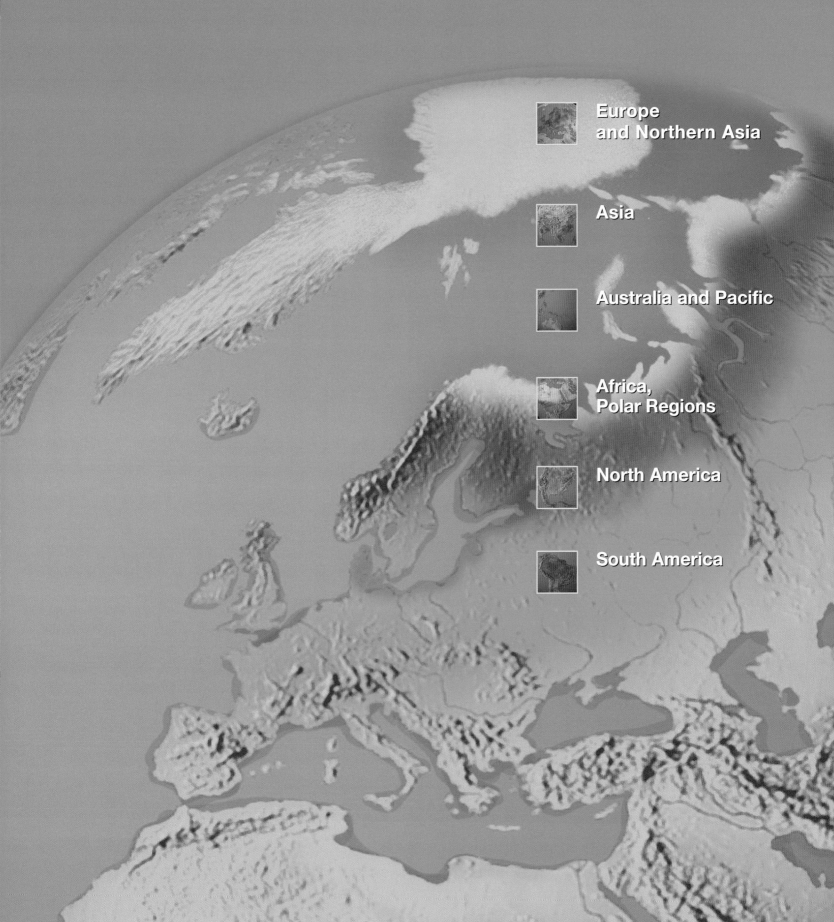

# Regional Maps

Europe
and Northern Asia

Asia

Australia and Pacific

Africa,
Polar Regions

North America

South America

# Europe - Physical

SCALE 1:21,000,000    OPTIMAL CONFORMAL PROJECTION

MILES       0        300        600        900
KILOMETERS  0   300        600        900

POPULATION OF CITIES AND TOWNS

| | | |
|---|---|---|
| ■ OVER 3,000,000 | ◉ 500,000 - 999,999 | ○ UNDER 100,000 |
| ▣ 1,000,000 - 2,999,999 | ⊙ 100,000 - 499,999 | |

► Europe Comparisons:  Pages 40 - 41
► Global relationships:  Pages 14 - 36
► Index of the World:  Pages 97 - 104

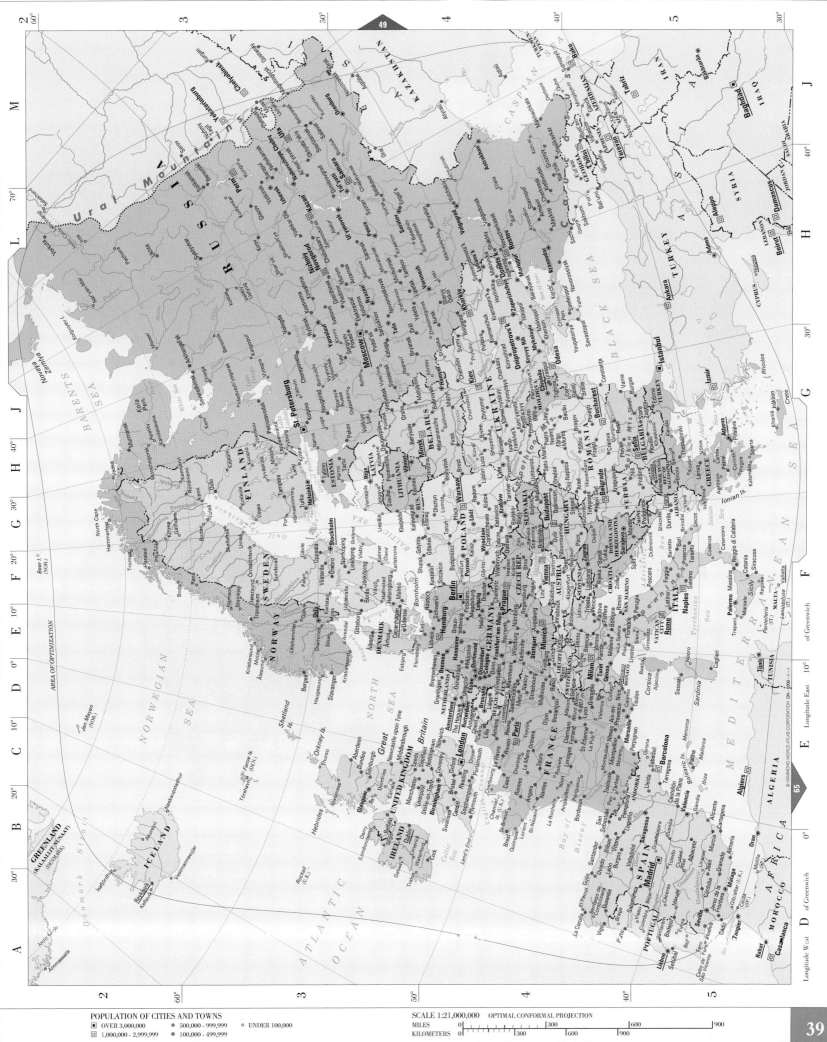

POPULATION OF CITIES AND TOWNS

▣ OVER 3,000,000          ● 500,000 - 999,999          ○ UNDER 100,000
▣ 1,000,000 - 2,999,999   ● 100,000 - 499,999

SCALE 1:21,000,000   OPTIMAL CONFORMAL PROJECTION

MILES          0      300          600          900
KILOMETERS  0        300      600      900

# Europe - Comparisons

► Europe Physical / Political: Pages 38 - 39
► Global Relationships: Pages 14 - 36
► Index of the World: Pages 97 - 104

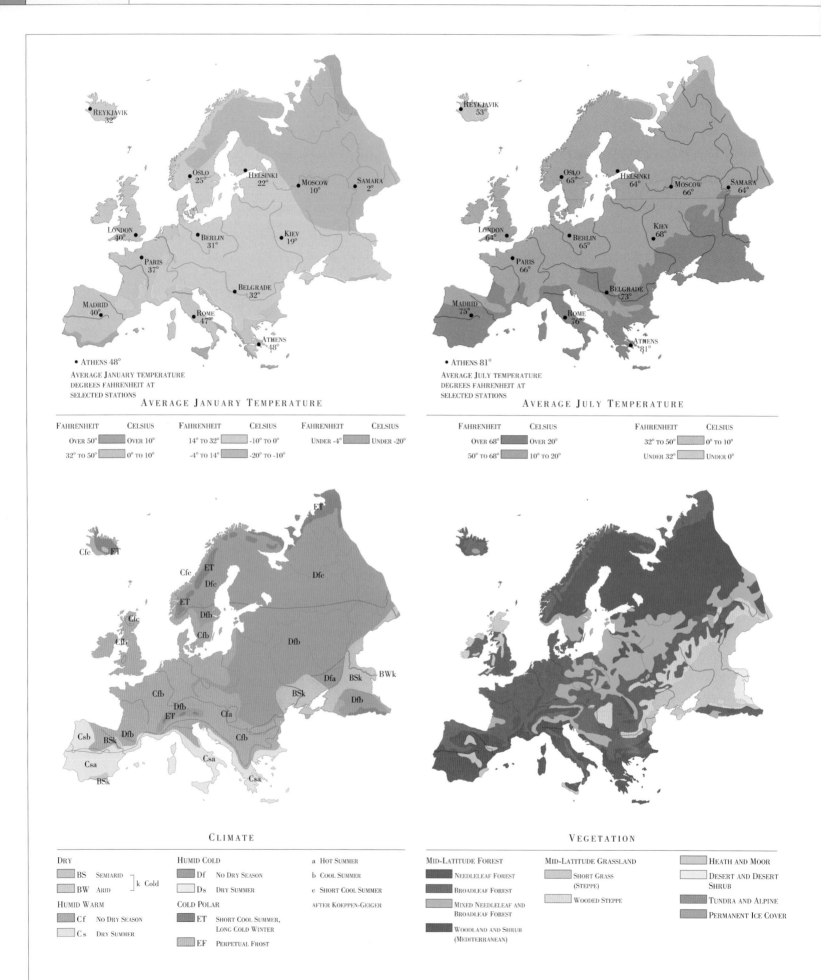

REYKJAVIK 32°
OSLO 25°
HELSINKI 22°
MOSCOW 10°
SAMARA 2°
LONDON 40°
BERLIN 31°
KIEV 19°
PARIS 37°
BELGRADE 32°
MADRID 40°
ROME 47°
ATHENS 48°

● ATHENS 48°
AVERAGE JANUARY TEMPERATURE
DEGREES FAHRENHEIT AT
SELECTED STATIONS

## AVERAGE JANUARY TEMPERATURE

| FAHRENHEIT | CELSIUS | FAHRENHEIT | CELSIUS | FAHRENHEIT | CELSIUS |
|---|---|---|---|---|---|
| OVER 50° | OVER 10° | 14° TO 32° | -10° TO 0° | UNDER -4° | UNDER -20° |
| 32° TO 50° | 0° TO 10° | -4° TO 14° | -20° TO -10° | | |

REYKJAVIK 53°
OSLO 65°
HELSINKI 64°
MOSCOW 66°
SAMARA 64°
LONDON 64°
BERLIN 65°
KIEV 68°
PARIS 66°
BELGRADE 73°
MADRID 75°
ROME 76°
ATHENS 81°

● ATHENS 81°
AVERAGE JULY TEMPERATURE
DEGREES FAHRENHEIT AT
SELECTED STATIONS

## AVERAGE JULY TEMPERATURE

| FAHRENHEIT | CELSIUS | FAHRENHEIT | CELSIUS |
|---|---|---|---|
| OVER 68° | OVER 20° | 32° TO 50° | 0° TO 10° |
| 50° TO 68° | 10° TO 20° | UNDER 32° | UNDER 0° |

## CLIMATE

(Climate map labels: ET, Cfc, Dfc, Dfb, Cfb, Dfa, BSk, BWk, BSk, Cfa, Csb, Csa, Cs, Csa)

AFTER KOEPPEN-GEIGER

| DRY | | HUMID COLD | | a HOT SUMMER |
|---|---|---|---|---|
| BS | SEMIARID | Df | NO DRY SEASON | b COOL SUMMER |
| BW | ARID | Ds | DRY SUMMER | c SHORT COOL SUMMER |

k Cold

| HUMID WARM | | COLD POLAR | |
|---|---|---|---|
| Cf | NO DRY SEASON | ET | SHORT COOL SUMMER, LONG COLD WINTER |
| Cs | DRY SUMMER | EF | PERPETUAL FROST |

## VEGETATION

| MID-LATITUDE FOREST | MID-LATITUDE GRASSLAND | HEATH AND MOOR |
|---|---|---|
| NEEDLELEAF FOREST | SHORT GRASS (STEPPE) | DESERT AND DESERT SHRUB |
| BROADLEAF FOREST | WOODED STEPPE | TUNDRA AND ALPINE |
| MIXED NEEDLELEAF AND BROADLEAF FOREST | | PERMANENT ICE COVER |
| WOODLAND AND SHRUB (MEDITERRANEAN) | | |

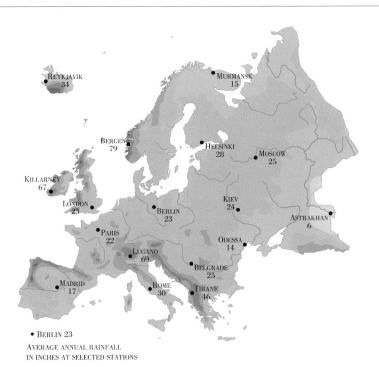

• BERLIN 23
AVERAGE ANNUAL RAINFALL
IN INCHES AT SELECTED STATIONS

## AVERAGE ANNUAL RAINFALL

| INCHES | CM | INCHES | CM | INCHES | CM |
|---|---|---|---|---|---|
| OVER 80 | OVER 200 | 40 TO 60 | 100 TO 150 | 10 TO 20 | 25 TO 50 |
| 60 TO 80 | 150 TO 200 | 20 TO 40 | 50 TO 100 | UNDER 10 | UNDER 25 |

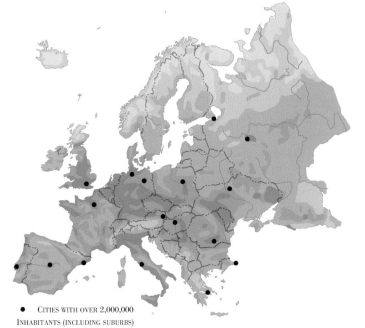

• CITIES WITH OVER 2,000,000
INHABITANTS (INCLUDING SUBURBS)

## POPULATION DISTRIBUTION

| DENSITY PER | | SQ. MI. | SQ. KM. | SQ. MI. | SQ. KM. |
|---|---|---|---|---|---|
| SQ. MI. | SQ. KM. | 130 TO 260 | 50 TO 100 | 3 TO 25 | 1 TO 10 |
| OVER 260 | OVER 100 | 25 TO 130 | 10 TO 50 | UNDER 3 | UNDER 1 |

## ENERGY SOURCES

 OIL REGION    COAL   HYDROELECTRICITY
NATURAL GAS REGION   LIGNITE   * URANIUM

## ENVIRONMENTAL CONCERNS

 POLLUTED RIVERS   AREAS SUBJECT TO DEFORESTATION   EXTENT OF ACID RAIN
 EXTENT OF COASTAL POLLUTION   AREAS SUBJECT TO DESERTIFICATION   • URBAN AREAS WITH SEVERE AIR POLLUTION

© Copyright by HAMMOND WORLD ATLAS CORPORATION, Union, N.J.

41

# Western Europe

► Europe Comparisons: Pages 40 - 41
► Global relationships: Pages 14 - 36
► Index of the World: Pages 97 - 104

Below Sea | 200 | 500 | 1,000 | 1,500 | 2,000 | 4,000 | 6,000 m.
Sea Lev. Level | 700 | 1,600 | 3,300 | 5,000 | 6,500 | 13,000 | 19,700 ft.

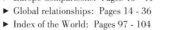

► Europe Comparisons: Pages 40 - 41
► Global relationships: Pages 14 - 36
► Index of the World: Pages 97 - 104

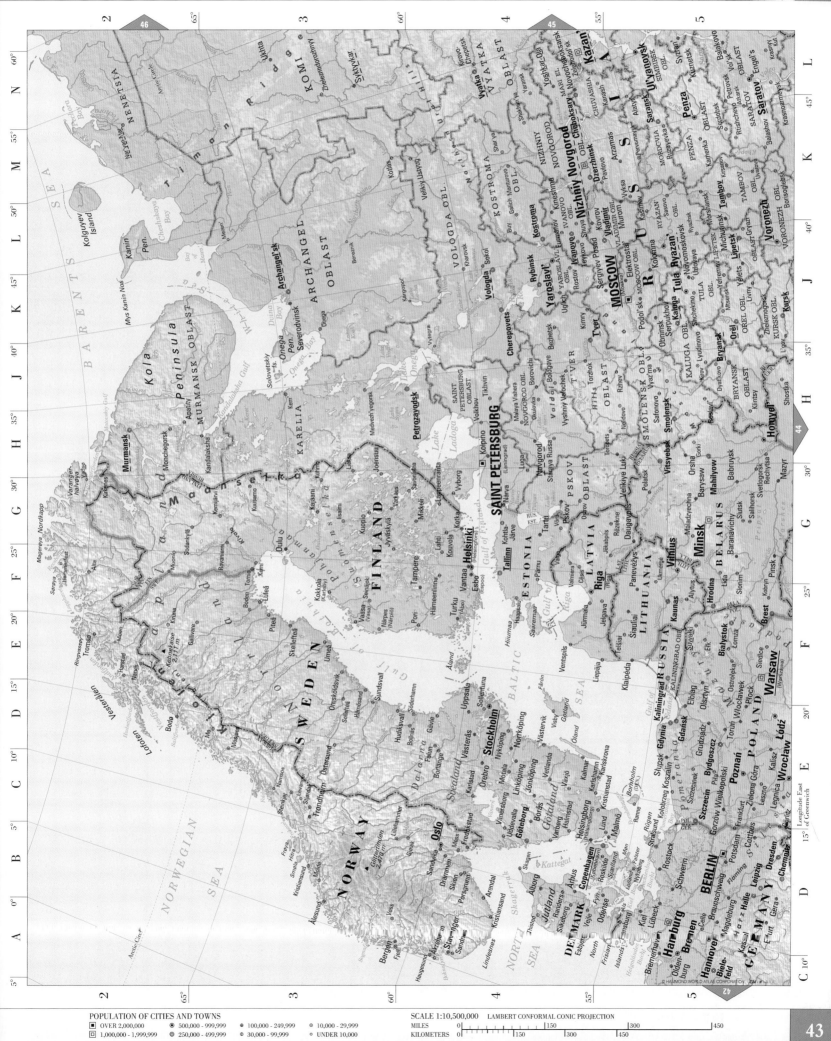

POPULATION OF CITIES AND TOWNS

| | |
|---|---|
| ■ OVER 2,000,000 | ⊛ 500,000 - 999,999 |
| ▣ 1,000,000 - 1,999,999 | ⊕ 250,000 - 499,999 |

| | |
|---|---|
| ⊕ 100,000 - 249,999 | ○ 10,000 - 29,999 |
| ⊙ 30,000 - 99,999 | ∘ UNDER 10,000 |

SCALE 1:10,500,000   LAMBERT CONFORMAL CONIC PROJECTION

MILES   0      150      300      450
KILOMETERS  0   150   300   450

# South Central Europe

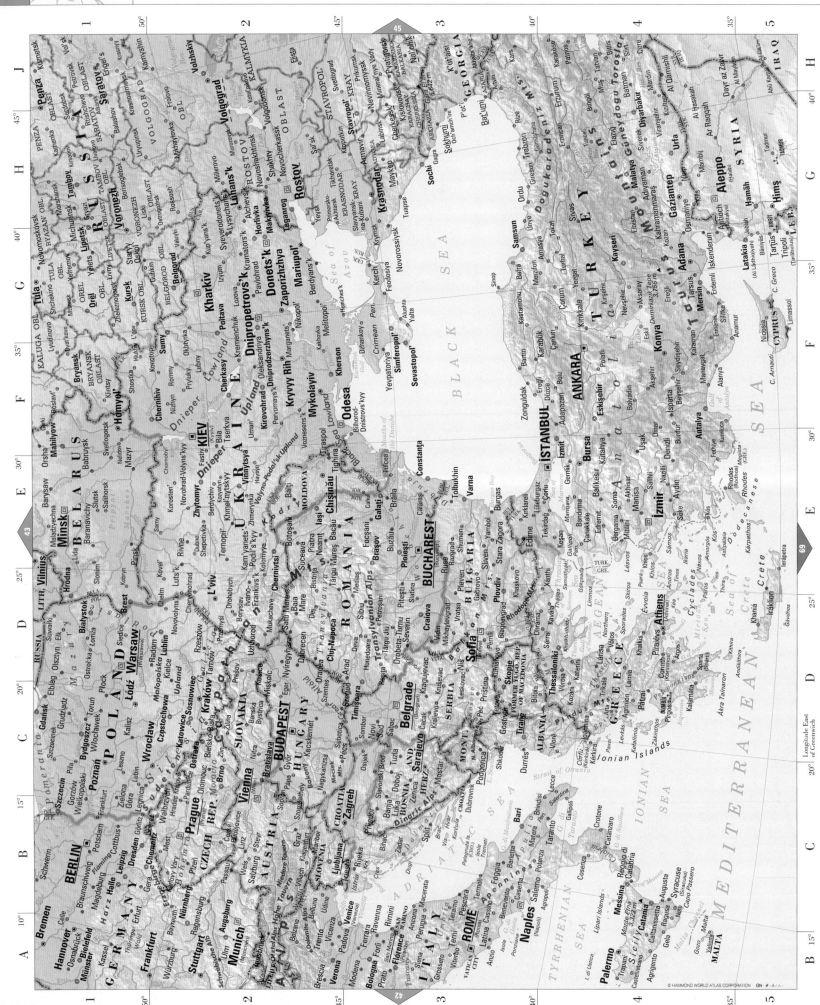

Below Sea 200 500 1,000 1,500 2,000 4,000 6,000 m.
Sea Lev. Level 700 1,600 3,300 5,000 6,500 13,000 19,700 ft.

► Europe Comparisons: Pages 40 - 41
► Global relationships: Pages 14 - 36
► Index of the World: Pages 97 - 104

POPULATION OF CITIES AND TOWNS

■ OVER 2,000,000  ◉ 500,000 - 999,999   ● 100,000 - 249,999   ◉ 10,000 - 29,999
▣ 1,000,000 - 1,999,999   ◎ 250,000 - 499,999   ● 30,000 - 99,999   ○ UNDER 10,000

SCALE 1:10,500,000   LAMBERT CONFORMAL CONIC PROJECTION

MILES    0        150        300        450
KILOMETERS  0   150   300   450

Below Sea Sea Lev. Level 200 500 1,000 1,500 2,000 4,000 6,000 m. 700 1,600 3,300 5,000 6,500 13,000 19,700 ft.

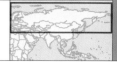

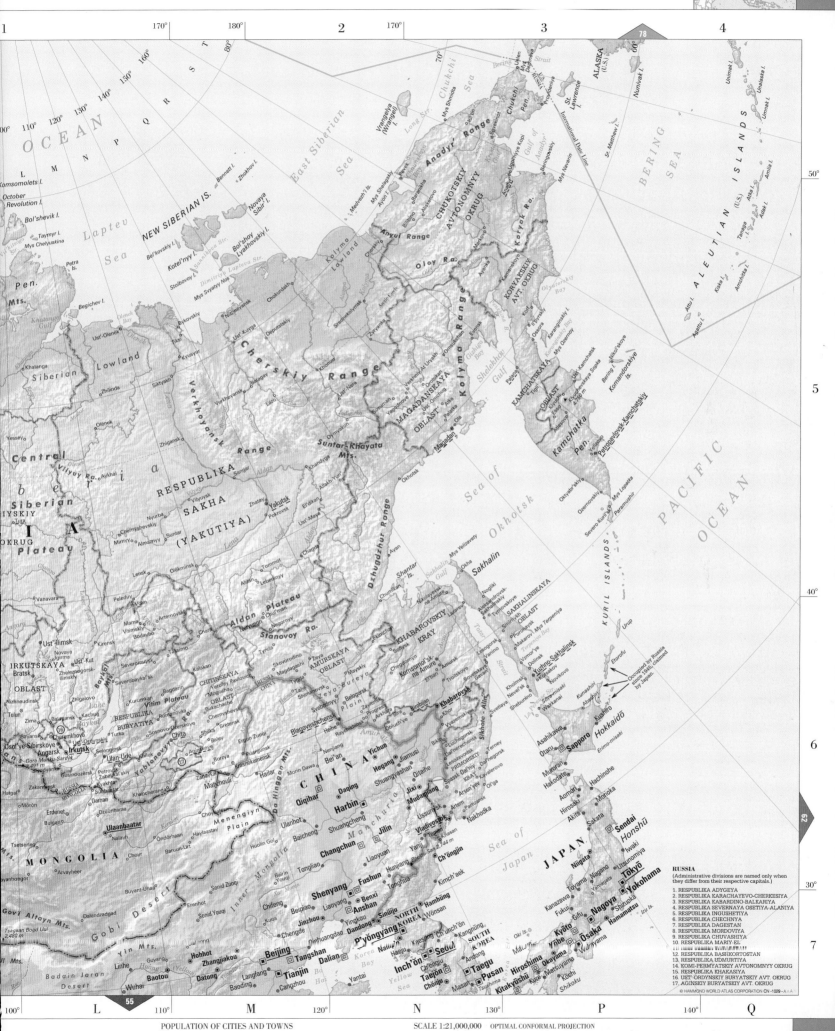

RUSSIA
(Administrative divisions are named only when they differ from their respective capitals.)

1. RESPUBLIKA ADYGEYA
2. RESPUBLIKA KARACHAYEVO-CHERKESIYA
3. RESPUBLIKA KABARDINO-BALKARIYA
4. RESPUBLIKA SEVERNAYA OSETIYA-ALANIYA
5. RESPUBLIKA INGUSHETIYA
6. RESPUBLIKA CHECHNYA
7. RESPUBLIKA DAGESTAN
8. RESPUBLIKA MORDOVIYA
9. RESPUBLIKA CHUVASHIYA
10. RESPUBLIKA MARIY-EL
11. RESPUBLIKA TATARSTAN
12. RESPUBLIKA BASHKORTOSTAN
13. RESPUBLIKA UDMURTIYA
14. KOMI-PERMYATSKIY AVTONOMNYY OKRUG
15. RESPUBLIKA KHAKASIYA
16. UST'-ORDYNSKIY BURYATSKIY AVT. OKRUG
17. AGINSKIY BURYATSKIY AVT. OKRUG

© HAMMOND WORLD ATLAS CORPORATION CN -1029 - A A A

POPULATION OF CITIES AND TOWNS

| ☐ OVER 2,000,000 | ◉ 500,000 - 999,999 | ◦ 50,000 - 99,999 |
| ☐ 1,000,000 - 1,999,999 | ● 100,000 - 499,999 | ○ UNDER 50,000 |

SCALE 1:21,000,000    OPTIMAL CONFORMAL PROJECTION

MILES       0                    300            600            900
KILOMETERS  0          300            600            900

# Asia-Physical

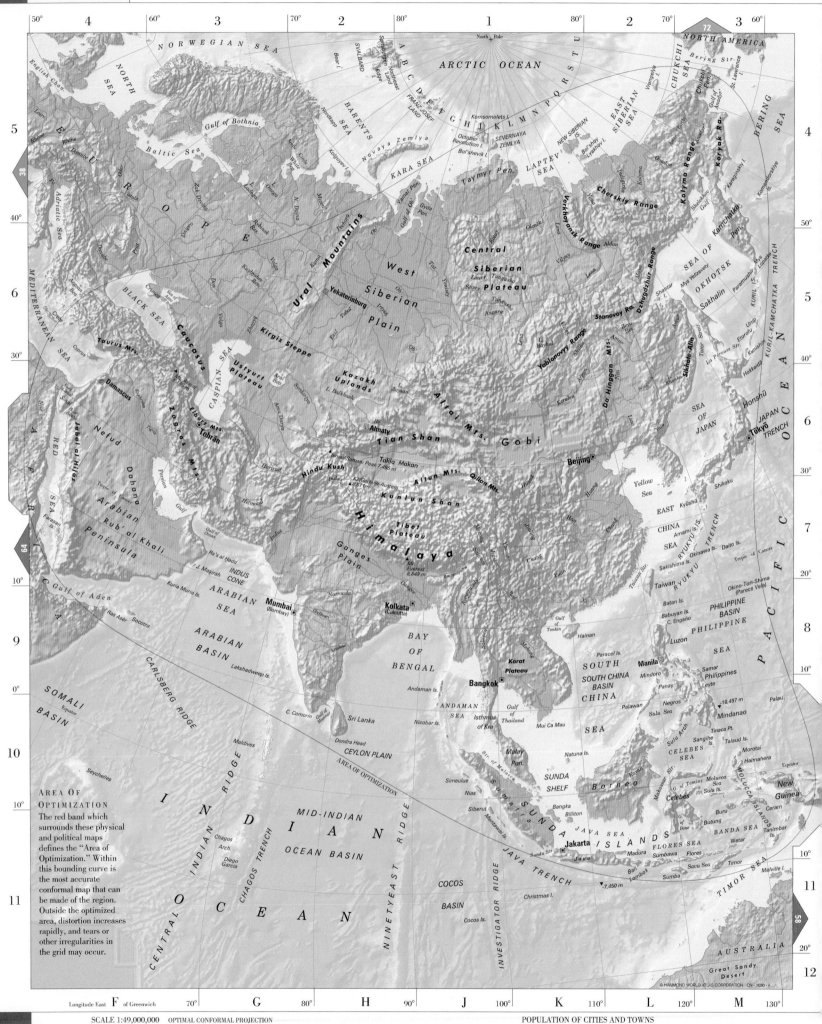

## AREA OF OPTIMIZATION

The red band which surrounds these physical and political maps defines the "Area of Optimization." Within this bounding curve is the most accurate conformal map that can be made of the region. Outside the optimized area, distortion increases rapidly, and tears or other irregularities in the grid may occur.

SCALE 1:49,000,000  OPTIMAL CONFORMAL PROJECTION

MILES 0    700    1400    2100

KILOMETERS 0    700    1400    2100

POPULATION OF CITIES AND TOWNS

- ◼ OVER 3,000,000
- ◻ 1,000,000 - 2,999,999
- ● 500,000 - 999,999
- ◉ 100,000 - 499,999
- ○ UNDER 100,000

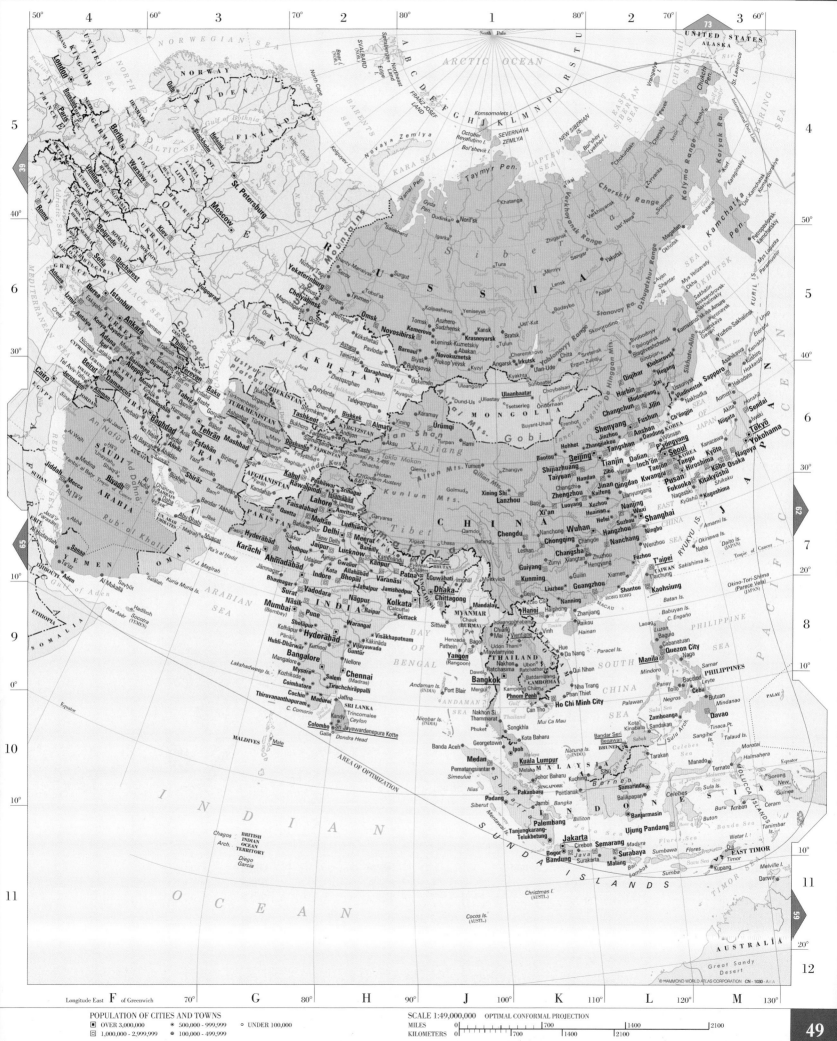

POPULATION OF CITIES AND TOWNS

■ OVER 3,000,000    ● 500,000 - 999,999    ○ UNDER 100,000
◪ 1,000,000 - 2,999,999    ◉ 100,000 - 499,999

SCALE 1:49,000,000    OPTIMAL CONFORMAL PROJECTION

MILES  0         700      1400      2100
KILOMETERS  0    700      1400      2100

© HAMMOND WORLD ATLAS CORPORATION  CN - 1030 - A - A A

# Asia - Comparisons

► Asia Physical / Political: Pages 48 - 49
► Global Relationships: Pages 14 - 36
► Index of the World: Pages 97 - 104

ASIA

• TOKYO 38°
AVERAGE JANUARY TEMPERATURE
DEGREES FAHRENHEIT AT
SELECTED STATIONS

**AVERAGE JANUARY TEMPERATURE**

| FAHRENHEIT | CELSIUS | FAHRENHEIT | CELSIUS | FAHRENHEIT | CELSIUS |
|---|---|---|---|---|---|
| OVER 68° | OVER 20° | 14° TO 32° | -10° TO 0° | -40° TO -22° | -40° TO -30° |
| 50° TO 68° | 10° TO 20° | -4° TO 14° | -20° TO -10° | UNDER -40° | UNDER -40° |
| 32° TO 50° | 0° TO 10° | -22° TO -4° | -30° TO -20° | | |

• TOKYO 77°
AVERAGE JULY TEMPERATURE
DEGREES FAHRENHEIT AT
SELECTED STATIONS

**AVERAGE JULY TEMPERATURE**

| FAHRENHEIT | CELSIUS | FAHRENHEIT | CELSIUS | FAHRENHEIT | CELSIUS |
|---|---|---|---|---|---|
| OVER 86° | OVER 30° | 50° TO 68° | 10° TO 20° | UNDER 32° | UNDER 0° |
| 68° TO 86° | 20° TO 30° | 32° TO 50° | 0° TO 10° | | |

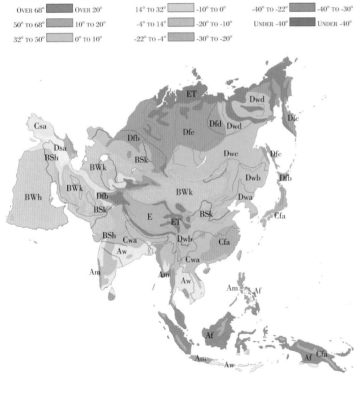

**CLIMATE**

HUMID TROPICAL
- Af NO DRY SEASON
- Am SHORT DRY SEASON
- Aw DRY WINTER

DRY
- BS SEMIARID ⎤ h HOT
- BW ARID ⎦ k COLD

AFTER KOEPPEN-GEIGER

HUMID WARM
- Cf NO DRY SEASON
- Cw DRY WINTER
- Cs DRY SUMMER

HUMID COLD
- Df NO DRY SEASON
- Dw DRY WINTER
- Ds DRY SUMMER

COLD POLAR
- ET SHORT COOL SUMMER, LONG COLD WINTER
- E COLD AND UNCLASSIFIED HIGHLANDS

a HOT SUMMER
b COOL SUMMER
c SHORT COOL SUMMER
d VERY COLD WINTER

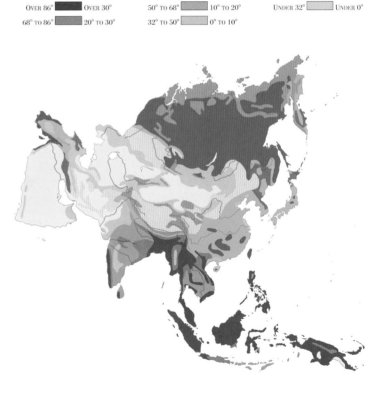

**VEGETATION**

TROPICAL FOREST
- TROPICAL RAINFOREST
- LIGHT TROPICAL FOREST
- WOODLAND AND SHRUB

TROPICAL GRASSLAND
- GRASS AND SHRUB (SAVANNA)
- WOODED SAVANNA

MID-LATITUDE FOREST
- NEEDLELEAF FOREST
- BROADLEAF FOREST
- MIXED NEEDLELEAF AND BROADLEAF FOREST
- WOODLAND AND SHRUB (MEDITERRANEAN)

MID-LATITUDE GRASSLAND
- SHORT GRASS (STEPPE)
- WOODED STEPPE
- DESERT AND DESERT SHRUB
- TUNDRA AND ALPINE
- UNCLASSIFIED HIGHLANDS

• TOKYO 62
AVERAGE ANNUAL RAINFALL
IN INCHES AT SELECTED STATIONS

● CITIES WITH OVER 3,000,000
INHABITANTS (INCLUDING SUBURBS)

## AVERAGE ANNUAL RAINFALL

| INCHES | CM | INCHES | CM | INCHES | CM |
|---|---|---|---|---|---|
| OVER 80 | OVER 200 | 40 TO 60 | 100 TO 150 | 10 TO 20 | 25 TO 50 |
| 60 TO 80 | 150 TO 200 | 20 TO 40 | 50 TO 100 | UNDER 10 | UNDER 25 |

## POPULATION DISTRIBUTION

| DENSITY PER | | SQ. MI. | SQ. KM. | SQ. MI. | SQ. KM. |
|---|---|---|---|---|---|
| SQ. MI. | SQ. KM. | 130 TO 260 | 50 TO 100 | 3 TO 25 | 1 TO 10 |
| OVER 260 | OVER 100 | 25 TO 130 | 10 TO 50 | UNDER 3 | UNDER 1 |

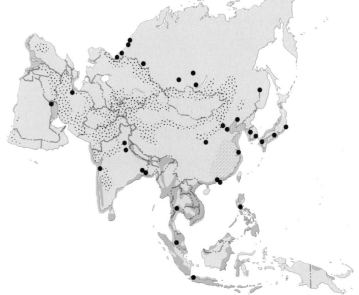

## ENERGY SOURCES

| | | |
|---|---|---|
| OIL REGION | ■ COAL | ● HYDROELECTRICITY |
| NATURAL GAS REGION | ■ LIGNITE | ✳ URANIUM |

## ENVIRONMENTAL CONCERNS

| POLLUTED RIVERS | AREAS SUBJECT TO DEFORESTATION | EXTENT OF ACID RAIN |
|---|---|---|
| EXTENT OF COASTAL POLLUTION | AREAS SUBJECT TO DESERTIFICATION | ● URBAN AREAS WITH SEVERE AIR POLLUTION |

© HAMMOND WORLD ATLAS CORPORATION   GN - # - A

| | Below Sea | 200 | 500 | 1,000 | 1,500 | 2,000 | 4,000 | 6,000 m. |
|---|---|---|---|---|---|---|---|---|
| | Sea Lev. Level | 700 | 1,600 | 3,300 | 5,000 | 6,500 | 13,000 | 19,700 ft. |

# Indian Subcontinent

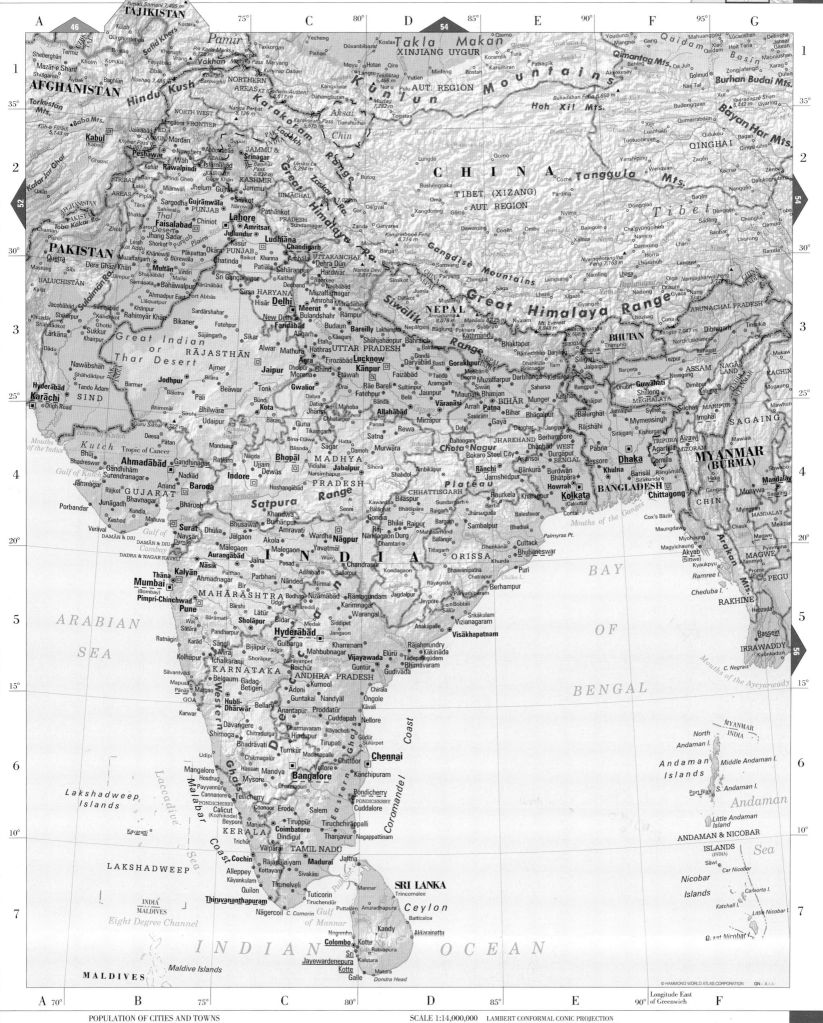

POPULATION OF CITIES AND TOWNS

- ▣ OVER 2,000,000
- ▣ 1,000,000 - 1,999,999
- ● 500,000 - 999,999
- ● 100,000 - 499,999
- ○ 50,000 - 99,999
- ○ UNDER 50,000

SCALE 1:14,000,000    LAMBERT CONFORMAL CONIC PROJECTION

MILES        0        200        400        600

KILOMETERS 0        200        400        600

© HAMMOND WORLD ATLAS CORPORATION        GN - A-A-A

Below Sea 200 500 1,000 1,500 2,000 4,000 6,000 m.
Sea Lev. Level 700 1,600 3,300 5,000 6,500 13,000 19,700 ft.

RUSSIA

SEA OF OKHOTSK

Khabarovsk

Sakhalin

Hokkaidō

Sapporo

Vladivostok

SEA OF JAPAN

HEILONGJIANG

Harbin

Qiqihar

Daqing

NEI MONGGOL ZIZHIQU

MONGOLIA

Changchun

Jilin

JILIN

NORTH KOREA

P'yŏngyang

Shenyang

LIAONING

Beijing

TIANJIN

HEBEI

SOUTH KOREA

Seoul

Inch'ŏn

Taejŏn

Taegu

Pusan

Tokyo

Yokohama

Nagoya

Ōsaka

Kōbe

Kyōto

Hiroshima

Fukuoka

Kitakyūshū

SHANXI

Taiyuan

SHANDONG

Jinan

Qingdao

Shijiazhuang

Zhengzhou

HENAN

YELLOW SEA

JIANGSU

Nanjing

Shanghai

ANHUI

Hefei

Wuhan

HUBEI

Changsha

HUNAN

Nanchang

JIANGXI

Hangzhou

ZHEJIANG

Ningbo

EAST CHINA SEA

FUJIAN

Fuzhou

T'aipei

TAIWAN

T'ainan

Kaohsiung

GUANGDONG

Guangzhou

HONG KONG

MACAU

PACIFIC OCEAN

Ryukyu Islands

Okinawa

Naha

Tropic of Cancer

SOUTH CHINA SEA

PHILIPPINES

© HAMMOND WORLD ATLAS CORPORATION  EM - 0001 - A.A.A

POPULATION OF CITIES AND TOWNS

| ■ OVER 2,000,000 | ● 500,000 - 999,999 | ○ 50,000 - 99,999 |
| □ 1,000,000 - 1,999,999 | ● 100,000 - 499,999 | ○ UNDER 50,000 |

SCALE 1:14,000,000   LAMBERT CONFORMAL CONIC PROJECTION

MILES 0   200   400   600
KILOMETERS 0   200   400   600

Maungdaw
Magyichaung
Akyab
(Sittwe)
Ramree I.
Cheduba I.
RAKHINE
Bay
of
Bengal
C. Negrais
Mouths of the Ayeyarwady

Myohaung Chauk Meiktila Taunggyi
MANDALAY
Yenangyaung Magwe
MAGWE
MYANMAR
(BURMA)
PEGU
Prome
(Pyel)
Henzada
Bassein
IRRAWADDY
Yangon
(Rangoon)
Kyônkadun

Shan Plateau
SHAN
Loi-Kaw
Chiang Rai
Chiang Mai
Doi Inthanon
2,600 m
Lampang
Phrae
KAYAH
KARAN
Pa-an
Moulmein
MON
Tak
Nakhon Sawan
Phitsanulok
Sara Buri
THAILAND
Nakhon Ratchasima
Bangkok
(Krung Thep)

Muang Xay
Louangphrabang
Ban Ban
Nan
Nong Khai
Vientiane
(Viangchan)
Udon Thani
Nakhon
Phanom
Savannakhet
Ubon Ratchathani
Phanom Dongrak Mts.

Xam Nua
Bai Thuong
Phou Bia
Leng 2,718 m
LAOS
Khammouan
Muang Khammouan

Haiphong
(Hai Phong)
Nam Dinh
Thanh Hoa
Vinh
Quang Tri
Hue
Da Nang
Hoi An
Tam Ky
Quang Ngai

Leizhou
Pen.
Dan Xian
Dongfang
Hainan
HAINAN
Yulin
Wenchang
Haikou
Xuwen
Haikang

CHINA

Gulf of
Tonkin

Dongsha I.
(CHINA)

Paracel Islands
(Sovereignty disputed)

SOUTH CHINA
SEA

Scarborough
Shoal

MYANMAR
INDIA
North
Andaman I.
Middle Andaman I.
Andaman
Islands
S. Andaman I.
Port Blair
Little Andaman
Island
ANDAMAN & NICOBAR
ISLANDS
(INDIA)
Car Nicobar
Nicobar
Islands
Camorta I.
Katchall I.
Little Nicobar I.
Great Nicobar I.

Tenasserim
Tavoy
Bilauktaung Ra.
Palaw
Mergui
Mergui
Archipelago
Chumphon
Isthmus
of Kra
Phangan I.
Samui I.
Nakhon Si
Thammarat

Chon Buri
Rat Buri
Phet Buri
Sa Kaeo
Chanthaburi
Chang I.
Kut I.
Gulf
of
Thailand

Battambang
Tonle
Sap
CAMBODIA
Phnum Aoral
1,771 m
Phnom Penh
(Phnum Penh)
Kampong
Saom
Kravanh Mts.
Kompong
Cham
Kompong
Loung Xuyen
Con Son

Pakxe
Muang
May
Champasak
Kon Tum
Pleiku
(Play Cu)
Tay Ninh
Bien Hoa
Ho Chi Minh City
(Saigon)
My Tho
Rach
Gia
Can Tho
Soc Trang
Bac Lieu
Ca Mau
Mui Ca Mau
Phu Quoc I.

Ngoc Linh
2,600 m
Qui Nhon
Tuy Hoa
Buon Me Thuot
Da Lat
Nha Trang
Cam Ranh
Phan Rang
Phan Thiet

VIETNAM

Spratly Islands
(Sovereignty disputed)

Roxas
Puerto
Princesa
Narra
Palawan
Brooke's Point
Balabac

Phuket
Trang
Hat Yai
Songkhla
Yala
Kota Baharu
Alor Setar
Langkawi I.
Sungai Petani
Georgetown
Pinang I.
Taiping
Ipoh
Telok Anson
Kuala Terengganu
Kuantan

Natuna
Is.
Bunguran I.
Anambas
Is.
Subi I.

Cagayan
Sulu I.
MALAYSIA
Gunung Kinabalu
4,101 m
Kota Kinabalu
Kampong
Telupid
Sukau
BRUNEI
Bandar Seri Begawan
Miri
Gunung
Murud 2,438 m

Sandakan
Tambisa
Lahad Datu
Pensiangan
Mostyn
Semporna
Sabah

We I.
Sabang
Banda Aceh
Pusat Gayo Mts.
Gunung Leuser
3,466 m
Langsa
Medan
Pematangsiantar
Tebingtinggi
Simeulue I.
Tuangku
Banyak
Islands
Nias I.
Sibolga
Barus
Padangsidempuan
Pakanbaru
Bengkalis I.

MALAYSIA
Malaya
Kelang
Shah Alam
Kuala Lumpur
Seremban
Melaka
Segamat
Keluang
Batu Pahat
Johor Baharu
Singapore
SINGAPORE

Tioman I.

Serasan
Tambelan
Is.
Riau Islands
Lingga
Is.
Singkep I.

Pamangkat
Singkawang
Pontianak
Ngabang
Sintang

Sibu
Saratok
Kuching
Sarawak
Borneo
Kapuas Hulu Mts.
Gunung Liangpran
2,240 m
Muller Mts.
Kalimantan
Schwaner Mts.
Bukit Raya 2,278 m

Kampong
Kuamut
Lumbis
Malinau
Banyu I.
Tarakan
Samarinda
Balikpapan
Kotabaru
Sebuku I.
Laut I.

Equator
Batu
Islands
Tanahbala I.
Siberut I.
Sipura I.
Mentawai
Islands
Gunung Pasaman
2,912 m
Bukittinggi
Payakumbuh
Padang
Gunung Kerinci
3,805 m
Barisan Mountains
Curup
Sumatra
Bengkulu
Gunung Dempo
3,159 m
Baturaja
Menggala
Kotabumi

Rengat
Jambi
Muntok
Pangkalpinang
Palembang
Bangka I.
Belitung I.
Tanjungpandan
Maya I.
Karimata I.

Sampit
Palangkaraya
Banjarmasin
Barabai
Meratus Mts.

IND
INDIAN
OCEAN

Enggano I.
Tanjungkarang
Serang
Jakarta
Bogor
Bandung
Panaitan I.
Sunda Strait

Greater
Sunda
Islands
JAVA SEA

Bawean I.
Kangean Is.
Madura

Cirebon
Pekalongan
Tegal
Gunung Galunggung
2,958 m
Surakarta
Cilacap
Yogyakarta
Semarang
Madiun
Kediri
Gunung
Kelud
3,676 m
Java
Gunung Agung
3,142 m
Malang
Gunung
Semeru
3,676 m
Surabaya
Probolinggo
Jember
Bali
Lesser
Moyo I.
Denpasar
Lombok
Sumbawa

Flo
Bali
Sea

Sumba

Below Sea    200    500    1,000  1,500  2,000  4,000  6,000 m.
Sea Lev. Level    700    1,600  3,300  5,000  6,500  13,000  19,700 ft.

▶ Asia Comparisons: Pages 50 - 51
▶ Global relationships: Pages 14 - 36
▶ Index of the World: Pages 97 - 104

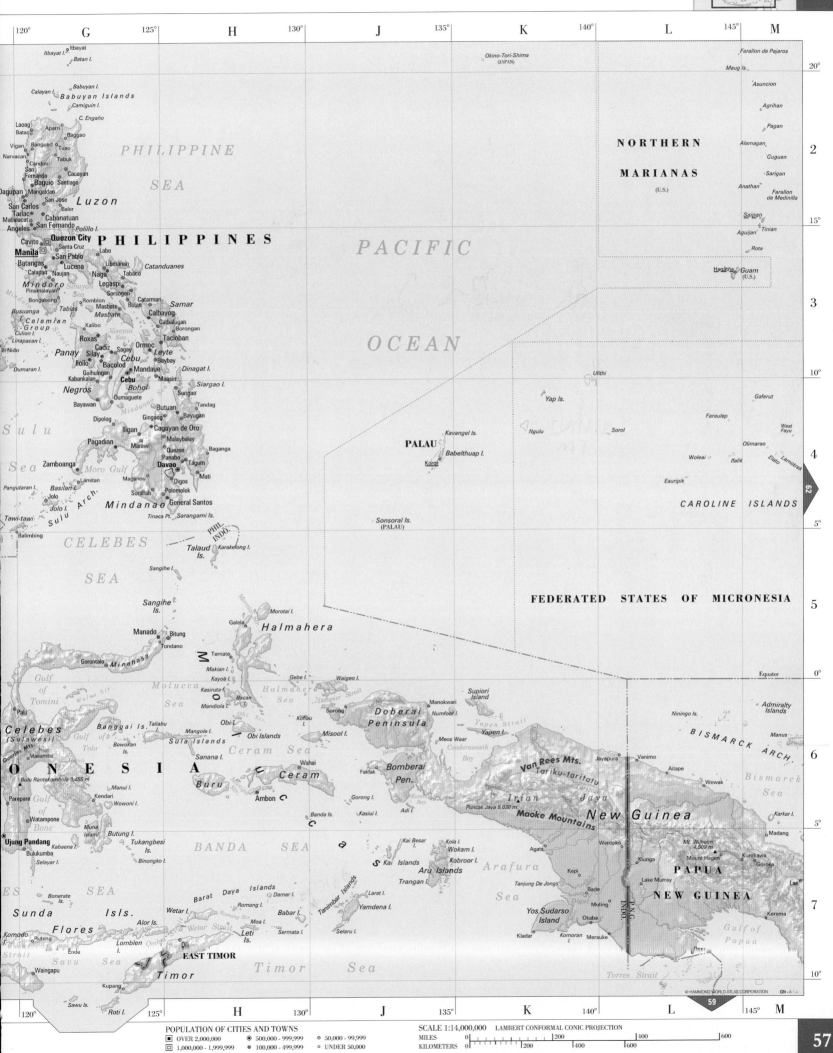

POPULATION OF CITIES AND TOWNS

■ OVER 2,000,000      ◉ 500,000 - 999,999      ⊙ 50,000 - 99,999
□ 1,000,000 - 1,999,999      ● 100,000 - 499,999      ○ UNDER 50,000

SCALE 1:14,000,000      LAMBERT CONFORMAL CONIC PROJECTION

MILES  0      200      400      600
KILOMETERS  0      200      400      600

# Australia, New Zealand - Physical

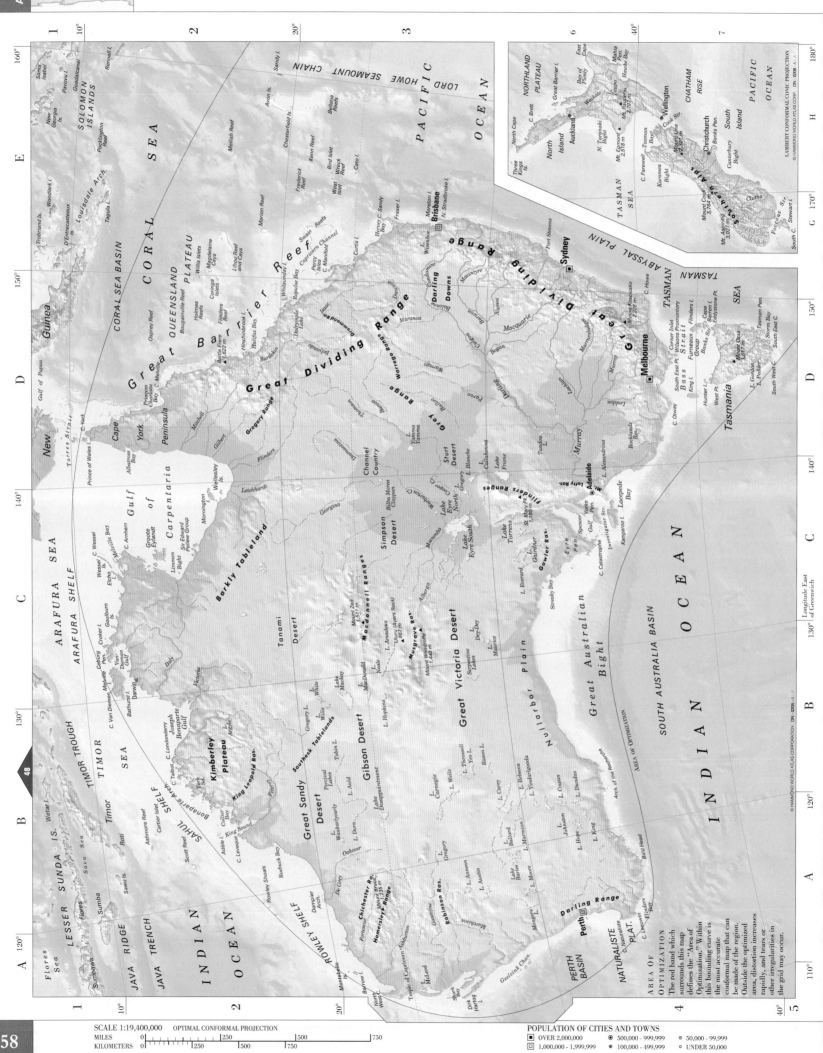

SCALE 1:19,400,000    OPTIMAL CONFORMAL PROJECTION

MILES    0      250      500      750

KILOMETERS    0    250    500    750

POPULATION OF CITIES AND TOWNS

▢ OVER 2,000,000          ● 500,000 - 999,999       ◦ 50,000 - 99,999
▢ 1,000,000 - 1,999,999   ● 100,000 - 499,999       ◦ UNDER 50,000

# Australia, New Zealand - Political

► Australia Comparisons: Pages 60 - 61
► Global relationships: Pages 14 - 36
► Index of the World: Pages 97 - 104

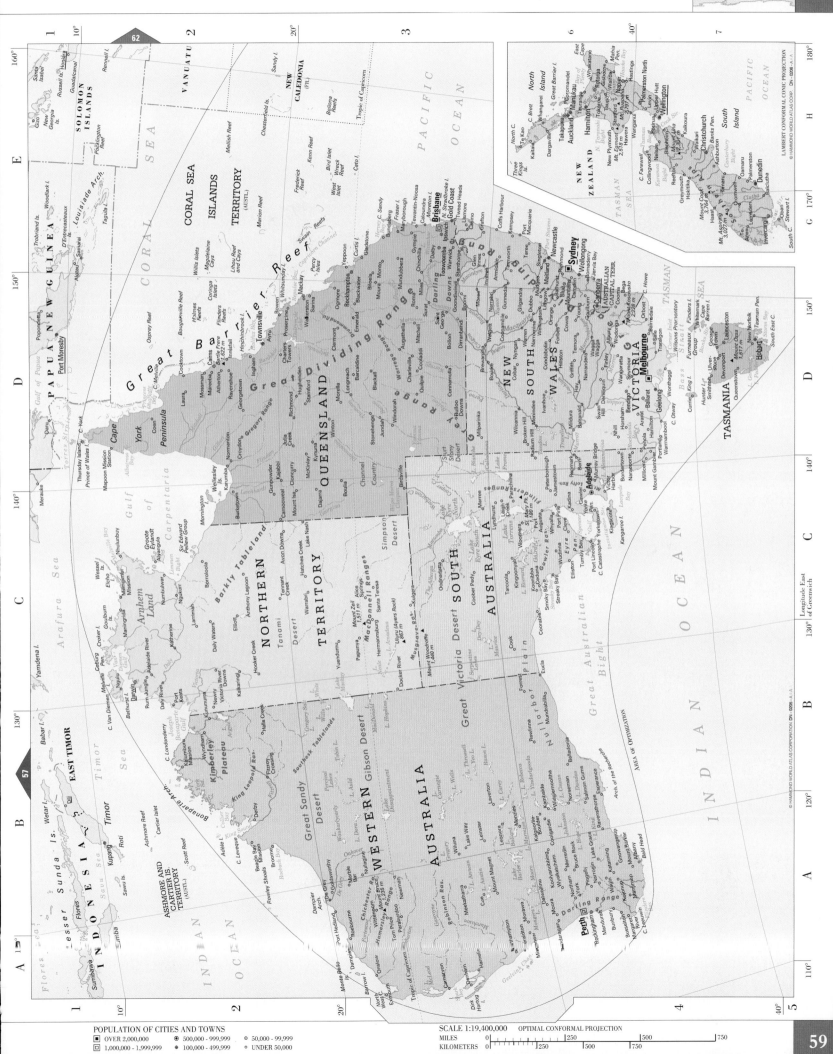

# Australia, New Zealand - Comparisons

AUSTRALIA

▶ Australia Physical / Political: Pages 58 - 59
▶ Global Relationships: Pages 14 - 36
▶ Index of the World: Pages 97 - 104

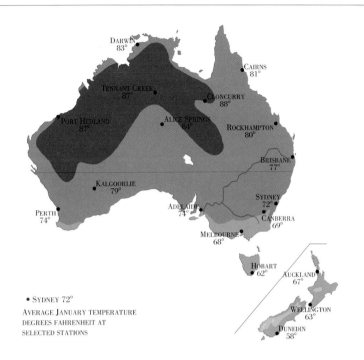

DARWIN 83°
CAIRNS 81°
TENNANT CREEK 87°
CLONCURRY 88°
PORT HEDLAND 87°
ALICE SPRINGS 84°
ROCKHAMPTON 80°
BRISBANE 77°
KALGOORLIE 79°
SYDNEY 72°
PERTH 74°
ADELAIDE 74°
CANBERRA 69°
MELBOURNE 68°
HOBART 62°
AUCKLAND 67°
WELLINGTON 63°
DUNEDIN 58°

• SYDNEY 72°
AVERAGE JANUARY TEMPERATURE
DEGREES FAHRENHEIT AT
SELECTED STATIONS

## AVERAGE JANUARY TEMPERATURE

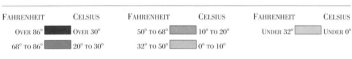

| FAHRENHEIT | CELSIUS | FAHRENHEIT | CELSIUS | FAHRENHEIT | CELSIUS |
|---|---|---|---|---|---|
| OVER 86° | OVER 30° | 50° TO 68° | 10° TO 20° | UNDER 32° | UNDER 0° |
| 68° TO 86° | 20° TO 30° | 32° TO 50° | 0° TO 10° | | |

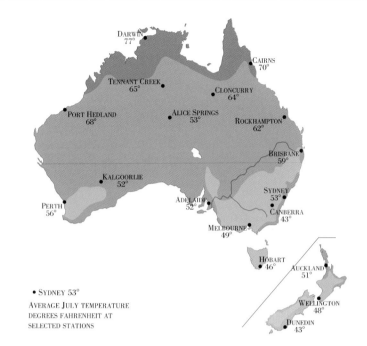

DARWIN 77°
CAIRNS 70°
TENNANT CREEK 65°
CLONCURRY 64°
PORT HEDLAND 68°
ALICE SPRINGS 53°
ROCKHAMPTON 62°
BRISBANE 59°
KALGOORLIE 52°
SYDNEY 53°
PERTH 56°
ADELAIDE 52°
CANBERRA 43°
MELBOURNE 49°
HOBART 46°
AUCKLAND 51°
WELLINGTON 48°
DUNEDIN 43°

• SYDNEY 53°
AVERAGE JULY TEMPERATURE
DEGREES FAHRENHEIT AT
SELECTED STATIONS

## AVERAGE JULY TEMPERATURE

| FAHRENHEIT | CELSIUS | FAHRENHEIT | CELSIUS |
|---|---|---|---|
| OVER 68° | OVER 20° | 32° TO 50° | 0° TO 10° |
| 50° TO 68° | 10° TO 20° | UNDER 32° | UNDER 0° |

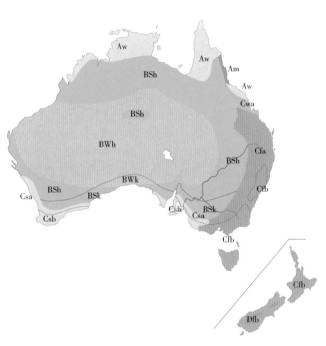

Aw
Aw
BSh
Am
Aw
BSh
Cwa
BWh
Cfa
BSh
BWk
Cfb
Csa
BSh
BSk
Csb
Csb
BSk
Csa
Cfb
Cfb
Dfb

## CLIMATE

HUMID TROPICAL
Am SHORT DRY SEASON
Aw DRY WINTER

DRY
BS SEMIARID ⌉ h HOT
BW ARID ⌋ k COLD

HUMID WARM
Cf NO DRY SEASON
Cw DRY WINTER
Cs DRY SUMMER

HUMID COLD
Df NO DRY SEASON
a HOT SUMMER
b COOL SUMMER

AFTER KOEPPEN-GEIGER

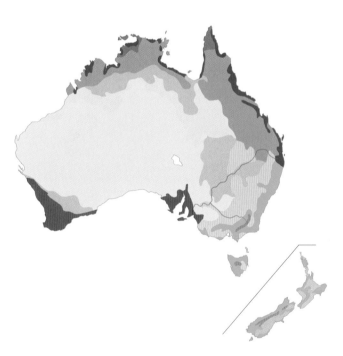

## VEGETATION

TROPICAL FOREST
TROPICAL RAINFOREST
LIGHT TROPICAL FOREST
WOODLAND AND SHRUB

TROPICAL GRASSLAND
GRASS AND SHRUB (SAVANNA)
WOODED SAVANNA

MID-LATITUDE FOREST
MIXED NEEDLELEAF AND BROADLEAF FOREST
MIXED WOODLAND
WOODLAND AND SHRUB (MEDITERRANEAN)

MID-LATITUDE GRASSLAND
SCRUB AND FERNLANDS
DESERT AND DESERT SHRUB
ALPINE

# Australia, New Zealand - Comparisons

► Australia Physical / Political: Pages 58 - 59
► Global Relationships: Pages 14 - 36
► Index of the World: Pages 97 - 104

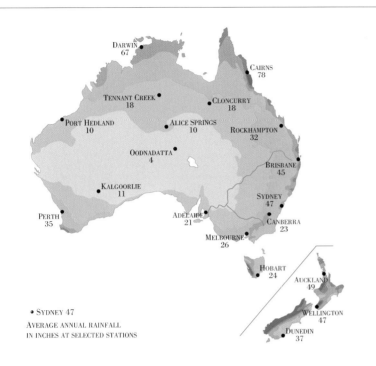

● SYDNEY 47
AVERAGE ANNUAL RAINFALL
IN INCHES AT SELECTED STATIONS

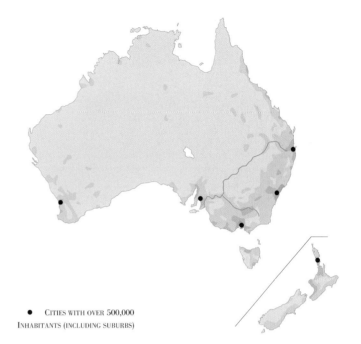

● CITIES WITH OVER 500,000
INHABITANTS (INCLUDING SUBURBS)

## AVERAGE ANNUAL RAINFALL

| INCHES | CM | INCHES | CM | INCHES | CM |
|---|---|---|---|---|---|
| OVER 80 | OVER 200 | 40 TO 60 | 100 TO 150 | 10 TO 20 | 25 TO 50 |
| 60 TO 80 | 150 TO 200 | 20 TO 40 | 50 TO 100 | UNDER 10 | UNDER 25 |

## POPULATION DISTRIBUTION

| DENSITY PER | | SQ. MI. | SQ. KM. | SQ. MI. | SQ. KM. |
|---|---|---|---|---|---|
| SQ. MI. | SQ. KM. | 25 TO 130 | 10 TO 50 | UNDER 3 | UNDER 1 |
| OVER 130 | OVER 50 | 3 TO 25 | 1 TO 10 | | |

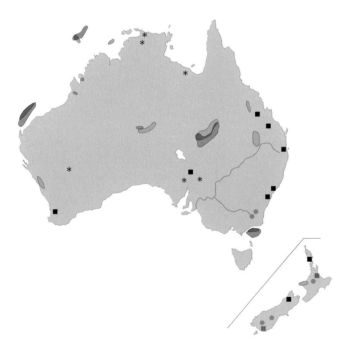

## ENERGY SOURCES

| | | |
|---|---|---|
| ▭ OIL REGION | ■ COAL | ● HYDROELECTRICITY |
| ▭ NATURAL GAS REGION | ■ LIGNITE | ✳ URANIUM |

## ENVIRONMENTAL CONCERNS

| | | |
|---|---|---|
| ∿ POLLUTED RIVERS | ▭ AREAS SUBJECT TO DEFORESTATION | ▦ AREAS SUBJECT TO DESERTIFICATION |
| ▦ EXTENT OF COASTAL POLLUTION | | |

Below Sea 200 500 1,000 1,500 2,000 4,000 6,000 m.
Sea Lev. Level 700 1,600 3,300 5,000 6,500 13,000 19,700 ft.

▶ Australia Comparisons:  Pages 60 - 61
▶ Global relationships:  Pages 14 - 36
▶ Index of the World:  Pages 97 - 104

POPULATION OF CITIES AND TOWNS

◼ OVER 3,000,000          ◉ 500,000 - 999,999          ○ UNDER 100,000
◪ 1,000,000 - 2,999,999   ◎ 100,000 - 499,999

SCALE 1:31,500,000    LAMBERT AZIMUTHAL EQUAL-AREA PROJECTION

MILES      0       400        800        1200
KILOMETERS 0   400      800     1200

© HAMMOND WORLD ATLAS CORPORATION    CN - 55 - A - A - A

# Africa - Physical

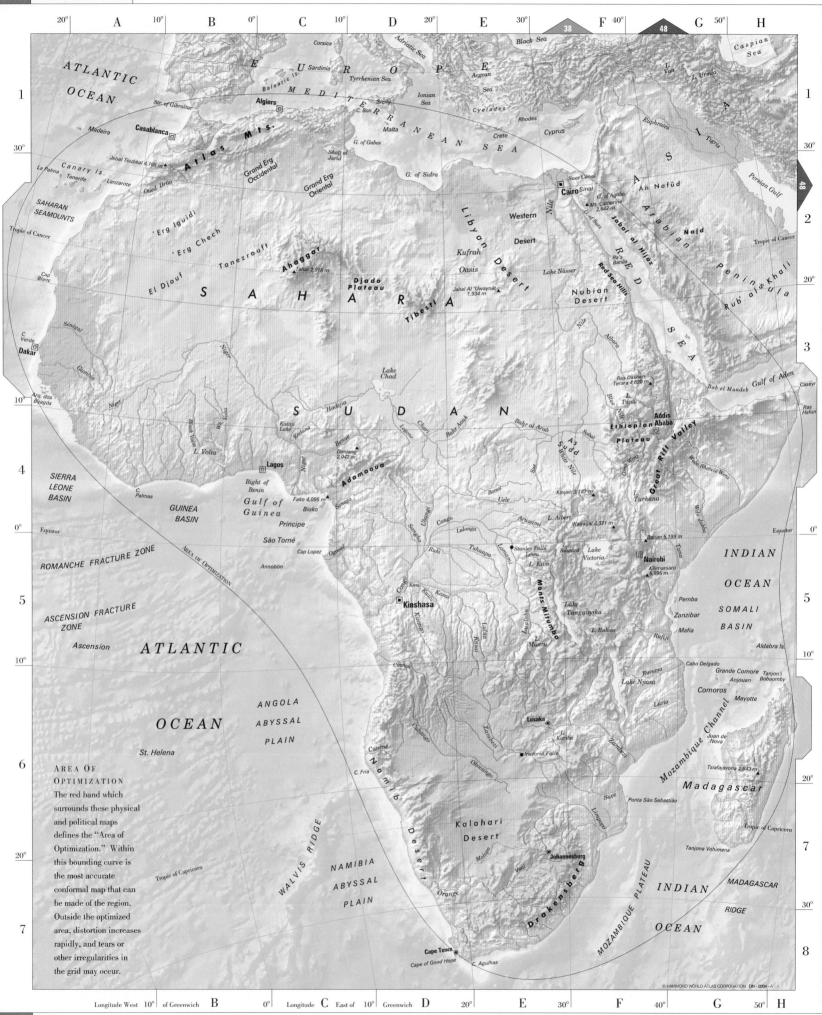

AREA OF OPTIMIZATION The red band which surrounds these physical and political maps defines the "Area of Optimization." Within this bounding curve is the most accurate conformal map that can be made of the region. Outside the optimized area, distortion increases rapidly, and tears or other irregularities in the grid may occur.

SCALE 1:35,000,000    OPTIMAL CONFORMAL PROJECTION

MILES   0 ___ 500 ___ 1000 ___ 1500

KILOMETERS   0 ___ 500 ___ 1000 ___ 1500

POPULATION OF CITIES AND TOWNS

▣ OVER 3,000,000          ● 500,000 - 999,999          ○ UNDER 100,000
▢ 1,000,000 - 2,999,999   ● 100,000 - 499,999

© HAMMOND WORLD ATLAS CORPORATION   DN - 0204 - A - A

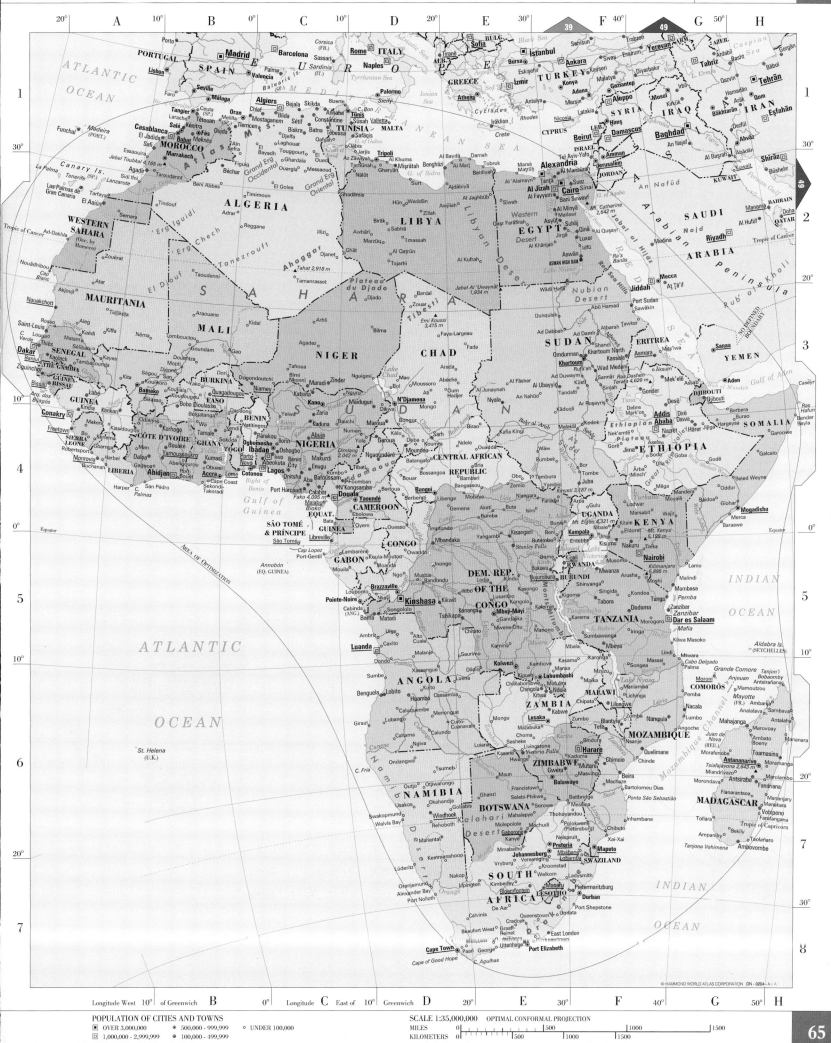

POPULATION OF CITIES AND TOWNS

☐ OVER 3,000,000        ● 500,000 - 999,999        ○ UNDER 100,000
☐ 1,000,000 - 2,999,999    ● 100,000 - 499,999

SCALE 1:35,000,000    OPTIMAL CONFORMAL PROJECTION

MILES 0 ____ 500 ____ 1000 ____ 1500
KILOMETERS 0 ___ 500 ___ 1000 ___ 1500

Longitude West 10° of Greenwich B    0° Longitude C East of 10° Greenwich D    20° E    30° F    40° G    50° H

© HAMMOND WORLD ATLAS CORPORATION   DN - 0204 - AAA

# Africa - Comparisons

● LAGOS 81°
AVERAGE JANUARY TEMPERATURE
DEGREES FAHRENHEIT AT
SELECTED STATIONS

### AVERAGE JANUARY TEMPERATURE

| FAHRENHEIT | CELSIUS | | FAHRENHEIT | CELSIUS |
|---|---|---|---|---|
| OVER 68° | OVER 20° | | 32° TO 50° | 0° TO 10° |
| 50° TO 68° | 10° TO 20° | | UNDER 32° | UNDER 0° |

● LAGOS 79°
AVERAGE JULY TEMPERATURE
DEGREES FAHRENHEIT AT
SELECTED STATIONS

### AVERAGE JULY TEMPERATURE

| FAHRENHEIT | CELSIUS | | FAHRENHEIT | CELSIUS |
|---|---|---|---|---|
| OVER 86° | OVER 30° | | 50° TO 68° | 10° TO 20° |
| 68° TO 86° | 20° TO 30° | | UNDER 50° | UNDER 10° |

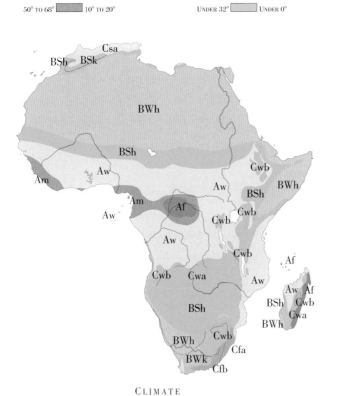

### CLIMATE

**HUMID TROPICAL**
- Af  NO DRY SEASON
- Am  SHORT DRY SEASON
- Aw  DRY WINTER

**DRY**
- BS  SEMIARID  ⎤ h HOT
- BW  ARID  ⎦ k COLD

**HUMID WARM**
- Cf  NO DRY SEASON
- Cw  DRY WINTER
- Cs  DRY SUMMER

a  HOT SUMMER
b  COOL SUMMER

AFTER KOEPPEN-GEIGER

### VEGETATION

**TROPICAL FOREST**
- TROPICAL RAINFOREST
- LIGHT TROPICAL FOREST
- WOODLAND AND SHRUB

**TROPICAL GRASSLAND**
- GRASS AND SHRUB (SAVANNA)
- WOODED SAVANNA

**MID-LATITUDE FOREST**
- MIXED NEEDLELEAF AND BROADLEAF FOREST
- WOODLAND AND SHRUB (MEDITERRANEAN)

**MID-LATITUDE GRASSLAND**
- SHORT GRASS (STEPPE)

- DESERT AND DESERT SHRUB
- RIVER VALLEY AND OASIS
- UNCLASSIFIED HIGHLANDS

# Africa - Comparisons

► Africa Physical / Political: Pages 64 - 65
► Global Relationships: Pages 14 - 36
► Index of the World: Pages 97 - 104

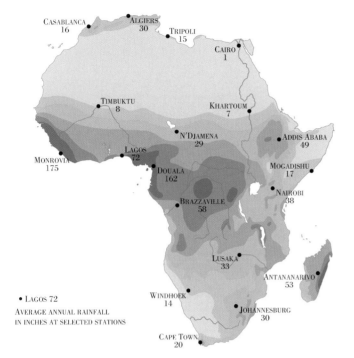

CASABLANCA 16
ALGIERS 30
TRIPOLI 15
CAIRO 1
TIMBUKTU 8
KHARTOUM 7
N'DJAMENA 29
ADDIS ABABA 49
LAGOS 72
MONROVIA 175
DOUALA 162
MOGADISHU 17
BRAZZAVILLE 58
NAIROBI 38
LUSAKA 33
ANTANANARIVO 53
WINDHOEK 14
JOHANNESBURG 30
CAPE TOWN 20

• LAGOS 72
AVERAGE ANNUAL RAINFALL
IN INCHES AT SELECTED STATIONS

## AVERAGE ANNUAL RAINFALL

| INCHES | CM | INCHES | CM | INCHES | CM |
|---|---|---|---|---|---|
| OVER 80 | OVER 200 | 40 TO 60 | 100 TO 150 | 10 TO 20 | 25 TO 50 |
| 60 TO 80 | 150 TO 200 | 20 TO 40 | 50 TO 100 | UNDER 10 | UNDER 25 |

• CITIES WITH OVER 1,000,000
INHABITANTS (INCLUDING SUBURBS)

## POPULATION DISTRIBUTION

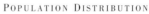

| DENSITY PER | | SQ. MI. | SQ. KM. | SQ. MI. | SQ. KM. |
|---|---|---|---|---|---|
| SQ. MI. | SQ. KM. | 130 TO 260 | 50 TO 100 | 3 TO 25 | 1 TO 10 |
| OVER 260 | OVER 100 | 25 TO 130 | 10 TO 50 | UNDER 3 | UNDER 1 |

## ENERGY SOURCES

OIL REGION  COAL  ✳ URANIUM

NATURAL GAS REGION  ● HYDROELECTRICITY

## ENVIRONMENTAL CONCERNS

POLLUTED RIVERS  AREAS SUBJECT TO DEFORESTATION  EXTENT OF ACID RAIN

EXTENT OF COASTAL POLLUTION  AREAS SUBJECT TO DESERTIFICATION

ATLANTIC OCEAN

ATLANTIC

OCEAN

Mediterranean Sea

MEDITE

M E D I T E R R A N E A N

SPAIN

Granada
Jerez
MÁLAGA
Cádiz
Marbella
Gibraltar (U.K.)
Almería
Cerro de Mulhacén
3,478 m
Cartagena
Bizerte
Cape Bon
Pantelleria (IT.)
MALTA
Valletta
Pelagie (IT.)

Algiers (El Djezair)
Skikda
Annaba
Ariana
TÚNIS
DJEMILA
DOUGGA
Constantine
Sousse
Mahdia
Sfax

Tangier
Ceuta (SP.)
Tétouan
Melilla (SP.)
Oran
Nador
Mostaganem
Chercell
Blida
Bouira
Sétif
Batna
Tébessa
El Kef
Kairouan

Larache
Ksar el Kebir
El Hoceima
Tlemcen
Sidi Bel Abbès
Relizane
Khemis Miliana
Saïda
Mascara
Tiaret
Barika
Djebel Mahmel
2,321 m

Kenitra
Mohammedia
Salé
Er Rif
Oujda
Taourirt
Bou Saâda
Biskra
Jabalah Sha'nabi
1,544 m
Gafsa

Casablanca
Rabat
Meknès
Fès
Taza
Djelfa
M'Sila
Tozeur
Gabès
Île de Jerba
Medenine

El Jadida
Khouribga
Moyen Atlas
Adrar bou Nasser
3,340 m
El Bayadh
Laghouat
El Oued
Chott el Jerid
Tataouine
Zarzis
Gulf of Gabes

MOROCCO
Safi
Beni Mellal
A t l a s
A t l a s   S a h a r i e n
Djamaa
El Golea
Touggourt
Grand Gabes
Tripoli (Tarabulus)
Zuwárah
LABDAH (LEPTIS MAGNA)
Gulf of Si

Essaouira
Oued Zem
Khenifra
Jebel Mesrouh
2,714 m
Ghardaïa
Ouargla
Nalút
Al Aziziyah
Gharyán
Tarhúnah
Mişrátah

Marrakech
Jebel Toubkal
4,165 m
H a u t   A t l a s
Er Rachidia
Djebel Aïssa
2,236 m
TUNISIA
Hassi Messaoud
Ghadámis
Al Hamádah al Hamra
Hún
Waddán

Agadir
Inezgane
A n t i - A t l a s
Adrar Mkorn
3,222 m
Tinrhir
Figuig
Béchar
Beni Ounit
Hassi Fahl
Hassi Khanem
TRIPOLITANIA
Bír 'Alláq

MOROCCO
Tata
Tiznit
Ouarzazate
Erfoud
Bou Dnib
Taghit
Grand   Erg   Occidental
Beni Abbès
Grand   Erg   Oriental
Al Hamádah al Hamra
Jabal as Sawdá
Zillah

Tan-Tan
Tarfaya
Anti-Atlas
Hamada du Dráa
Tabelbala
Kerzaz
Timimoun
Adrar
Plateau du Tademaït
In Salah
Ohanet
Hamada du Tinrhert
Hamadat Tinghert
Fezzan
Awbári
Marzúq
Majdúl

El Aaiún
Cabo Bojador
Smara
Tindouf
Erg   Iguidi
El Eglab
Chenachane
Tidikelt
Aoulef
Reggane
Bordj Omar Driss
In Amenas
Şahrá' Awbári
Birák
Sabhá
Tmassah

WESTERN SAHARA
(Occupied by Morocco)
Guelta Zemmur
Tifariti
Ain Ben Tili
Erg   Chech
El Mzereb
POSTE WEYGAND
Garet el Djenoún
2,327 m
Djebel Telertheba
2,456 m
Djanet
In Ezzane
Al Qaţrún
Tajarhí
Sarir

Ad Dakhla
Zouérat
Kediet Ijill
915 m
'Ayoûn 'Abd El Mâlek
Tanezrouft
POSTE MAURICE CORTIER
I-n-Dagouber
Silet
Idèles
In Alkoum
Tahat 2,918 m
Tamanrasset
A h a g g a r
Azao 2,158 m
Al Kuri
Djado
Chirfa
Pic Toussidé
3,315 m
Bardaï
Aozou

Nouâdhibou
Cap Blanc
Fdérik
Aguènit
Tichla
Zug
Atar
Ouadane
Quarane
Bir Ounâne
Taoudenni
Adrar
Toummo
Plateau du Djado
Madama
Passe de Korizo

PARC NATIONAL DU BANC D'ARGUIN
Akjoujt
Adrar   des   Iforas
Aguelhok
In Guezzam
Timia
Ténéré   du   Tafassasset
Séguédine
Achegour
Dirkou
Bilma

Nouakchott
Trarza
Boutilimit
Tidjikdja
Tichît
Néma
Araouane
Tessalit
Kidal
Arhli
Mont Tamgak
1,988 m
Aïr
Mont Bagane
2,022 m
Fachi
Grand Erg de Bilma
Modjigo
Bodélé
Siltou

MAURITANIA
Aleg
Boûmdeïd
AOUDAGHOST
'Ayoûn el Atroûs
Aoukar
Boû Djébéha
Azaouâd
Anefis In-Darane
Talak
Agadem
Erg   du   Ténéré

Saint-Louis
Rosso
Dagana
Bogué
Kaédi
Kiffa
Lac Faguibine
Gourma Rharous
Bourem
MALI
NIGER
Agadez
N'guigmi
Kanem
Lake Chad
Mao
Bol

Louga
Thiès
Diourbel
Linguère
Matam
Selibabi
Touil
MAURITANIA / MALI
Fassala-Néré
Tombouctou (Timbuktu)
Gao
Ménaka
Chin Tabaradene
Tahoua
Tânout
Bedouaram
Sogolé

Dakar
Kaolack
Kaffrine
SENEGAL
Bakel
Nioro du Sahel
Diéma
Nara
Niafounké
Niangay
Hombori Tondo
1,155 m
Ansongo
Bani-Bangou
Iliéla
Dakoro
Gouré
Goudoumaria
Diffa
Bornu Plains

Banjul
THE GAMBIA
Brikama
Tambacounda
Bafoulabé
Kayes
Diéma
Ségou
Djenné
Douentza
Mopti
Bandiagara
Gorom Gorom
Dori
Filingué
Ouallam
Tillabéri
Birni Nkonni
Madaoua
Tessaoua
Magaria
Nguru
Gashua
Maïné-Soroa
Ngala
N'DJAMENA
PARC NATIONAL DE KALAMALOUÉ

Ziguinchor
Bignona
Kolda
Basse Santa Su
Koundara
Kédougou
PN DE LA BOUCLE DU BAOULÉ
Koulikoro
Kolokani
Koutiala
San
Koro
Ouahigouya
Teo
NIGER
Niamey
Filingué
Sokoto
Maradi
Zinder
SENEGAL / NIGER
Baguirmi
Bokoro

Cap Roxo
GUINEA-BISSAU
Bafatá
Bissau
PN DU NIOKOLO-KOBA
Kéniéba
Kita
Bamako
Dioïla
Bougouni
Sikasso
Bobo Dioulasso
BURKINA FASO
Dédougou
Ouagadougou
Kaya
Fada-N'Gourma
Diapaga
PN DU "W" DU NIGER
PN DU "W" DU BURKINA FASO
PN DU "W" DU BENIN
Dosso
Gaya
Birnin Kebbi
Gusau
Talata Mafara
Katsina
Daura
Kano
Dutse
Hadejia
Potiskum
Damaturu
Maiduguri
Dikwa
Mora
Bama
CAMEROON

Bubaque
Arquipélago dos Bijagós
Boké
Télimélé
Dabola
Kangaba
Yanfolila
Orodara
Banfora
Léo
Ouahigouya
Yako
NIGERIA
Sokoto Plains
Kaduna
Zaria
Funtua
Kontagora
Minna
Abuja
Bauchi
Deba Habe
Biu
Gombe
Kumo
YANKARI GAME RESERVE
Gubio
Kaélé
Guider
Maroua

GUINEA
Kindia
Mamou
Faranah
Kankan
Odienné
Korhogo
PN DE LA COMOÉ
Bondoukou
Bole
Wa
Bolgatanga
Navrongo
Tenkodogo
PN DE LA PENDJARI
Natitingou
Kandi
BENIN
Parakou
Shaki
Ilorin
Oyo
Birnin Gwari
Jos
Plateau
Panshin
Jalingo
Yola
BARRAGE DE LAGDO
Garoua
Tchollíré
PN DU FARO
Ngaoundéré
Mont Kaveagaroup
420 m

Conakry
Moussayah
Kabala
PORT LOKO
Kissidougou
Macenta
Loma Mts.
Loma Marisa
1,948 m
Pic de Tibé
1,504 m
Man
Nzérékoré
Touba
Séguéla
Katiola
Bouaké
Mankono
PN DE LA MARAHOUÉ
Bouaflé
Sunyani
Wenchi
Mampong
Kintampo
Yendi
Bassari
Sokodé
Kara-Kara
Djougou
Plateau of Yorubaland
Iseyin
Ado Ekiti
Oshogbo
Ilesha
Ikare
Okene
Lokoja
Makurdi
Otukpo
Wukari
Gembu
Dimlang
2,042 m
Tibati
Adamaoua
Banyo
Meiganga
Tchabal Mbabo
2,460 m
Garoua Boulaï

SIERRA LEONE
Freetown
Kenema
Bo
Kabala
Kailahun
C. Sierra Leone
Bong Range
GUINEA
Danané
Mont Nimba
1,752 m
Guiglo
Duékoué
Daloa
CÔTE D'IVOIRE
Sinfra
Yamoussoukro
Bouaké
Dimbokro
Abengourou
Agnibilékrou
BARRAGE DE KOSSOU
GHANA
Ashanti
Kumasi
Obuasi
DIGYA NP
AKOSOMBO DAM
Kpalimé
Atakpamé
TOGO
Savè
Abeokuta
Ogbomosho
Ede
Ibadan
Ife
Benin City
Onitsha
Warri
Owerri
Aba
Calabar
Kumba
Bafia
Fako 4,095 m
Buea
Douala
Yaoundé
CAMEROON
Bertoua
Batouri
Bafoussam
Bamenda
Foumban
Kumbo
Mont Cameroun
Ngaoundéré
PN DU DJA
Abong Mbang

LIBERIA
Monrovia
Harbel
Buchanan
Robertsport
Zwedru
Tabou
C. Palmas
Harper
Grain Coast
Gagnoa
Divo
Abidjan
San Pédro
Sassandra
Grand-Bassam
Sekondi-Takoradi
Cape Coast
Accra
Tema
Lomé
Cotonou
Porto-Novo
Lagos
Bight of Benin
Mouths of the Niger
Port Harcourt
Bonny
Bioko
Malabo
Pico de Santa Isabel
3,008 m
EQUATORIAL GUINEA
Bight of Biafra
Bata
Ebebiyin
Bitam
Mbini
Monte Mitra
1,200 m
Mekambo
Makokou

Gulf of Guinea

SÃO TOMÉ AND PRÍNCIPE
Príncipe
Santo António
São Tomé
Libreville
GABON
N'Djolé
Booué
Lambaréné
Cap Esterias
Cap Lopez
Port-Gentil
Mont Boundji
980 m
Yombi
Mbigou
Mouila
Koula-Moutou
Franceville
Omboué
Moanda
M'Binda
Bakoumba
CONGO
Owando
Mongoumou
Ngo
Plateau Batéké
Tchibanga
Makabana

Equator

ATLANTIC OCEAN

Annobón
(EQ. G.)
Palé

Below Sea Level     Sea Lev. Level     200 / 700     500 / 1,600     1,000 / 3,300     1,500 / 5,000     2,000 / 6,500     4,000 / 13,000     6,000 m. / 19,700 ft.

A 20°     B 15°     C 10°     Longitude West of Greenwich     5°     E 0°     F     Longitude East of Greenwich     5°     G 10°     H 15°     J

► Africa Comparisons: Pages 66 - 67
► Global relationships: Pages 14 - 36
► Index of the World: Pages 97 - 104

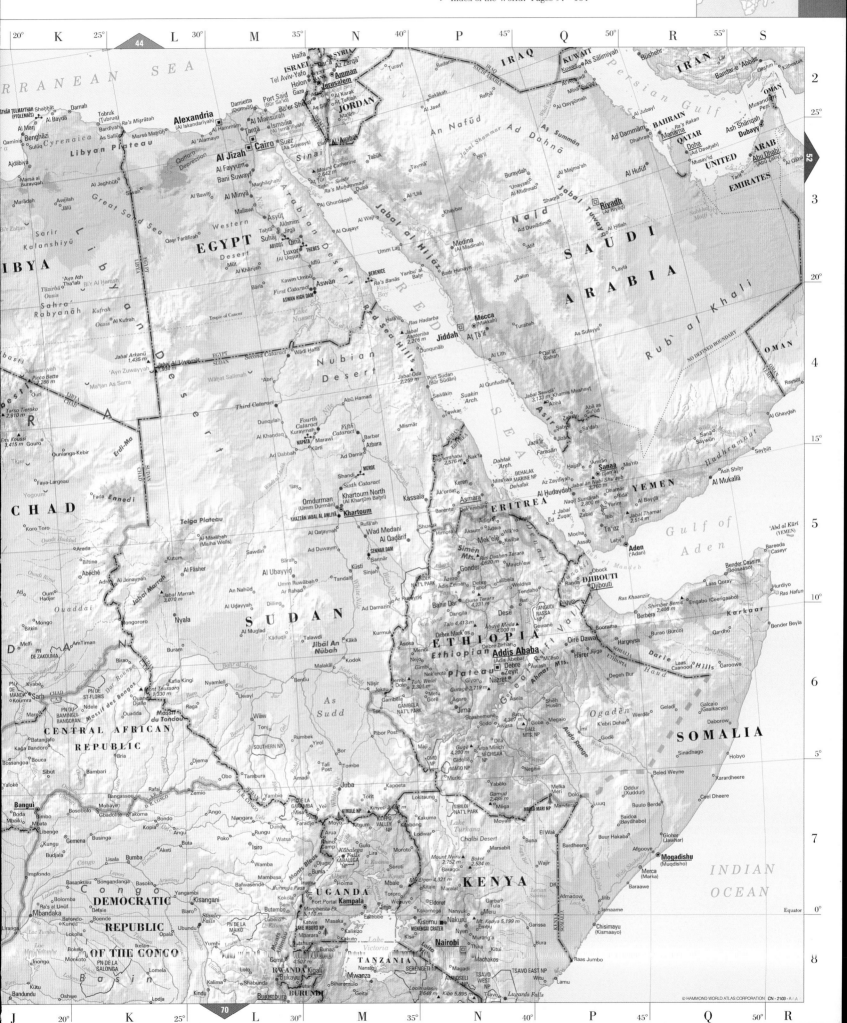

POPULATION OF CITIES AND TOWNS

| ■ OVER 2,000,000 | ● 500,000 - 999,999 | ○ 50,000 - 99,999 |
| □ 1,000,000 - 1,999,999 | ● 100,000 - 499,999 | ○ UNDER 50,000 |

SCALE 1:17,500,000   POLYCONIC PROJECTION

MILES  0         250         500         750
KILOMETERS  0    250    500    750

© HAMMOND WORLD ATLAS CORPORATION   CN - 2103 - A - A

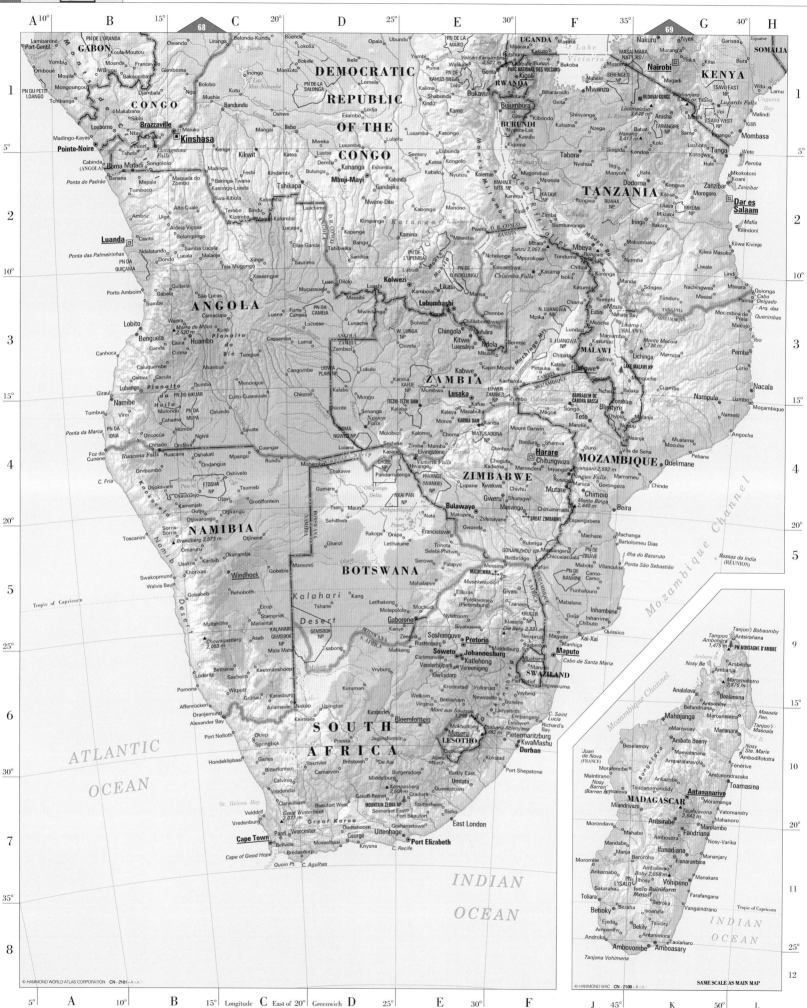

SCALE 1:17,500,000   POLYCONIC PROJECTION

MILES 0 | 250 | 500 | 750
KILOMETERS 0 | 250 | 500 | 750

POPULATION OF CITIES AND TOWNS
▪ OVER 2,000,000          ● 500,000 - 999,999          ◦ 50,000 - 99,999
□ 1,000,000 - 1,999,999   ◦ 100,000 - 499,999          ◦ UNDER 50,000

© HAMMOND WORLD ATLAS CORPORATION   CN - 2101 - A - A

► World Physical: Pages 10 - 11
► World Political: Pages 12 - 13
► Index of the World: Pages 97 - 104

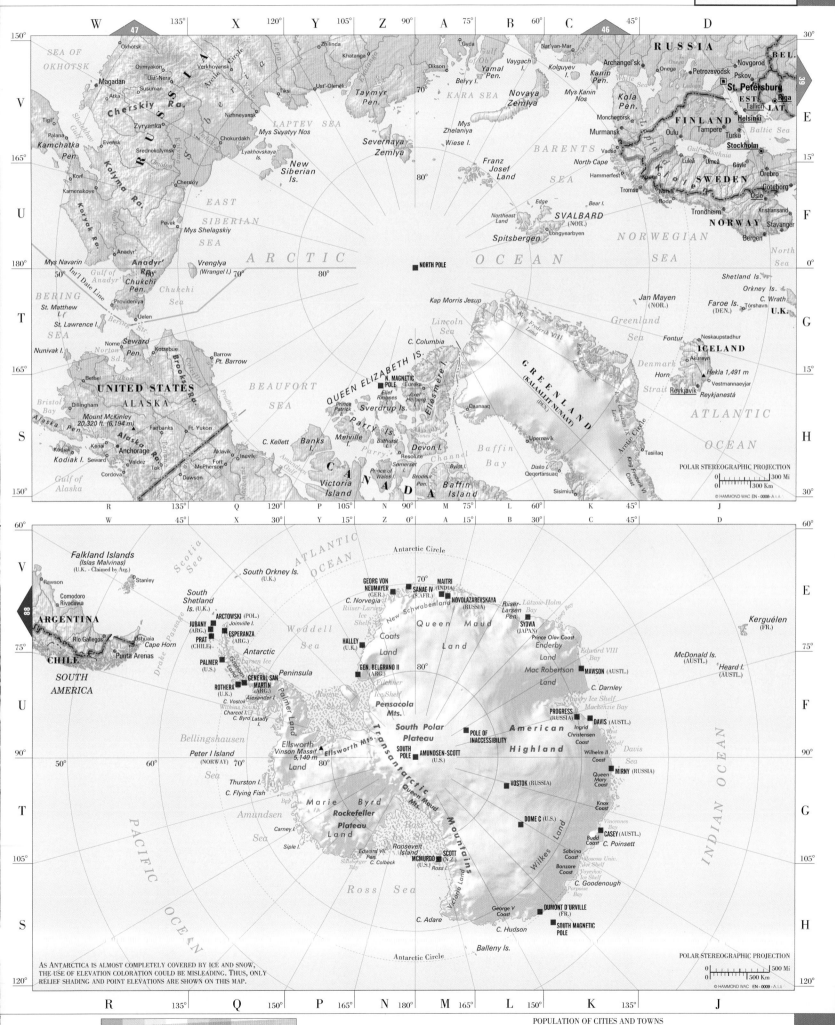

As Antarctica is almost completely covered by ice and snow, the use of elevation coloration could be misleading. Thus, only relief shading and point elevations are shown on this map.

POLAR STEREOGRAPHIC PROJECTION

| Below Sea | Sea | 200 | 500 | 1,000 | 1,500 | 2,000 | 4,000 | 6,000 m. |
| Sea Lev. Level | | 700 | 1,600 | 3,300 | 5,000 | 6,500 | 13,000 | 19,700 ft. |

**POPULATION OF CITIES AND TOWNS**

■ OVER 2,000,000        ● 500,000 - 999,999      ○ 50,000 - 99,999
□ 1,000,000 - 1,999,999  ● 100,000 - 499,999      ○ UNDER 50,000

# North America - Physical

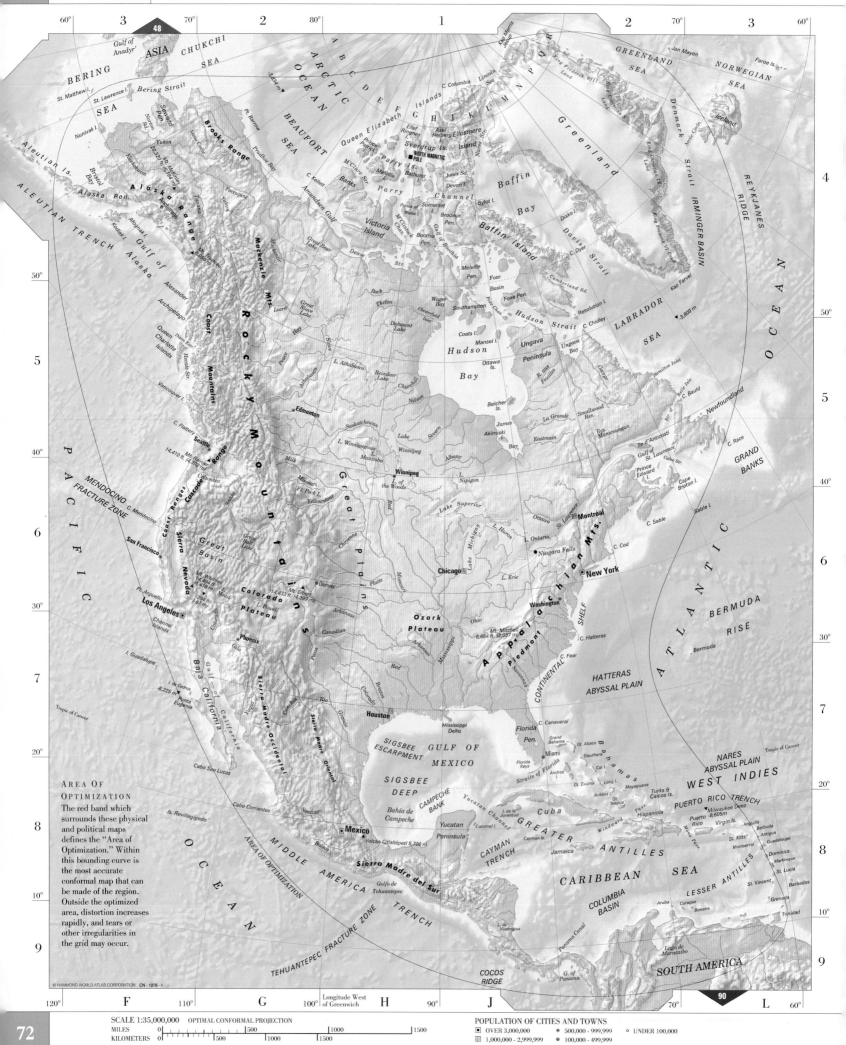

AREA OF OPTIMIZATION
The red band which surrounds these physical and political maps defines the "Area of Optimization." Within this bounding curve is the most accurate conformal map that can be made of the region. Outside the optimized area, distortion increases rapidly, and tears or other irregularities in the grid may occur.

© HAMMOND WORLD ATLAS CORPORATION    CN - 1076 - A

SCALE 1:35,000,000    OPTIMAL CONFORMAL PROJECTION

MILES 0 | 500 | 1000 | 1500
KILOMETERS 0 | 500 | 1000 | 1500

POPULATION OF CITIES AND TOWNS
■ OVER 3,000,000          ✱ 500,000 - 999,999          ○ UNDER 100,000
▣ 1,000,000 - 2,999,999   ● 100,000 - 499,999

# North America - Political

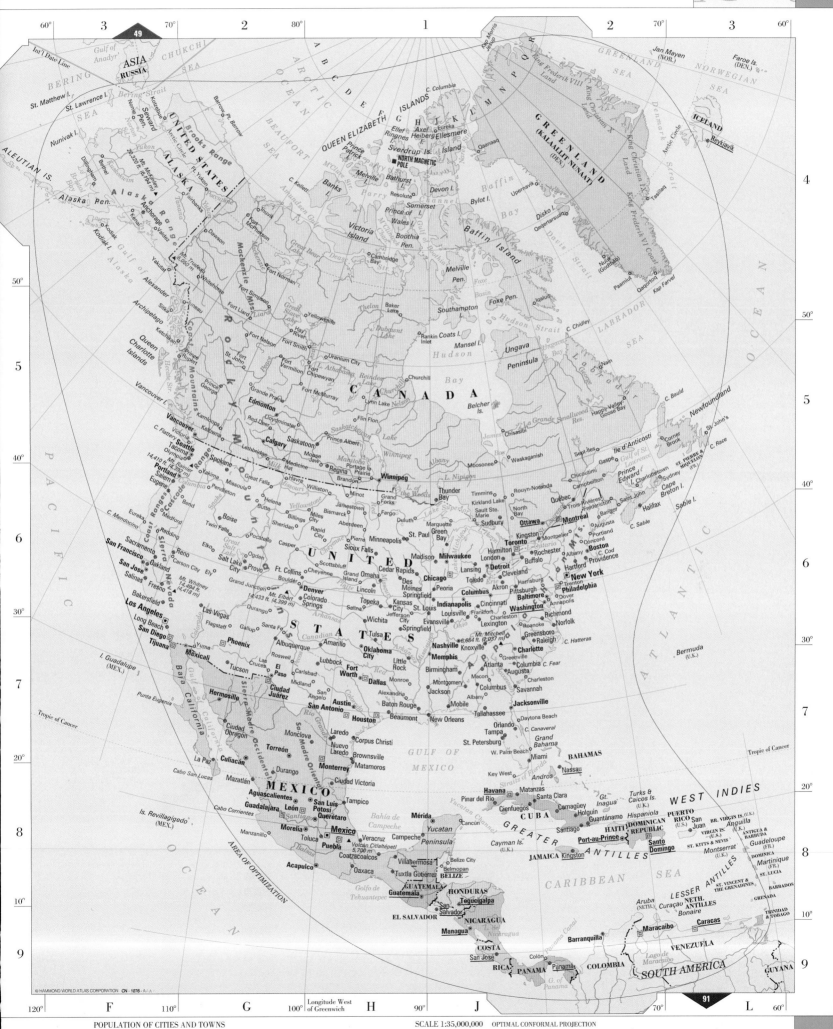

POPULATION OF CITIES AND TOWNS

■ OVER 3,000,000     ⊡ 500,000 - 999,999     ○ UNDER 100,000
⊡ 1,000,000 - 2,999,999     ● 100,000 - 499,999

SCALE 1:35,000,000     OPTIMAL CONFORMAL PROJECTION

MILES  0          500          1000          1500
KILOMETERS  0     500     1000     1500

# North America - Comparisons

**AVERAGE JANUARY TEMPERATURE**

• NEW YORK 34°
AVERAGE JANUARY TEMPERATURE
DEGREES FAHRENHEIT AT
SELECTED STATIONS

FAIRBANKS -11°
JUNEAU 25°
NUUK 18°
EDMONTON 6°
VANCOUVER 37°
WINNIPEG -3°
QUÉBEC 10°
DENVER 29°
CHICAGO 26°
NEW YORK 34°
LOS ANGELES 55°
PHOENIX 50°
NEW ORLEANS 55°
LA PAZ 65°
TAMPICO 67°
HAVANA 72°
SAN JUAN 74°
MEXICO 54°
BELIZE CITY 74°
COLÓN 80°

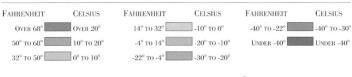

| FAHRENHEIT | CELSIUS | FAHRENHEIT | CELSIUS | FAHRENHEIT | CELSIUS |
|---|---|---|---|---|---|
| OVER 68° | OVER 20° | 14° TO 32° | -10° TO 0° | -40° TO -22° | -40° TO -30° |
| 50° TO 68° | 10° TO 20° | -4° TO 14° | -20° TO -10° | UNDER -40° | UNDER -40° |
| 32° TO 50° | 0° TO 10° | -22° TO -4° | -30° TO -20° | | |

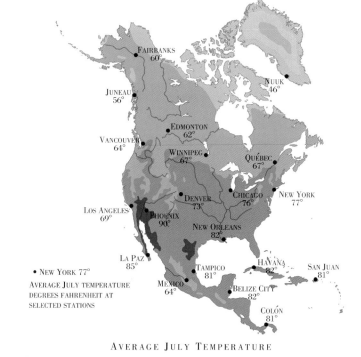

**AVERAGE JULY TEMPERATURE**

• NEW YORK 77°
AVERAGE JULY TEMPERATURE
DEGREES FAHRENHEIT AT
SELECTED STATIONS

FAIRBANKS 60°
JUNEAU 56°
NUUK 46°
EDMONTON 62°
VANCOUVER 64°
WINNIPEG 67°
QUÉBEC 67°
DENVER 73°
CHICAGO 76°
NEW YORK 77°
LOS ANGELES 69°
PHOENIX 90°
NEW ORLEANS 82°
LA PAZ 85°
TAMPICO 81°
HAVANA 82°
SAN JUAN 81°
MEXICO 64°
BELIZE CITY 82°
COLÓN 81°

| FAHRENHEIT | CELSIUS | FAHRENHEIT | CELSIUS | FAHRENHEIT | CELSIUS |
|---|---|---|---|---|---|
| OVER 86° | OVER 30° | 50° TO 68° | 10° TO 20° | 14° TO 32° | -10° TO 0° |
| 68° TO 86° | 20° TO 30° | 32° TO 50° | 0° TO 10° | UNDER 14° | UNDER -10° |

**CLIMATE**

ET
Dfc
ET
Cfc
Dfc
ET
ET
Cfb
Dfc
BSk
Dsb Dfb
Dfb
Csa
BWk
Dfa
Cfb
Dfb
Cfa
BWh
BSk
BSh BWh
BSh
Aw
Cw
Aw
Am
Af
Aw
Af
BSh

**VEGETATION**

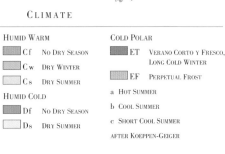

| HUMID TROPICAL | | HUMID WARM | | COLD POLAR | |
|---|---|---|---|---|---|
| Af | NO DRY SEASON | Cf | NO DRY SEASON | ET | VERANO CORTO Y FRESCO, LONG COLD WINTER |
| Am | SHORT DRY SEASON | Cw | DRY WINTER | EF | PERPETUAL FROST |
| Aw | DRY WINTER | Cs | DRY SUMMER | a | HOT SUMMER |
| DRY | | HUMID COLD | | b | COOL SUMMER |
| BS | SEMIARID | Df | NO DRY SEASON | c | SHORT COOL SUMMER |
| BW | ARID | Ds | DRY SUMMER | | |

h HOT
k COLD

AFTER KOEPPEN-GEIGER

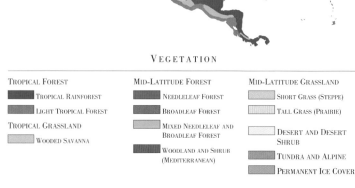

| TROPICAL FOREST | MID-LATITUDE FOREST | MID-LATITUDE GRASSLAND |
|---|---|---|
| TROPICAL RAINFOREST | NEEDLELEAF FOREST | SHORT GRASS (STEPPE) |
| LIGHT TROPICAL FOREST | BROADLEAF FOREST | TALL GRASS (PRAIRIE) |
| TROPICAL GRASSLAND | MIXED NEEDLELEAF AND BROADLEAF FOREST | DESERT AND DESERT SHRUB |
| WOODED SAVANNA | WOODLAND AND SHRUB (MEDITERRANEAN) | TUNDRA AND ALPINE |
| | | PERMANENT ICE COVER |

► North America Physical / Political: Pages 72 - 73
► Global Relationships: Pages 14 - 36
► Index of the World: Pages 97 - 104

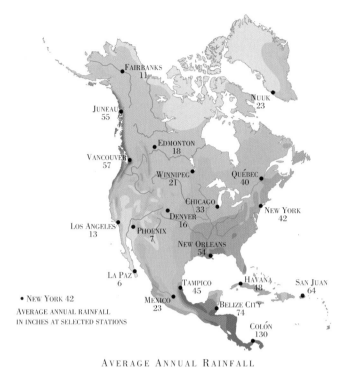

● NEW YORK 42
AVERAGE ANNUAL RAINFALL
IN INCHES AT SELECTED STATIONS

## AVERAGE ANNUAL RAINFALL

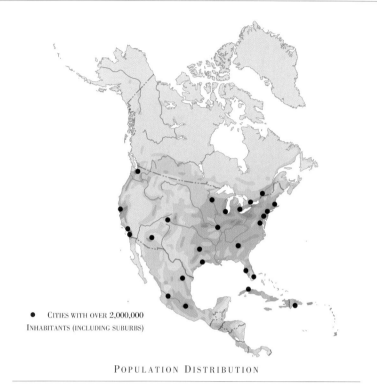

● CITIES WITH OVER 2,000,000
INHABITANTS (INCLUDING SUBURBS)

## POPULATION DISTRIBUTION

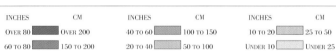

| INCHES | CM | | INCHES | CM | | INCHES | CM |
|---|---|---|---|---|---|---|---|
| OVER 80 | OVER 200 | | 40 TO 60 | 100 TO 150 | | 10 TO 20 | 25 TO 50 |
| 60 TO 80 | 150 TO 200 | | 20 TO 40 | 50 TO 100 | | UNDER 10 | UNDER 25 |

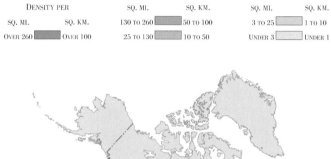

| DENSITY PER | | SQ. MI. | SQ. KM. | | SQ. MI. | SQ. KM. |
|---|---|---|---|---|---|---|
| SQ. MI. | SQ. KM. | 130 TO 260 | 50 TO 100 | | 3 TO 25 | 1 TO 10 |
| OVER 260 | OVER 100 | 25 TO 130 | 10 TO 50 | | UNDER 3 | UNDER 1 |

## ENERGY SOURCES

| | OIL REGION | ■ COAL | * URANIUM |
|---|---|---|---|
| | NATURAL GAS REGION | ● HYDROELECTRICITY | |

## ENVIRONMENTAL CONCERNS

| POLLUTED RIVERS | AREAS SUBJECT TO DEFORESTATION | EXTENT OF ACID RAIN |
|---|---|---|
| EXTENT OF COASTAL POLLUTION | AREAS SUBJECT TO DESERTIFICATION | ● URBAN AREAS WITH SEVERE AIR POLLUTION |

Below Sea | 200 | 500 | 1,000 | 1,500 | 2,000 | 4,000 | 6,000 m.
Sea Lev. Level | 700 | 1,600 | 3,300 | 5,000 | 6,500 | 13,000 | 19,700 ft.

► North America Comparisons: Pages 74 - 75
► Global relationships: Pages 14 - 36
► Index of the World: Pages 97 - 104

POPULATION OF CITIES AND TOWNS

| ■ OVER 2,000,000 | ● 500,000 - 999,999 | ◉ 50,000 - 99,999 |
| □ 1,000,000 - 1,999,999 | ○ 100,000 - 499,999 | ○ UNDER 50,000 |

SCALE 1:14,000,000    LAMBERT CONFORMAL CONIC PROJECTION

▶ North America Comparisons: Pages 74 - 75
▶ Global relationships: Pages 14 - 36
▶ Index of the World: Pages 97 - 104

POPULATION OF CITIES AND TOWNS

■ OVER 2,000,000    ● 500,000 - 999,999    ○ 50,000 - 99,999
▣ 1,000,000 - 1,999,999    ● 100,000 - 499,999    ○ UNDER 50,000

SCALE 1:14,000,000    LAMBERT CONFORMAL CONIC PROJECTION
MILES 0 | 200 | 400 | 600
KILOMETERS 0 | 200 | 400 | 600

© HAMMOND WORLD ATLAS CORPORATION

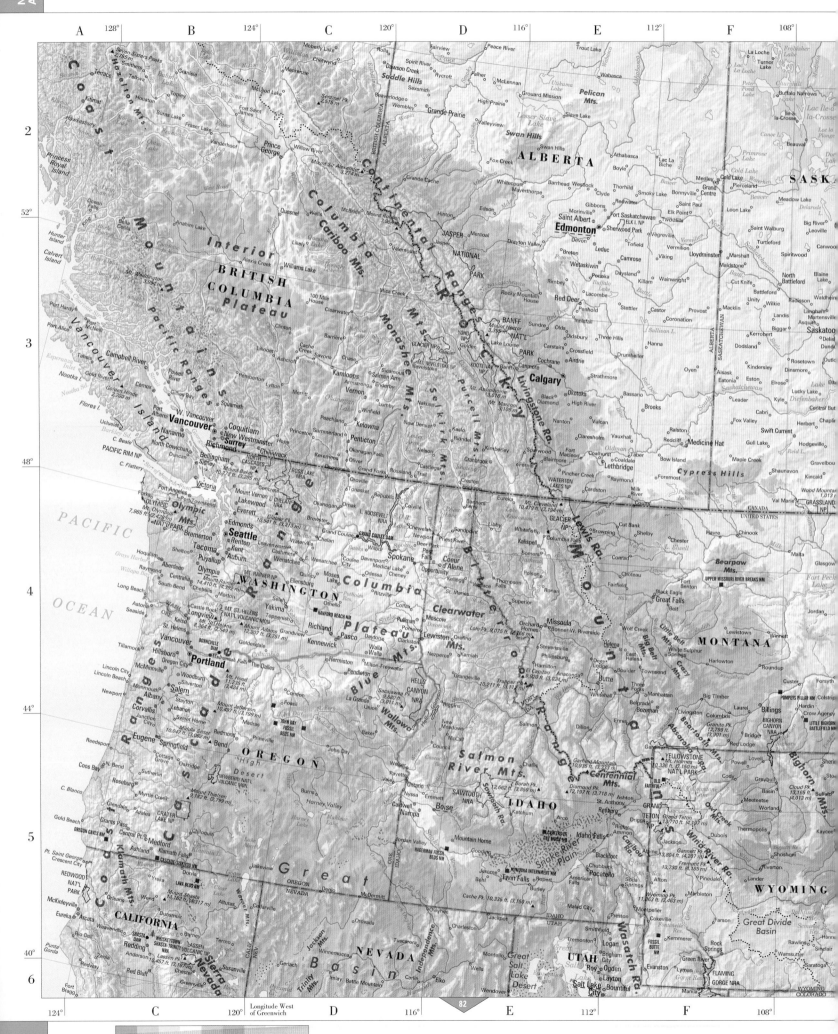

► North America Comparisons: Pages 74 - 75
► Global relationships: Pages 14 - 36
► Index of the World: Pages 97 - 104

NORTH AMERICA

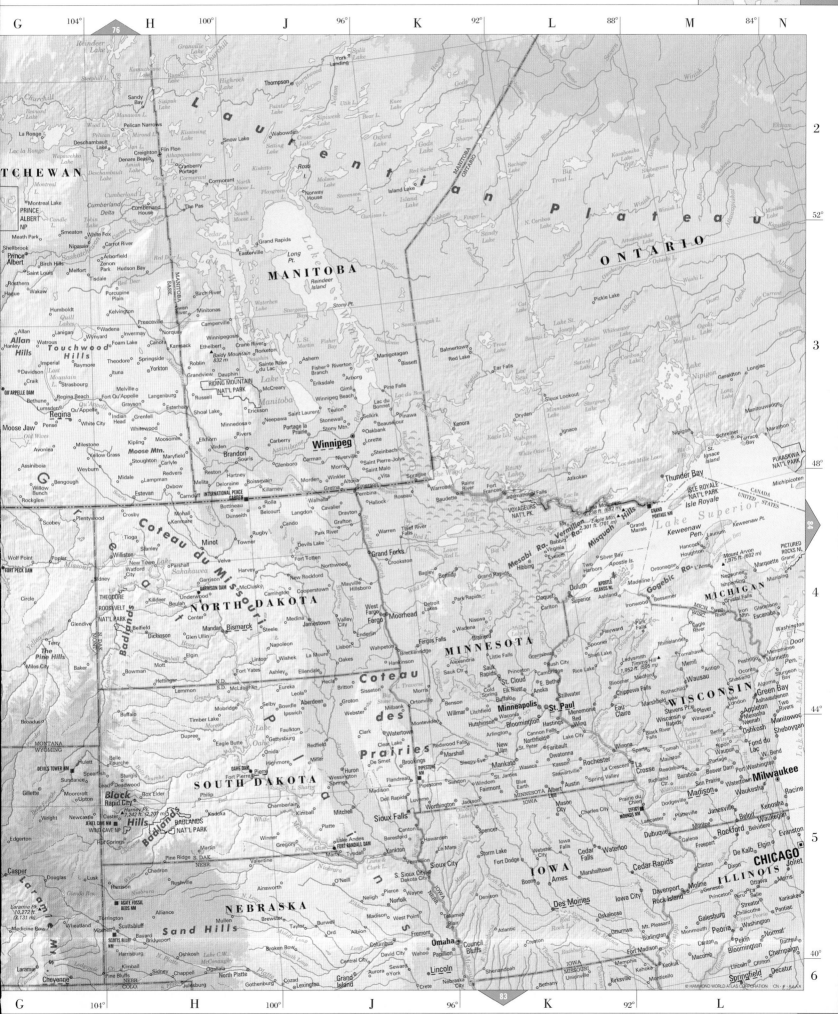

POPULATION OF CITIES AND TOWNS

| | | |
|---|---|---|
| ▣ OVER 2,000,000 | ⊙ 500,000 - 999,999 | ⊙ 100,000 - 249,999 | ○ 10,000 - 29,999 |
| ▢ 1,000,000 - 1,999,999 | ⊙ 250,000 - 499,999 | ⊙ 30,000 - 99,999 | ○ UNDER 10,000 |

SCALE 1:10,500,000    LAMBERT CONFORMAL CONIC PROJECTION

MILES 0 — 150 — 300 — 450

KILOMETERS 0 — 150 — 300 — 450

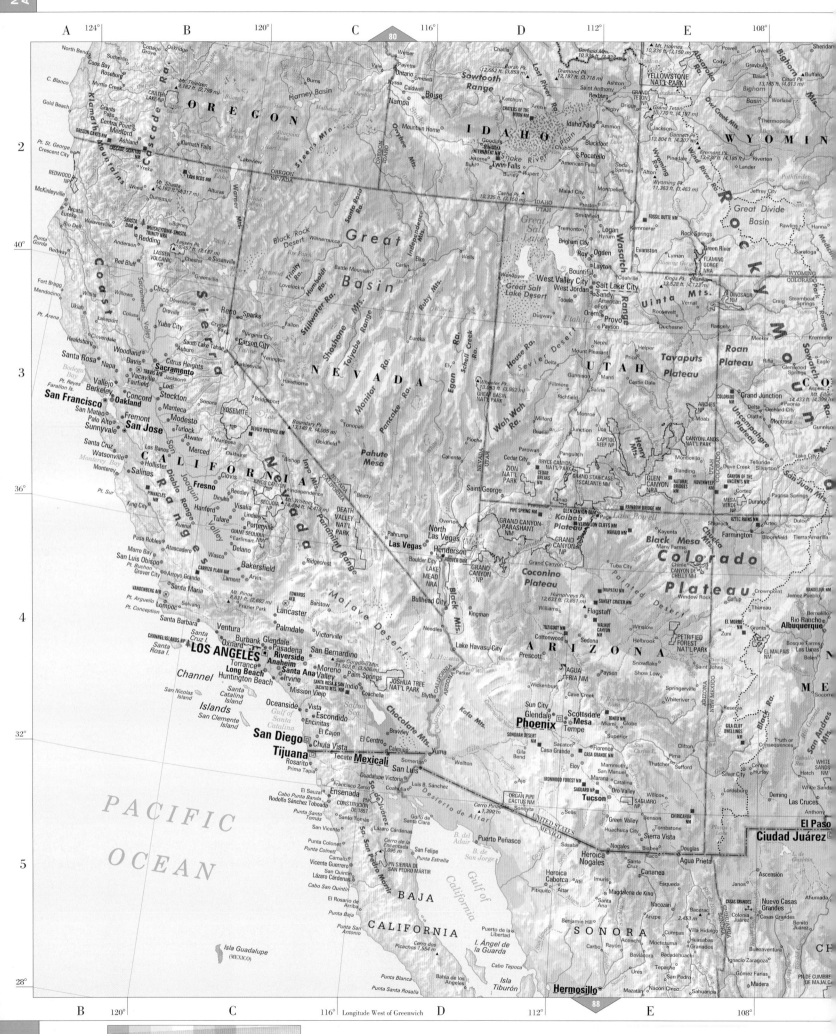

POPULATION OF CITIES AND TOWNS

■ OVER 2,000,000   ◉ 500,000 - 999,999   ● 100,000 - 249,999   ○ 10,000 - 29,999
▣ 1,000,000 - 1,999,999   ◉ 250,000 - 499,999   ◉ 30,000 - 99,999   ○ UNDER 10,000

SCALE 1:7,000,000    LAMBERT CONFORMAL CONIC PROJECTION

MILES    0    100    200    300
KILOMETERS    0    100    200    300

# Southeastern Canada, Northeastern United States

▶ North America Comparisons: Pages 74 - 75
▶ Global relationships: Pages 14 - 36
▶ Index of the World: Pages 97 - 104

| Below Sea | 200 | 500 | 1,000 | 1,500 | 2,000 | 4,000 | 6,000 m. |
|---|---|---|---|---|---|---|---|
| Sea Lev. Level | 700 | 1,600 | 3,300 | 5,000 | 6,500 | 13,000 | 19,700 ft. |

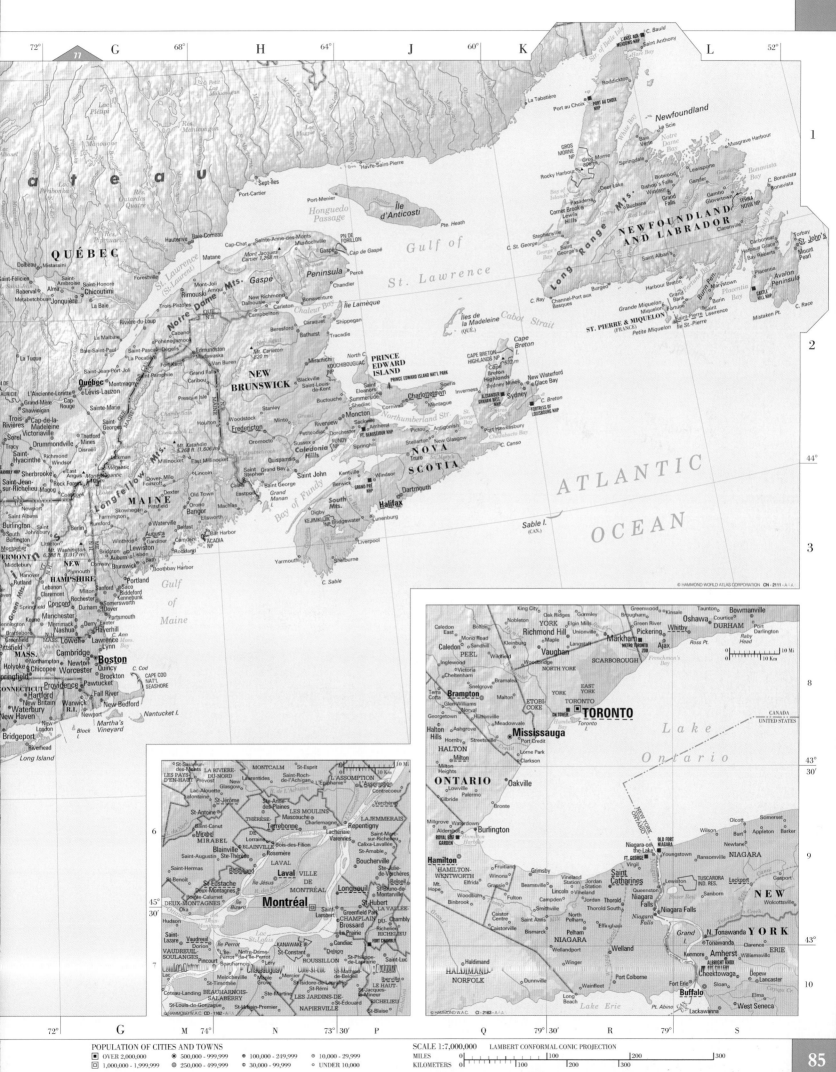

## POPULATION OF CITIES AND TOWNS

- ■ OVER 2,000,000
- ☐ 1,000,000 - 1,999,999
- ⬤ 500,000 - 999,999
- ◉ 250,000 - 499,999
- ● 100,000 - 249,999
- ⬤ 30,000 - 99,999
- ◯ 10,000 - 29,999
- ○ UNDER 10,000

SCALE 1:7,000,000    LAMBERT CONFORMAL CONIC PROJECTION

MILES  0    100    200    300
KILOMETERS  0    100    200    300

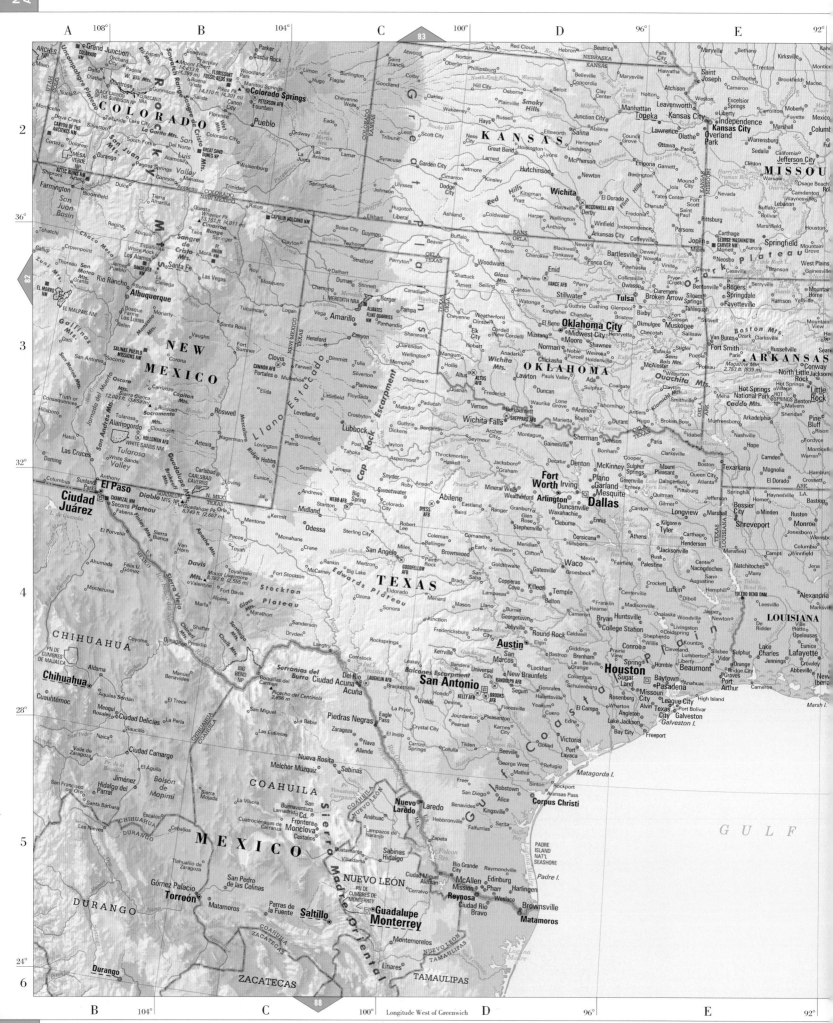

Below Sea  200   500   1,000  1,500  2,000  4,000  6,000 m.
Sea Lev. Level 700 1,600 3,300 5,000 6,500 13,000 19,700 ft.

Longitude West of Greenwich

▶ North America Comparisons: Pages 74 - 75
▶ Global relationships: Pages 14 - 36
▶ Index of the World: Pages 97 - 104

POPULATION OF CITIES AND TOWNS

| Symbol | Population |
|---|---|
| ■ | OVER 2,000,000 |
| ⊚ | 500,000 - 999,999 |
| ⬤ | 100,000 - 249,999 |
| ○ | 10,000 - 29,999 |
| ▫ | 1,000,000 - 1,999,999 |
| ⊙ | 250,000 - 499,999 |
| ◉ | 30,000 - 99,999 |
| ○ | UNDER 10,000 |

SCALE 1:7,000,000    LAMBERT CONFORMAL CONIC PROJECTION

MILES 0 | 100 | 200 | 300
KILOMETERS 0 | 100 | 200 | 300

© HAMMOND WORLD ATLAS CORPORATION

POPULATION OF CITIES AND TOWNS

| | |
|---|---|
| ■ OVER 2,000,000 | ◉ 500,000 - 999,999 | ⊕ 100,000 - 249,999 | ◦ 10,000 - 29,999 |
| □ 1,000,000 - 1,999,999 | ◎ 250,000 - 499,999 | ⊙ 30,000 - 99,999 | ∘ UNDER 10,000 |

Below Sea    200   500   1,000  1,500  2,000  4,000  6,000 m.
Sea Lev. Level  700  1,600  3,300  5,000  6,500  13,000  19,700 ft.

ATLANTIC OCEAN

PACIFIC OCEAN

CARIBBEAN SEA

**UNITED STATES / MEXICO**

CALIF. · El Centro · Gila Bend · Casa Grande · Casa Grande Ruins NM · Thatcher · Clifton · Hillsboro · WHITE SANDS · Alamogordo · Artesia · Seminole
San Diego · Chula Vista · Yuma · ARIZONA · Safford · Silver City · NEW MEXICO · Hobbs · Andrews
Mexicali · San Luis Río Colorado · SAGUARO NP · Tucson · CHIRICAHUA NM · Mt. Graham 10,713 ft. (3,265 m) · Las Cruces · White Sands · CARLSBAD CAVERNS NP · Midland · Odessa
Tijuana · SAGUARO NP · Benson · Green Valley · Sierra Vista · Tombstone · Douglas · El Paso · GUADALUPE MTS. NP · Kermit · Monahans · Rankin
Ensenada · Ojos Negros · ORGAN PIPE CACTUS NM · Nogales · TUMACACORI NHP · Ciudad Juárez · Mt. Lemmon 9,157 ft. (2,791 m) · Mentone · McCamey · Ft. Stockton
Punta Santo Tomás · Cerro Pinacate 1,390 m · Sonoyta · Heroica Nogales · Agua Prieta · Sierra Blanca · Van Horn · TEXAS
San Vicente · La Libertad · Heroica Caborca · Cananea · Nuevo Casas Grandes · Chinati Pk. 7,730 ft. (2,356 m) · Marfa · Alpine · Sanderson

**BAJA CALIFORNIA / SONORA / CHIHUAHUA**

Hermosillo · SONORA · Chihuahua · CHIHUAHUA · COAHUILA
Guaymas · Ciudad Obregón · Ciudad Delicias · Ciudad Camargo · ZARAGOZA
Ciudad Rosalia · Los Mochis · Gómez Palacio · Ciudad Lerdo · Torreón · Matamoros
La Paz · SINALOA · Culiacán · DURANGO · Durango · ZACATECAS
Mazatlán · Zacatecas · Aguascalientes
San José del Cabo · San Lucas · Cabo San Lucas · Tepic · NAYARIT · Tepic · JALISCO · Guadalajara
Puerto Vallarta · COLIMA · Colima · MICHOACÁN

Tropic of Cancer

SCALE 0 — 100 Mi · 0 — 100 Km
© HAMMOND W.A.C. DI-0004-AAA

**BAHAMAS / CUBA / JAMAICA**

Hilton Head Island · C. Canaveral · Melbourne · Vero Beach · Fort Pierce · Port St. Lucie · Stuart · West Palm Beach · Coral Springs · Fort Lauderdale · Hollywood · Miami · Coral Gables · Hialeah · Biscayne NP · Key Largo · Florida Keys
Grand Bahama · Freeport · Great Abaco · Bimini Is. · Berry Is. · BAHAMAS · Eleuthera · Nassau · New Providence I. · Andros I. · Cat I. · Exuma Sound · San Salvador (Watling I.) · Great Exuma · Rum Cay · Long I. · Clarence Town · Crooked I. · Acklins I. · Abraham's Bay · Mayaguana · Turks and Caicos Is. (U.K.) · Caicos Is. · Grand Turk · Turks Is.
Sagua la Grande · Caibarién · Santa Clara · Cienfuegos · Sancti Spíritus · CUBA · Ciego de Ávila · Morón · Camagüey · Victoria de las Tunas · Holguín · Bayamo · Guantánamo · Santiago de Cuba · Pico Turquino 4,131 m · GUANTANAMO BAY U.S. NAVAL BASE
Little Cayman · Cayman Brac · JAMAICA · Montego Bay · Ocho Rios · Saint Ann's Bay · Spanish Town · Mandeville · May Pen · Kingston · Blue Mtn. Pk. 2,256 m · Pedro Cays (JAM.)

**HISPANIOLA**

HAITI · Port-de-Paix · Cap-Haïtien · Santiago · Monte Cristi · Puerto Plata · Sosúa · Cabo Francés Viejo · San Francisco de Macorís · DOMINICAN REPUBLIC · Cabo Samaná
Gonaïves · La Vega · El Seibo · Higüey
Jérémie · Port-au-Prince · Pico Duarte 3,175 m · San Juan · Hato Mayor · San Pedro de Macorís
Les Cayes · Jacmel · Azua · Bani · SANTO DOMINGO · La Romana
Pic de Macaya 2,300 m · Neiba · Barahona · Pedernales · Cabo Beata

**PUERTO RICO / LESSER ANTILLES**

PUERTO RICO (U.S.) · Aguadilla · Arecibo · San Juan · Bayamón · Carolina · Caguas · Mayagüez · Ponce · Guayama
Virgin Is. · St. Thomas (U.S.) · St. John (U.S.) · Tortola I. (U.K.) · Anegada (U.K.) · Road Town · The Valley · Anguilla (U.K.) · St.-Martin (FR.) · Philipsburg · St. Maarten (N.A.) · Saba (N.A.) · ST. KITTS AND NEVIS · Basseterre · Charlestown · Barbuda · Codrington · ANTIGUA AND BARBUDA · Antigua · Saint John's
Montserrat · Plymouth · GUADELOUPE (FRANCE) · Basse-Terre · Soufrière 1,467 m · Grande-Terre · Pointe-à-Pitre · Marie-Galante
DOMINICA · Roseau · Marigot
MARTINIQUE (FRANCE) · Mont Pelée 1,397 m · Saint-Pierre · Fort-de-France
ST. LUCIA · Castries · Vieux Fort · Soufrière 1,234 m
ST. VINCENT AND THE GRENADINES · Kingstown · BARBADOS · Bridgetown
GRENADA · Mt. St. Catherine 840 m · Saint George's · Carriacou · Leeward Is. · Windward Is.

**VENEZUELA / COLOMBIA / TRINIDAD**

Aruba (NETH.) · Oranjestad · Curaçao (NETH.) · Willemstad · Bonaire (NETH.) · Kralendijk · NETH. ANTILLES · El Roque · I. La Orchila (VEN.) · Islas Las Aves (VEN.) · Islas Los Roques (VEN.) · I. Blanquilla (VEN.) · I. La Tortuga (VEN.) · I. de Margarita · Porlamar · La Asunción
TRINIDAD AND TOBAGO · Charlotteville · Roxborough · Scarborough · Tobago · Port-of-Spain · TRINIDAD
Punta Gallinas · Cabo de la Vela · Guajira · Pen. de Paraguaná · Santa Marta · Barranquilla · Soledad · Maracaibo · Coro · Puerto Cabello · Maracay · Caracas · Cumaná · Barcelona · Maturín
Cartagena · COLOMBIA · Valledupar · Cabimas · Ciudad Ojeda · Valencia · Barquisimeto · Acarigua · VENEZUELA · Ciudad Guayana · Ciudad Bolívar
Pico Cristóbal Colón 5,775 m · Lago de Maracaibo · Mérida · Pico Bolívar 5,007 m · Barinas · San Fernando de Apure

**PANAMA**

Isthmus of Panama · Colón · La Chorrera · Panamá · Gulf of Panama · PN DARIÉN

SCALE 1:10,500,000 · LAMBERT CONFORMAL CONIC PROJECTION
MILES 0 — 150 — 300 — 450
KILOMETERS 0 — 150 — 300 — 450

# South America - Physical

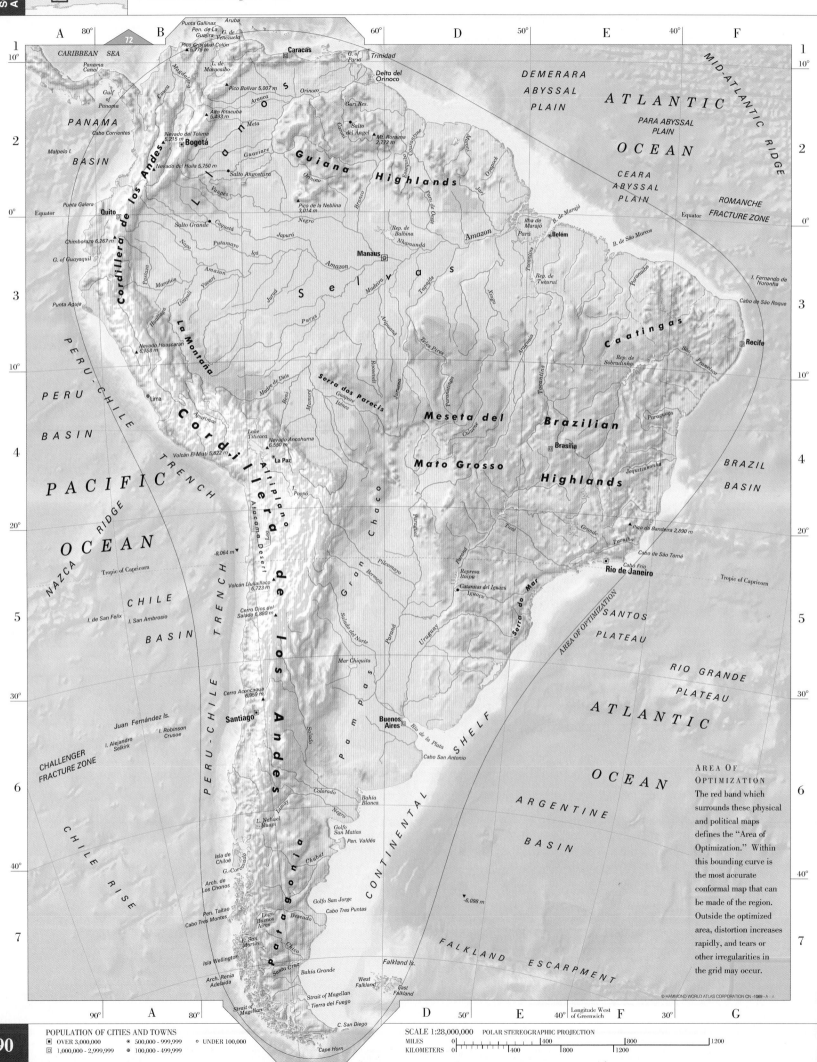

AREA OF OPTIMIZATION
The red band which surrounds these physical and political maps defines the "Area of Optimization." Within this bounding curve is the most accurate conformal map that can be made of the region. Outside the optimized area, distortion increases rapidly, and tears or other irregularities in the grid may occur.

© HAMMOND WORLD ATLAS CORPORATION CN -1069 - A - A

POPULATION OF CITIES AND TOWNS
- ■ OVER 3,000,000
- ▣ 1,000,000 - 2,999,999
- ◉ 500,000 - 999,999
- ● 100,000 - 499,999
- ○ UNDER 100,000

SCALE 1:28,000,000    POLAR STEREOGRAPHIC PROJECTION

MILES   0        400        800        1200
KILOMETERS 0     400    800   1200

► South America Comparisons: Pages 92 - 93
► Global relationships: Pages 14 - 36
► Index of the World: Pages 97 - 104

POPULATION OF CITIES AND TOWNS

■ OVER 3,000,000      ● 500,000 - 999,999      ○ UNDER 100,000
▣ 1,000,000 - 2,999,999      ◉ 100,000 - 499,999

SCALE 1:28,000,000      POLAR STEREOGRAPHIC PROJECTION

MILES    0          400          800          1200
KILOMETERS 0          400          800          1200

© HAMMOND WORLD ATLAS CORPORATION CN -1069 - A-A-A

# South America - Comparisons

► South America Physical / Political: Pages 90 - 91
► Global Relationships: Pages 14 - 36
► Index of the World: Pages 97 - 104

• LIMA 74°
AVERAGE JANUARY TEMPERATURE
DEGREES FAHRENHEIT AT
SELECTED STATIONS

• LIMA 62°
AVERAGE JULY TEMPERATURE
DEGREES FAHRENHEIT AT
SELECTED STATIONS

## AVERAGE JANUARY TEMPERATURE

| FAHRENHEIT | CELSIUS | FAHRENHEIT | CELSIUS | FAHRENHEIT | CELSIUS |
|---|---|---|---|---|---|
| OVER 86° | OVER 30° | 50° TO 68° | 10° TO 20° | UNDER 32° | UNDER 0° |
| 68° TO 86° | 20° TO 30° | 32° TO 50° | 0° TO 10° | | |

## AVERAGE JULY TEMPERATURE

| FAHRENHEIT | CELSIUS | FAHRENHEIT | CELSIUS | FAHRENHEIT | CELSIUS |
|---|---|---|---|---|---|
| OVER 86° | OVER 30° | 50° TO 68° | 10° TO 20° | UNDER 32° | UNDER 0° |
| 68° TO 86° | 20° TO 30° | 32° TO 50° | 0° TO 10° | | |

## CLIMATE

HUMID TROPICAL
- Af  NO DRY SEASON
- Am  SHORT DRY SEASON
- Aw  DRY WINTER

DRY
- BS  SEMIARID  ⎤ h HOT
- BW  ARID       ⎦ k COLD

HUMID WARM
- Cf  NO DRY SEASON
- Cw  DRY WINTER
- Cs  DRY SUMMER

COLD POLAR
- ET  SHORT COOL SUMMER,
      LONG COLD WINTER

a  HOT SUMMER
b  COOL SUMMER
c  SHORT COOL SUMMER
AFTER KOEPPEN-GEIGER

## VEGETATION

TROPICAL FOREST
- TROPICAL RAINFOREST
- LIGHT TROPICAL FOREST
- WOODLAND AND SHRUB

TROPICAL GRASSLAND
- GRASS AND SHRUB (SAVANNA)
- WOODED SAVANNA

MID-LATITUDE FOREST
- NEEDLELEAF FOREST
- MIXED NEEDLELEAF AND BROADLEAF FOREST
- WOODLAND AND SHRUB (MEDITERRANEAN)

MID-LATITUDE GRASSLAND
- SHORT GRASS (STEPPE)
- TALL GRASS (PRAIRIE) AND WOODED STEPPE

- DESERT AND DESERT SHRUB
- TUNDRA AND ALPINE
- UNCLASSIFIED HIGHLANDS

# South America - Comparisons

► South America Physical / Political: Pages 90 - 91
► Global Relationships: Pages 14 - 36
► Index of the World: Pages 97 - 104

• MANAUS 71
AVERAGE ANNUAL RAINFALL
IN INCHES AT SELECTED STATIONS

● CITIES WITH OVER 1,000,000
INHABITANTS (INCLUDING SUBURBS)

## AVERAGE ANNUAL RAINFALL

| INCHES | CM | INCHES | CM | INCHES | CM |
|--------|-----|--------|-----|--------|-----|
| OVER 80 | OVER 200 | 40 TO 60 | 100 TO 150 | 10 TO 20 | 25 TO 50 |
| 60 TO 80 | 150 TO 200 | 20 TO 40 | 50 TO 100 | UNDER 10 | UNDER 25 |

## POPULATION DISTRIBUTION

| DENSITY PER | | SQ. MI. | SQ. KM. | SQ. MI. | SQ. KM. |
|-------------|---------|---------|---------|---------|---------|
| SQ. MI. | SQ. KM. | 130 TO 260 | 50 TO 100 | 3 TO 25 | 1 TO 10 |
| OVER 260 | OVER 100 | 25 TO 130 | 10 TO 50 | UNDER 3 | UNDER 1 |

## ENERGY SOURCES

| ▬ OIL REGION | ■ COAL | ✳ URANIUM |
|---|---|---|
| ▬ NATURAL GAS REGION | ● HYDROELECTRICITY | |

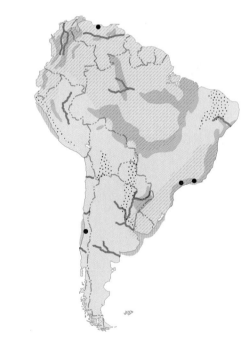

## ENVIRONMENTAL CONCERNS

| 〜 POLLUTED RIVERS | ▨ AREAS SUBJECT TO DEFORESTATION | ☐ EXTENT OF ACID RAIN |
|---|---|---|
| ▤ EXTENT OF COASTAL POLLUTION | ⠿ AREAS SUBJECT TO DESERTIFICATION | ● URBAN AREAS WITH SEVERE AIR POLLUTION |

| | Below Sea | 200 | 500 | 1,000 | 1,500 | 2,000 | 4,000 | 6,000 m. |
|---|---|---|---|---|---|---|---|---|
| | Sea Lev. Level | 700 | 1,600 | 3,300 | 5,000 | 6,500 | 13,000 | 19,700 ft. |

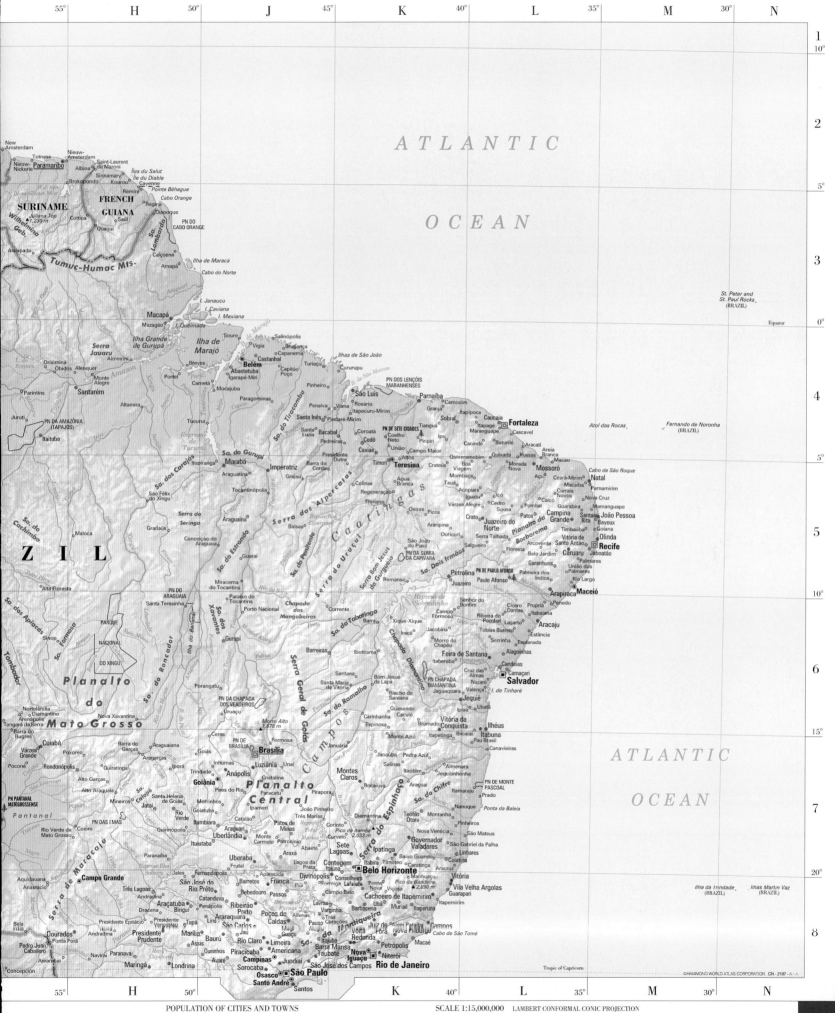

# Southern South America

► South America Comparisons: Pages 92 - 93
► Global relationships: Pages 14 - 36
► Index of the World: Pages 97 - 104

POPULATION OF CITIES AND TOWNS
- ◻ OVER 2,000,000
- ◻ 1,000,000 - 1,999,999
- ● 500,000 - 999,999
- ● 100,000 - 499,999
- ⊙ 50,000 - 99,999
- ○ UNDER 50,000

SCALE 1:15,000,000    LAMBERT CONFORMAL CONIC PROJECTION

| | | | | | |
|---|---|---|---|---|---|
| MILES | 0 | 200 | 400 | | 600 |
| KILOMETERS | 0 | 200 | 400 | 600 | |

Below Sea | 200 | 500 | 1,000 | 1,500 | 2,000 | 4,000 | 6,000 m.
Sea Lev. Level | 700 | 1,600 | 3,300 | 5,000 | 6,500 | 13,000 | 19,700 ft.

© HAMMOND WORLD ATLAS CORPORATION    CN - 2105 - A - A

This alphabetical list gives countries, cities, regions, political divisions, and physical features for the world. Latitude/longitude coordinates are given for each entry, where possible, followed by the page number for the map on which the entry appears to the best advantage. The entry may be located on other maps as well by the use of the coordinates given. Capitals are designated by asterisks (*).

## ▶ INDEX ABBREVIATIONS

| | | | | | | | | | |
|---|---|---|---|---|---|---|---|---|---|
| Afghan. | Afghanistan | D.R. Congo | Democratic Republic of the Congo | Miss. | Mississippi | N.Z. | New Zealand | S.D. | South Dakota |
| Ala. | Alabama | E. | East, Eastern | Mo. | Missouri | Nun. | Nunavut | Serb. | Serbia |
| Alg. | Algeria | El Sal. | El Salvador | Mont. | Montana | Okla. | Oklahoma | S. Korea | South Korea |
| Alta. | Alberta | Eng. | England | Monte. | Montenegro | Ont. | Ontario | Sol. Is. | Solomon Islands |
| Amer. | America | Eq. Guin. | Equatorial Guinea | Moz. | Mozambique | Ore. | Oregon | St. Ste. | Saint, Sainte |
| arch. | archipelago | Falk. Is. | Falkland Islands | mt., mts. | mountain, mountains | Pa. | Pennsylvania | Switz. | Switzerland |
| Arg. | Argentina | Fla. | Florida | N., No. | North, Northern | Pak. | Pakistan | Tajik. | Tajikistan |
| Ariz. | Arizona | Fr. | France, French | Namb. | Namibia | P.E.I. | Prince Edward Island | Tanz. | Tanzania |
| Ark. | Arkansas | Ga. | Georgia | Nat'l Pk | National Park | Phil. | Philippines | Tenn. | Tennessee |
| Austl. | Australia | Ger. | Germany | N.B. | New Brunswick | plat. | plateau | Terr. | Territory |
| Azer. | Azerbaijan | Guat. | Guatemala | N.C. | North Carolina | P.N.G. | Papua New Guinea | Thai. | Thailand |
| Belg. | Belgium | Ill. | Illinois | N.D. | North Dakota | Port. | Portugal | Trkm. | Turkmenistan |
| Bots. | Botswana | Ind. | Indiana | Neb. | Nebraska | P.R. | Puerto Rico | U.K. | United Kingdom |
| Br. Col. | British Columbia | Indon. | Indonesia | Neth. | Netherlands | prom. | promontory | Un. | United |
| Calif. | California | isl., isls. | island, islands | Neth. Ant. | Netherlands Antilles | prov. | province, provincial | U.S. | United States |
| Can. | Canada | Kans. | Kansas | Nev. | Nevada | Qué. | Québec | Uzb. | Uzbekistan |
| CAfr. | Central A]an Republic | Kazak. | Kazakhstan | New Cal. | New Caledonia | Rep. | Republic | Va. | Virginia |
| chan. | channel | Ky. | Kentucky | Newf. | Newfoundland and Labrador | res. | reservoir | Ven. | Venezuela |
| Col. | Colombia | La. | Louisiana | N.H. | New Hampshire | R.I. | Rhode Island | Vt. | Vermont |
| Colo. | Colorado | Lux. | Luxembourg | Nic. | Nicaragua | Rom. | Romania | W. | West, Western |
| Conn. | Connecticut | Man. | Manitoba | N.J. | New Jersey | S., So. | South, Southern | Wash. | Washington |
| C.R. | Costa Rica | Mart. | Martinique | N. Korea | North Korea | S. Afr. | South Africa | Wis. | Wisconsin |
| Czech Rep. | Czech Republic | Mass. | Massachusetts | N.M. | New Mexico | S. Ar. | Saudi Arabia | W. Va. | West Virginia |
| D.C. | District of Columbia | Md. | Maryland | No. Ire. | Northern Ireland | Sask. | Saskatchewan | Wyo. | Wyoming |
| Del. | Delaware | Mex. | Mexico | N.S. | Nova Scotia | S.C. | South Carolina | Zim. | Zimbabwe |
| Den. | Denmark | Mich. | Michigan | N.W. Terrs. | Northwest Territories (Canada) | Scot. | Scotland | | |
| Dom. Rep. | Dominican Republic | Minn. | Minnesota | N.Y. | New York | | | | |

| NAME | POPULATION | LATITUDE | LONGITUDE | PAGE |
|---|---|---|---|---|
| **A** | | | | |
| Aberdeen, Scot. | 219,120 | 57° 09′ N | 02° 06′ W | 42 |
| Abidjan, Côte d'Ivoire | 1,929,079 | 05 20 N | 04 01 W | 68 |
| Abilene, Texas, U.S. | 115,930 | 32 27 N | 99 44 W | 83 |
| Abitibi (lake), Ont.,Qué., Can. | | 48 30 N | 79 30 W | 84 |
| Abitibi (river), Ont., Can. | | 49 00 N | 81 00 W | 84 |
| Abu Dhabi,* United Arab Emirates | 398,695 | 24 28 N | 54 22 E | 52 |
| Abuja,* Nigeria | 305,900 | 09 05 E | 68 | |
| Acadia Nat'l Pk., Maine, U.S. | | 44 30 N | 68 30 W | 85 |
| Acapulco, Mex. | 620,656 | 16 51 N | 99 55 W | 88 |
| Accra,* Ghana | 953,500 | 05 33 N | 00 12 W | 68 |
| Aconcagua (mt.), Arg.,Chile | | 32 45 S | 70 14 W | 96 |
| Adair, (cape), Nun., Can. | | 72 00 N | 71 30 W | 77 |
| Adana, Turkey | 1,133,028 | 37 00 N | 35 15 E | 44 |
| Ad Dahna′ (desert), S. Ar. | | 27 30 N | 45 00 E | 52 |
| Addis Ababa,* Ethiopia | 2,534,000 | 09 01 N | 38 45 E | 69 |
| Adelaide, Austl. | 995,955 | 34 55 S | 138 37 E | 59 |
| Aden, Yemen | 562,000 | 12 45 N | 45 05 E | 52 |
| Adirondack (mts.), N.Y., U.S. | | 44 00 N | 74 00 W | 84 |
| Admiralty (inlet), Nun., Can. | | 73 00 N | 86 00 W | 77 |
| Adrar de Iforas (plat.), Alg.,Mali. | | 20 00 N | 02 00 E | 68 |
| Adriatic (sea), Europe | | 42 50 N | 15 40 E | 44 |
| Aegean (sea), Greece,Turkey | | 40 23 N | 25 00 E | 44 |
| **Afghanistan** | **31,056,997** | **34 00 N** | **65 00 E** | **49** |
| Africa (cont.) | 910,849,725 | | | 65 |
| Āgra, India | 1,259,979 | 27 10 N | 78 08 E | 53 |
| Aguascalientes, Mex. | 594,092 | 21 53 N | 102 18 W | 88 |
| Agulhas (cape), S. Afr. | | 34 51 S | 19 59 E | 70 |
| Ahaggar (mts.), Alg. | | 23 00 N | 05 00 E | 68 |
| Ahmadabad, India | 3,515,361 | 23 00 N | 72 44 E | 53 |
| Ahvāz, Iran | 804,980 | 31 19 N | 48 42 E | 52 |
| Aklavik, N.W. Terrs., Can. | 632 | 68 12 N | 135 00 W | 76 |
| Akron, Ohio, U.S. | 217,074 | 41 05 N | 81 31 W | 84 |
| Alabama (state), U.S. | 4,447,100 | 33 00 N | 87 00 W | 87 |
| Åland (isls.), Finland | | 60 15 N | 20 00 E | 43 |
| Alaska (gulf), Alaska, U.S. | | 59 00 N | 145 00 W | 78 |
| Alaska (pen.), Alaska, U.S. | | 57 00 N | 158 00 W | 78 |
| Alaska (range), Alaska, U.S. | | 63 00 N | 151 00 W | 78 |
| Alaska (state), U.S. | 626,932 | 65 00 N | 154 00 W | 78 |
| **Albania** | **3,581,655** | **41 00 N** | **20 00 E** | **44** |
| Albany (river), On., Can. | | 52 16 N | 81 30 W | 77 |
| Albany, Ga., U.S. | 76,939 | 31 34 N | 84 09 W | 87 |
| Albany,* N.Y., U.S. | 95,658 | 42 39 N | 73 45 W | 84 |
| Albert (lake), D.R. Congo,Uganda | | 01 45 N | 31 00 E | 69 |
| Alberta (prov.), Can. | 2,974,810 | 54 00 N | 115 00 W | 76 |
| Albuquerque, N.M., U.S. | 448,607 | 35 05 N | 106 39 W | 82 |
| Aleppo, Syria | 1,542,000 | 36 12 N | 37 10 E | 52 |
| Aleutian (isls.), Alaska, U.S. | | 52 00 N | 175 00 W | 78 |
| Alexandria, Egypt | 3,339,076 | 31 12 N | 29 55 E | 69 |
| Alexandria, La., U.S. | 46,342 | 31 18 N | 92 26 W | 83 |
| Alexandria, Va., U.S. | 128,283 | 38 48 N | 77 03 W | 84 |
| **Algeria** | **32,930,091** | **30 00 N** | **04 00 E** | **68** |
| Algiers,* Alg. | 1,569,897 | 36 45 N | 03 04 E | 68 |
| Alicante, Spain | 284,580 | 38 21 N | 00 29 W | 42 |
| Al Jīsah, Egypt | 2,221,817 | 30 01 N | 31 13 E | 69 |
| Allahabad, India | 990,298 | 25 30 N | 81 58 E | 69 |
| Allentown, Pa., U.S. | 106,632 | 40 36 N | 75 28 W | 84 |
| Almaty, Kazak. | 1,135,400 | 43 15 N | 76 57 E | 54 |
| Alps (mts.), Europe | | 46 40 N | 10 00 E | 42 |
| Altai (mts.), China,Mongolia | | 47 00 N | 92 00 E | 54 |
| Altun (mts.), China | | 37 30 N | 88 00 E | 54 |
| Amarillo, Texas, U.S. | 173,627 | 25 12 N | 101 50 W | 82 |
| Amazon (river), Brazil,Peru | | 00 00 | 49 00 W | 95 |
| American Highland (upland), Antarctica | | 72 30 S | 78 00 E | 71 |
| American Samoa, U.S. | 68,688 | 14 20 S | 170 00 W | 63 |
| Ames, Iowa, U.S. | 50,731 | 42 01 N | 93 37 W | 81 |
| Amherst, N.S., Can. | 9,502 | 45 50 N | 64 12 W | 85 |
| Amman,* Jordan | 969,598 | 31 57 N | 35 56 E | 52 |
| Amritsar, India | 975,695 | 31 45 N | 74 58 E | 53 |
| Amsterdam,* Neth. | 735,526 | 52 20 N | 04 50 E | 42 |
| Amu Darya (river), Trkm.,Uzb. | | 43 40 N | 59 01 E | 46 |
| Amundsen (sea), Antarctica | | 72 00 S | 109 00 W | 71 |
| Amur (river), China,Russia | | 52 56 N | 141 10 E | 55 |
| Anadyr′ (mts.), Russia | | 67 00 N | 176 00 E | 47 |
| Anaheim, Calif., U.S. | 328,014 | 33 50 N | 117 55 E | 82 |
| Anatolia (region), Turkey | | 39 00 N | 30 00 E | 44 |
| Anchorage, Alaska, U.S. | 260,283 | 61 10 N | 149 55 W | 78 |
| Andaman (isls.), India | 317,057 | 12 00 N | 92 45 E | 53 |
| Anderson, Ind., U.S. | 59,734 | 40 06 N | 85 40 W | 84 |
| Andes (mts.), S. America | | 27 00 S | 69 00 W | 91 |
| **Andorra** | **71,201** | **42 34 N** | **01 35 E** | **42** |
| Andorra la Vella,* Andorra | 18,142 | 01 32 N | 42 30 E | 42 |
| Angara (river), Russia | | 56 05 N | 101 48 E | 47 |
| **Angola** | **12,127,071** | **12 00 S** | **17 00 E** | **70** |
| Anguilla, U.K. | 11,561 | 18 13 N | 63 03 W | 89 |
| Ankara,* Turkey | 3,203,362 | 39 55 N | 32 52 E | 44 |
| Annapolis,* Md., U.S. | 35,838 | 38 58 N | 76 29 W | 84 |
| Ann Arbor, Mich., U.S. | 114,024 | 42 17 N | 83 44 W | 84 |
| Anshan, China | 1,556,285 | 41 08 N | 122 59 E | 55 |
| Antananarivo,* Madagascar | 710,236 | 18 54 S | 47 30 E | 70 |
| Antarctic (pen.), Antarctica | | 69 30 S | 65 00 W | 71 |
| Antarctica (cont.) | | | | 71 |
| Anticosti (isl.), Qué., Can. | | 49 30 N | 63 00 W | 85 |
| **Antigua and Barbuda** | **69,108** | **17 05 N** | **61 48 W** | **89** |
| Antwerp, Belg. | 467,518 | 51 20 N | 04 25 E | 42 |
| Apennines (mts.), Italy | | 43 00 N | 13 00 E | 44 |
| Apia,* Samoa | 38,836 | 13 56 S | 171 45 W | 63 |
| Appalachian (mts.), U.S. | | 40 00 N | 78 00 W | 79 |
| Appleton, Wis., U.S. | 70,087 | 44 15 N | 88 25 W | 84 |
| Aqaba (gulf), S. Ar.,Egypt | | 29 30 N | 35 05 E | 52 |
| Aqtöbe, Kazakhstan | 249,200 | 50 17 N | 57 10 E | 45 |
| Arafura (sea), Indon. | | 09 00 S | 134 00 E | 57 |
| Arakan (mts.), Myanmar | | 19 00 N | 94 00 E | 53 |
| Aral (sea) Kazak.,Uzb. | | 44 46 N | 60 00 E | 45 |
| Ararat (mt.), Turkey | | 39 42 N | 44 18 E | 45 |
| Aras (river), Azer.,Iran | | 39 56 N | 48 20 E | 45 |
| Archangel'sk, Russia | 364,985 | 64 34 N | 40 32 E | 43 |
| Ardennes (region), Belg. | | 50 10 N | 05 30 E | 42 |
| Arequipa, Peru | 624,500 | 16 24 S | 71 33 W | 94 |
| **Argentina** | **39,921,833** | **35 00 S** | **65 00 W** | **96** |
| Århus, Den. | 209,404 | 56 11 N | 10 15 E | 43 |
| Arizona (state), U.S. | 5,130,632 | 34 00 N | 112 00 W | 82 |
| Arkansas (river), U.S. | | 33 48 N | 91 07 W | 83 |
| Arkansas (state), U.S. | 2,673,400 | 34 45 N | 92 30 W | 83 |
| Arlington, Texas, U.S. | 332,969 | 32 44 N | 97 06 W | 83 |
| Arlington, Va., U.S. | 189,453 | 38 53 N | 77 05 W | 84 |
| **Armenia** | **2,976,372** | **40 15 N** | **45 00 E** | **45** |
| Aruba (isl.) Neth. | 71,566 | 12 30 N | 69 58 W | 89 |
| Ascension (isl.), U.K. | 1,117 | 07 57 S | 14 22 W | 12 |
| Asheville, N.C., U.S. | 68,889 | 35 36 N | 82 33 W | 87 |
| Ashgabat,* Trkm. | 525,000 | 37 57 N | 58 23 E | 45 |
| Asia (cont.) | 3,958,768,088 | | | 49 |
| Asir (region), S. Ar. | | 18 00 N | 42 00 E | 52 |
| Asmara,* Eritrea | 500,600 | 15 20 N | 38 57 E | 69 |
| Assiniboine, (riv.), Man.,Sask., Can. | | 51 30 N | 99 00 W | 83 |
| Astana,* Kazakhstan | 322,400 | 34 45 N | 71 30 E | 62 |
| Astrakhan′, Russia | 482,402 | 46 21 N | 48 03 E | 69 |
| Asunción,* Paraguay | 513,399 | 25 16 S | 57 40 W | 96 |
| Atacama (desert), Chile | | 24 00 S | 70 00 W | 96 |
| Atatürk (res.), Turkey | | 37 30 N | 38 30 E | 44 |
| Athabasca, (lake), Alta.,Sask., Can. | | 59 20 N | 109 00 W | 76 |
| Athabasca (river), Alta., Can. | | 58 30 N | 111 00 W | 76 |
| Athens, Ga., U.S. | 101,489 | 33 57 N | 83 23 W | 87 |
| Athens,* Greece | 789,166 | 37 59 N | 23 44 E | 44 |
| Atlanta,* Ga., U.S. | 416,474 | 33 45 N | 84 24 W | 87 |
| Atlantic City, N.J., U.S. | 40,517 | 39 21 N | 74 27 W | 84 |
| Atlas (mts.), Alg.,Morocco | | 34 00 N | 00 01 W | 68 |
| Attu (isl.), Alaska, U.S. | | 52 55 N | 172 55 E | 78 |
| Auckland, N.Z. | 367,737 | 36 53 S | 174 45 E | 61 |
| Augsburg, Germany | 254,867 | 48 20 N | 10 53 E | 42 |
| Augusta, Ga., U.S. | 199,775 | 33 28 N | 81 58 W | 87 |
| Augusta,* Maine, U.S. | 18,560 | 44 18 N | 69 46 W | 85 |
| Aurora, Co., U.S. | 276,393 | 39 44 N | 104 50 W | 83 |
| Aurora, Ill., U.S. | 142,990 | 41 45 N | 88 19 W | 84 |
| Austin,* Texas, U.S. | 656,562 | 30 16 N | 97 44 W | 86 |
| **Australia (cont.)** | **20,264,082** | **25 00 S** | **135 00 E** | **59** |
| Australian Capital Terr., Austl. | 311,947 | 35 18 S | 149 07 E | 59 |
| **Austria** | **8,192,880** | **47 15 N** | **14 00 E** | **42** |
| Auyuittuq Nat'l Pk., Nun., Can. | | 67 00 N | 66 00 W | 77 |
| Avalon (pen.), Newf., Can. | | 46 30 N | 53 30 W | 85 |
| Axel Heiberg (isl.), Nun., Can | | 79 00 N | 90 00 W | 76 |
| Ayeyarwady (river), Myanmar | | 23 19 N | 96 00 E | 53 |
| **Azerbaijan** | **7,961,619** | **40 30 N** | **48 00 E** | **45** |
| Azores (isls.), Port. | 241,763 | 38 30 N | 28 00 W | 12 |
| Azov (sea), Russia, Ukraine | | 46 00 N | 37 00 E | 44 |
| **B** | | | | |
| Back (river), Nun., Can. | | 66° 00′ N | 96° 00′ W | 76 |
| Badlands Nat'l Pk., S.D., U.S. | | 43 00 N | 102 00 W | 81 |
| Baffin (bay), Can. | | 74 00 N | 68 00 W | 77 |
| Baffin (isl.), Nun., Can. | | 68 30 N | 70 00 W | 77 |
| Baghdad,* Iraq | 3,841,268 | 33 21 N | 44 24 E | 52 |
| **Bahamas, The** | **303,770** | **24 00 N** | **76 00 W** | **89** |
| **Bahrain** | **698,585** | **26 00 N** | **50 40 E** | **52** |
| Baie-Comeau, Qué., Can. | 23,079 | 49 12 N | 68 12 W | 85 |
| Baja California (pen.), Mex. | | 28 00 N | 114 00 W | 89 |
| Bakersfield, Calif., U.S. | 247,057 | 35 22 N | 119 01 W | 82 |
| Bākhtarān, Iran | 665,636 | 34 19 N | 47 04 E | 52 |
| Baku,* Azer. | 1,823,300 | 40 23 N | 49 51 E | 45 |
| Balaton (lake), Hungary | | 46 50 N | 17 50 E | 44 |
| Balearic (isls.), Spain | 841,669 | 39 30 N | 03 00 E | 42 |
| Bali (isl.), Indon. | 3,151,162 | 08 30 S | 115 30 E | 56 |
| Balkan (mts.), Europe | | 43 15 N | 23 00 E | 44 |
| Balkhash (lake), Kazak. | | 46 00 N | 74 00 E | 54 |
| Baltic (sea), Europe | | 56 30 N | 19 00 E | 43 |
| Baltimore, Md., U.S. | 651,154 | 39 17 N | 76 36 W | 84 |
| Bamako,* Mali | 1,016,167 | 12 38 N | 07 59 W | 68 |
| Banaba (isl.) Kiribati | | 00 52 S | 169 35 E | 62 |
| Banda (sea), Indon. | | 06 00 S | 128 00 E | 57 |
| Bandar Seri Begawan,* Brunei.. | 27,285 | 04 55 N | 114 55 E | 56 |
| Bandung, Indon. | 2,138,066 | 06 56 S | 107 36 E | 56 |
| Banff, Alta., Can. | 7,135 | 51 10 N | 115 34 W | 80 |
| Banff Nat'l Pk., Alta., Can. | | 51 30 N | 115 45 W | 80 |
| Bangalore, India | 4,292,223 | 12 59 N | 77 28 E | 53 |
| Bangka (isl.), Indon. | | 02 22 S | 106 08 E | 56 |
| Bangkok,* Thai. | 6,355,100 | 13 45 N | 100 30 E | 56 |
| **Bangladesh** | **147,365,352** | **23 30 N** | **90 00 E** | **53** |
| Bangor, Maine, U.S. | 31,473 | 44 48 N | 68 46 W | 85 |
| Bangui,* CAfr. | 451,690 | 04 22 N | 18 36 E | 69 |
| Bangweulu (lake), Zambia | | 11 00 S | 29 45 E | 70 |
| Banjul,* Gambia | 42,326 | 13 28 N | 16 35 W | 68 |
| Banks (isl.) N.W. Terrs., Can. | | 73 00 N | 122 00 W | 76 |
| Baotou, China | 1,671,181 | 40 40 N | 109 59 E | 55 |
| **Barbados** | **279,912** | **13 10 N** | **59 30 W** | **89** |
| Barcelona, Spain | 1,503,884 | 41 38 N | 02 10 E | 42 |
| Bareilly, India | 699,839 | 28 21 N | 79 25 E | 53 |
| Barents (sea), Russia | | 70 00 N | 45 00 E | 46 |
| Bari, Italy | 332,143 | 41 07 N | 16 52 E | 44 |
| Barisan (mts.), Indon. | | 03 00 S | 102 15 E | 56 |
| Barkly Tableland (plat.), Austl. | | 20 00 C | 130 00 C | 60 |
| Baroda, India | 1,306,035 | 22 18 N | 73 12 E | 53 |
| Barquisimeto, Ven. | 625,450 | 10 04 N | 69 19 W | 94 |
| Barranquilla, Col. | 1,000,283 | 10 59 N | 74 50 W | 94 |
| Barrie, Ont., Can. | 103,710 | 44 24 N | 79 40 W | 84 |
| Barrow (strait), Nun., Can. | | 74 00 N | 94 00 W | 76 |
| Basel, Switz. | 166,558 | 47 35 N | 07 32 E | 42 |

# Index of the World


| NAME | POPULATION | LATITUDE | LONGITUDE | PAGE |
|---|---|---|---|---|
| Bass (strait), Austl. | | 40 15 S | 146 00 E | 59 |
| Basseterre,* St. Kitts & Nevis | 12,605 | 17 18 N | 62 43 W | 89 |
| Bathurst, N.B., Can. | 12,924 | 47 36 N | 65 39 W | 85 |
| Bathurst (inlet), Nun., Can. | | 67 30 N | 99 00 W | 76 |
| Baton Rouge,* La., U.S. | 227,818 | 30 27 N | 91 09 W | 87 |
| Battle Creek, Mich., U.S. | 53,364 | 42 19 N | 85 10 W | 84 |
| Baykal (lake), Russia | | 54 00 N | 109 00 E | 47 |
| Beaufort (sea), Can., U.S. | | 71 00 N | 140 00 W | 76 |
| Beaumont, Texas, U.S. | 113,866 | 30 05 N | 94 05 W | 86 |
| Beersheba, Israel | 152,645 | 31 14 N | 34 47 E | 52 |
| Beijing (Peking),* China | 11,509,595 | 39 56 N | 116 24 E | 55 |
| Beira, Moz. | 397,368 | 19 50 S | 34 50 E | 70 |
| Beirut,* Lebanon | 1,000,000 | 33 55 N | 35 30 E | 52 |
| **Belarus** | **10,293,011** | **53 00 N** | **28 00 E** | **43** |
| Belcher (isls.), Nun., Can. | | 56 00 N | 79 30 W | 77 |
| Belém, Brazil | 1,280,614 | 01 28 S | 48 27 W | 95 |
| Belfast,* No. Ire. | 279,237 | 54 35 N | 05 55 W | 42 |
| **Belgium** | **10,379,067** | **50 45 N** | **04 30 E** | **42** |
| Belgrade,* Serb. | 1,119,642 | 44 48 N | 20 29 E | 44 |
| Belitung (isl.), Indon. | | 02 54 S | 107 58 E | 56 |
| **Belize** | **287,730** | **17 00 N** | **88 45 W** | **88** |
| Belize City, Belize | 49,050 | 17 30 N | 88 12 W | 88 |
| Bell (pen.), Nun., Can. | | 64 00 N | 80 30 W | 77 |
| Belle Isle (strait), Newf., Can. | | 51 30 N | 56 30 W | 77 |
| Bellingham, Wash., U.S. | 67,171 | 48 45 N | 122 29 W | 80 |
| Bellingshausen (sea), Antarctica | | 69 00 S | 81 00 E | 71 |
| Belmopan,* Belize | 8,130 | 17 15 N | 88 47 W | 88 |
| Belo Horizonte, Brazil | 2,238,526 | 19 56 S | 43 57 W | 95 |
| Bend, Ore., U.S. | 52,029 | 44 03 N | 121 19 W | 80 |
| Bengal (bay), Asia | | 18 00 N | 90 00 E | 53 |
| Benghazi, Libya | 446,000 | 32 07 N | 20 03 E | 69 |
| **Benin** | **7,862,944** | **09 00 N** | **02 00 E** | **68** |
| Benin, Bight of (bay), Africa | | 05 00 N | 04 00 E | 68 |
| Ben Nevis (mt.), Scot., U.K. | | 56 48 N | 04 59 W | 42 |
| Bergen, Norway | 209,375 | 60 25 N | 05 20 E | 43 |
| Bering (sea), Russia,U.S. | | 55 00 N | 180 00 | 47 |
| Bering (strait), Russia,U.S. | | 67 00 N | 170 00 W | 78 |
| Berkeley, Calif., U.S. | 102,743 | 37 52 N | 122 16 W | 82 |
| Berlin,* Germany | 3,386,667 | 52 30 N | 13 20 E | 42 |
| Bermuda, U.K. | 65,365 | 32 20 N | 64 40 W | 73 |
| Bern,* Switz. | 128,634 | 47 00 N | 07 30 E | 42 |
| Bethlehem, Pa., U.S. | 71,329 | 40 37 N | 75 22 W | 84 |
| Bhopāl, India | 1,433,875 | 23 16 N | 77 24 E | 53 |
| **Bhutan** | **2,279,723** | **27 15 N** | **90 00 E** | **53** |
| Bialystok, Poland | 291,383 | 53 09 N | 23 09 E | 44 |
| Bienville (lake), Qué., Can. | | 55 00 N | 73 00 W | 77 |
| Bikini (isl.), Marshall Islands | | 11 37 N | 165 33 E | 62 |
| Bilbao, Spain | 349,972 | 43 16 N | 03 05 W | 42 |
| Billings, Mont., U.S. | 89,847 | 45 47 N | 108 30 W | 80 |
| Biloxi, Miss., U.S. | 50,644 | 30 23 N | 88 52 W | 87 |
| Binghamton, N.Y., U.S. | 47,380 | 42 06 N | 75 55 W | 84 |
| Birmingham, Ala., U.S. | 242,820 | 33 31 N | 86 48 W | 87 |
| Birmingham, Eng., U.K. | 965,928 | 52 30 N | 01 55 W | 42 |
| Biscay (bay), Fr. | | 45 00 N | 05 00 W | 42 |
| Bishkek,* Kyrgyzstan | 781,800 | 42 54 N | 74 36 E | 54 |
| Bismarck (arch.), P.N.G. | | 04 00 S | 150 00 E | 62 |
| Bismarck,* N.D., U.S. | 55,532 | 46 48 N | 100 47 W | 81 |
| Bissau,* Guinea-Bissau | 109,214 | 11 51 N | 15 35 W | 68 |
| Bitterroot (mts.), Idaho,Mont., U.S. | | 46 30 N | 114 25 W | 80 |
| Black (sea), Asia,Europe | | 42 30 N | 35 00 E | 44 |
| Black Hills (mts.), S.D. U.S. | | 44 00 N | 103 30 W | 81 |
| Blanc (mt.), Fr.,Italy | | 45 50 N | 06 51 E | 42 |
| Blantyre, Malawi | 502,053 | 15 49 S | 35 00 E | 70 |
| Bloemfontein,* S. Afr. | 111,698 | 29 07 S | 26 14 E | 70 |
| Bloomington, Ill., U.S. | 64,808 | 40 29 N | 88 59 W | 84 |
| Bloomington, Ind., U.S. | 69,291 | 39 10 N | 86 31 W | 84 |
| Blue Nile (river), Egypt,Ethiopia | | 15 37 N | 32 31 E | 69 |
| Boca Raton, Fla., U.S. | 74,764 | 26 21 N | 80 05 W | 87 |
| Bogotá,* Col. | 5,698,566 | 04 36 N | 74 05 W | 94 |
| Boise,* Idaho, U.S. | 185,787 | 43 36 N | 116 12 W | 80 |
| **Bolivia** | **8,989,046** | **16 00 S** | **64 00 W** | **94** |
| Bologna, Italy | 379,964 | 44 30 N | 11 20 E | 42 |
| Bonaire (isl.), Neth. Ant. | 14,218 | 12 12 N | 68 15 W | 89 |
| Bonifacio (strait), Fr.,Italy | | 41 18 N | 09 15 E | 42 |
| Bonn, Germany | 301,048 | 50 44 N | 07 06 E | 42 |
| Boothia (gulf), Nun., Can. | | 70 00 N | 91 00 W | 76 |
| Boothia (pen.), Nun., Can. | | 70 00 N | 95 00 W | 76 |
| Bordeaux, Fr. | 218,948 | 44 50 N | 00 35 W | 42 |
| Borden (pen.), Nun., Can. | | 74 00 N | 83 00 W | 77 |
| Borneo (isl.), Asia | 16,254,358 | 00 00 | 113 00 E | 56 |
| Bornholm (isl.), Den. | | 55 10 N | 15 00 E | 43 |
| **Bosnia and Herzegovina** | **4,498,976** | **44 00 N** | **18 00 E** | **44** |
| Bosporus (strait), Turkey | | 41 15 N | 29 10 E | 44 |
| Boston,* Mass., U.S. | 589,141 | 42 21 N | 71 03 W | 85 |
| Bothnia (gulf), Finland,Sweden | | 62 00 N | 20 00 E | 43 |
| Botou, China | 550,888 | 38 05 N | 116 30 E | 55 |
| **Botswana** | **1,639,833** | **22 00 S** | **24 00 E** | **70** |
| Bougainville (isl.), P.N.G. | | 06 10 S | 155 15 E | 62 |
| Boulder, Colo., U.S. | 94,673 | 40 01 N | 105 16 W | 83 |
| Bouvet (isl.), Norway | | 54 26 S | 03 24 E | 12 |
| Bozeman, Mont., U.S. | 27,509 | 45 41 N | 111 02 W | 80 |
| Bradford, Eng., U.K. | 289,376 | 53 47 N | 01 45 W | 42 |
| Brahmaputra (river), Bangladesh,India | | 29 30 N | 95 00 E | 53 |
| Brăila, Rom. | 216,292 | 45 15 N | 27 58 E | 44 |
| Brampton, Ont., Can. | 325,428 | 43 41 N | 79 45 W | 84 |
| Brandon, Man., Can. | 39,716 | 49 50 N | 99 57 W | 81 |
| Brasília,* Brazil | 2,051,146 | 15 47 S | 47 55 W | 95 |
| Braşov, Rom. | 284,246 | 45 39 N | 25 37 E | 44 |
| Bratislava,* Slovakia | 427,425 | 48 09 N | 17 07 E | 44 |
| Braunschweig, Germany | 246,322 | 52 22 N | 10 42 E | 42 |
| **Brazil** | **188,078,227** | **14 00 S** | **50 00 W** | **91** |
| Brazos (river), Texas, U.S. | | 28 57 N | 95 18 W | 86 |
| Brazzaville,* Congo | 937,500 | 04 17 S | 15 14 E | 70 |
| Bremen, Germany | 540,330 | 53 10 N | 08 40 E | 42 |
| Brescia, Italy | 194,697 | 45 30 N | 10 15 E | 42 |
| Breton (cape), N.S., Can. | | 45 56 N | 59 48 W | 85 |
| Bridgeport, Conn., U.S. | 139,529 | 41 11 N | 73 11 W | 85 |
| Bridgetown,* Barbados | 6,700 | 13 06 N | 59 37 W | 89 |
| Brisbane, Austl. | 1,490,475 | 27 25 S | 153 05 E | 59 |

| NAME | POPULATION | LATITUDE | LONGITUDE | PAGE |
|---|---|---|---|---|
| Bristol (bay), Alaska, U.S. | | 57 45 N | 160 00 W | 78 |
| Bristol, Eng., U.K. | 407,992 | 51 28 N | 02 35 W | 42 |
| Britanny (region), Fr. | | 48 00 N | 03 00 W | 42 |
| British Columbia (prov.), Can. | 3,907,735 | 55 00 N | 125 00 W | 76 |
| British Indian Ocean Terr., U.K. | 3,200 | 06 00 S | 72 00 E | 13 |
| Brno, Czech Rep. | 379,185 | 49 10 N | 16 30 E | 42 |
| Brockton, Mass., U.S. | 94,304 | 42 05 N | 71 01 W | 85 |
| Brockville, Ont., Can. | 23,014 | 44 36 N | 75 41 W | 84 |
| Brodeaur (pen.), Nun., Can. | | 73 00 N | 89 30 W | 76 |
| Brooks (mts.), Alaska, U.S. | | 68 30 N | 153 00 W | 78 |
| Brownsville, Texas, U.S. | 139,722 | 25 54 N | 97 30 W | 86 |
| **Brunei** | **379,444** | **04 30 N** | **115 00 E** | **56** |
| Brussels,* Belg. | 964,405 | 50 50 N | 04 22 E | 42 |
| Bryan, Texas, U.S. | 65,660 | 30 40 N | 96 22 W | 86 |
| Bucharest,* Rom. | 1,926,334 | 44 25 N | 26 06 E | 44 |
| Budapest,* Hungary | 1,729,456 | 47 30 N | 19 10 E | 44 |
| Buenos Aires,* Arg. | 2,776,138 | 34 36 S | 58 26 W | 96 |
| Buffalo, N.Y., U.S. | 292,648 | 42 53 N | 78 52 W | 84 |
| Bujumbura,* Burundi | 235,440 | 03 23 S | 29 22 E | 70 |
| Bulawayo, Zimbabwe | 621,742 | 20 09 S | 28 36 E | 70 |
| **Bulgaria** | **7,385,367** | **42 30 N** | **25 30 E** | **44** |
| Burbank, Calif., U.S. | 100,316 | 34 11 N | 118 18 W | 82 |
| Burgundy (region), Fr. | | 47 00 N | 05 00 E | 42 |
| **Burkina Faso** | **13,902,972** | **12 00 N** | **01 30 W** | **68** |
| Burlington, Ont., Can. | 150,836 | 43 19 N | 79 47 W | 84 |
| Burlington, Vt., U.S. | 38,889 | 44 28 N | 73 12 W | 85 |
| **Burma (Myanmar)** | **42,720,196** | **20 00 N** | **96 00 E** | **49** |
| Bursa, Turkey | 1,184,144 | 40 11 N | 29 04 E | 44 |
| **Burundi** | **8,090,068** | **03 30 S** | **30 00 E** | **70** |
| Bydgoszcz, Poland | 373,804 | 53 50 N | 27 35 E | 42 |


## C


| NAME | POPULATION | LATITUDE | LONGITUDE | PAGE |
|---|---|---|---|---|
| Caatingas (region), Brazil | | 07° 00′ N | 43° 00′ W | 95 |
| Cabonga (res.), Qué., Can. | | 47 30 N | 76 30 W | 84 |
| Cádiz, Spain | 133,363 | 36 32 N | 06 18 W | 42 |
| Cagliari, Italy | 162,993 | 39 13 N | 09 07 E | 42 |
| Cairo,* Egypt | 6,800,992 | 30 03 N | 31 15 E | 69 |
| Calgary, Alta., Can. | 878,866 | 51 03 N | 114 05 W | 80 |
| Cali, Col. | 1,624,937 | 03 28 N | 76 30 W | 94 |
| California (gulf), Mex. | | 28 00 N | 112 00 W | 89 |
| California (state), U.S. | 33,871,648 | 37 00 N | 120 00 W | 82 |
| Callao, Peru | 515,200 | 12 03 S | 77 10 W | 94 |
| Camagüey, Cuba | 249,332 | 21 53 N | 77 55 W | 89 |
| **Cambodia** | **13,881,427** | **12 00 N** | **105 00 E** | **56** |
| Cambridge, Ont., Can. | 110,372 | 43 23 N | 80 19 W | 84 |
| Cambridge, Mass., U.S. | 101,355 | 43 22 N | 71 06 W | 85 |
| Camden, N.J., U.S. | 79,904 | 39 56 N | 75 06 W | 84 |
| **Cameroon** | **17,340,702** | **05 00 N** | **13 00 E** | **68** |
| Campbell River, Br. Col., Can. | 31,294 | 50 02 N | 125 15 W | 80 |
| Campbellton, N.B., Can. | 7,798 | 48 00 N | 66 40 W | 85 |
| Campeche (bay), Mex. | | 20 00 N | 93 00 W | 88 |
| Campinas, Brazil | 969,396 | 22 54 S | 47 05 W | 95 |
| **Canada** | **33,098,932** | **60 00 N** | **100 00 W** | **76** |
| Canadian (river), U.S. | | 35 28 N | 95 04 W | 83 |
| Canary (isls.), Spain | 1,694,477 | 28 00 N | 16 00 W | 68 |
| Canaveral (cape), Fla., U.S. | | 28 27 N | 80 31 W | 87 |
| Canberra,* Austl. | 307,053 | 35 18 S | 149 07 E | 61 |
| Caniapiscau (lake), Qué., Can. | | 54 00 N | 70 00 W | 77 |
| Caniapiscau (river), Qué., Can. | | 55 00 N | 69 30 W | 77 |
| Cannes, Fr. | 68,214 | 43 33 N | 07 01 E | 42 |
| Cantabrica (mts.), Spain | | 43 15 N | 05 00 W | 42 |
| Canton (Guangzhou), China | 8,524,826 | 23 07 N | 113 15 E | 55 |
| Canton, Ohio, U.S. | 80,806 | 40 48 N | 81 22 W | 84 |
| Cape Breton (isl.), N.S., Can. | | 46 00 N | 61 00 W | 85 |
| Cape Breton Highlands Nat'l Pk., N.S., Can. | | 47 00 N | 61 00 W | 85 |
| Cape Town,* S. Afr. | 987,007 | 33 57 S | 18 28 E | 70 |
| **Cape Verde** | **420,979** | **16 00 N** | **24 00 W** | **12** |
| Cape York (pen.), Austl. | | 13 00 S | 142 30 E | 59 |
| Caprivi Strip (region), Namibia | | 18 00 S | 23 00 E | 70 |
| Caracas,* Ven. | 1,822,465 | 10 30 N | 66 55 W | 94 |
| Cardiff,* Wales | 272,129 | 51 30 N | 03 12 W | 42 |
| Caribbean (sea) | | 15 00 N | 75 00 W | 89 |
| Caribou (mts.), Alta., Can. | | 59 00 N | 115 00 W | 76 |
| Caroline (isls.), Micronesia | | 08 00 N | 150 00 E | 62 |
| Carpathian (mts.), Europe | | 48 00 N | 23 00 E | 44 |
| Carpentaria (gulf), Austl. | | 15 00 S | 139 00 E | 59 |
| Carson City,* Nev., U.S. | 52,457 | 39 10 N | 119 46 W | 82 |
| Cartegena, Spain | 184,686 | 37 36 N | 00 59 W | 42 |
| Casablanca, Morocco | 2,946,440 | 33 36 N | 07 38 W | 68 |
| Cascades (mts.), U.S. | | 45 00 N | 122 00 W | 80 |
| Casper, Wyo., U.S. | 49,644 | 42 51 N | 106 19 W | 81 |
| Caspian (sea) | | 42 00 N | 50 00 E | 44 |
| Castries,* St. Lucia | 11,092 | 14 00 N | 60 59 W | 89 |
| Catalonia (region), Spain | | 41 15 N | 02 00 E | 42 |
| Caucasus (mts.), Europe | | 42 30 N | 45 00 E | 45 |
| Cayenne,* Fr. Guiana | 50,395 | 04 56 N | 52 20 W | 95 |
| Cayman (isls.), U.K. | 39,410 | 19 30 N | 80 40 W | 88 |
| Cebu, Phil. | 662,299 | 10 18 N | 123 54 E | 57 |
| Cebu (isl.), Phil. | | 10 18 N | 123 54 E | 57 |
| Cedar Rapids, Iowa, U.S. | 120,758 | 41 59 N | 91 40 W | 83 |
| Celebes (isl.), Indon. | 14,111,444 | 02 00 S | 121 00 E | 57 |
| **Central African Republic** | **4,303,356** | **06 00 N** | **20 00 E** | **69** |
| Ceuta, Spain | 71,505 | 35 52 N | 05 20 W | 68 |
| Ceylon (isl.), Sri Lanka | | 07 00 N | 81 00 E | 53 |
| **Chad** | **9,944,201** | **15 00 N** | **18 00 E** | **69** |
| Chad (lake), Africa | | 13 15 N | 14 30 E | 68 |
| Chaleur (bay), N.B.,Qué., Can. | | 48 00 N | 65 00 W | 85 |
| Champaign, Ill., U.S. | 67,518 | 40 07 N | 88 14 W | 84 |
| Champlain (lake), Can.,U.S. | | 44 30 N | 73 20 W | 84 |
| Changchun, China | 3,225,557 | 43 53 N | 125 18 E | 55 |
| Chang (Yangtze) (river), China | | 31 48 N | 121 10 E | 55 |
| Changsha, China | 2,122,873 | 28 12 N | 112 59 E | 55 |
| Channel (isls.), U.K. | 150,000 | 49 30 N | 02 30 W | 42 |
| Chaozhou, China | 363,582 | 23 40 N | 116 38 E | 55 |
| Chapel Hill, N.C., U.S. | 48,715 | 35 54 N | 79 03 W | 87 |
| Charleston, S.C., U.S. | 96,650 | 32 47 N | 79 56 W | 87 |
| Charleston,* W. Va., U.S. | 53,421 | 38 21 N | 81 38 W | 87 |
| Charlotte, N.C., U.S. | 540,828 | 35 13 N | 80 50 W | 87 |
| Charlottesville, Va., U.S. | 45,049 | 38 02 N | 78 29 W | 87 |
| Charlottetown,* P.E.I., Can. | 32,245 | 46 14 N | 63 08 W | 85 |

| NAME | POPULATION | LATITUDE | LONGITUDE | PAGE |
|---|---|---|---|---|
| Chattanooga, Tenn., U.S. | 155,554 | 35 02 N | 85 18 W | 87 |
| Chelyabinsk, Russia | 1,084,208 | 55 10 N | 61 24 E | 45 |
| Chelyuskin (cape), Russia | | 77 45 N | 104 30 E | 47 |
| Chemnitz, Germany | 263,222 | 50 40 N | 12 55 E | 42 |
| Chengdu, China | 4,333,541 | 30 40 N | 104 04 E | 54 |
| Chesapeake (bay), Md.,Va., U.S. | | 38 35 N | 76 25 W | 84 |
| Chennai (Madras), India | 4,216,268 | 13 05 N | 80 15 E | 53 |
| Cheshskaya (bay), Russia | | 67 30 N | 47 00 E | 43 |
| Chesterfield (inlet), Nun., Can. | | 63 40 N | 91 45 W | 76 |
| Cheyenne,* Wyo., U.S. | 53,011 | 41 08 N | 104 49 W | 81 |
| Chiba, Japan | 887,164 | 35 36 N | 140 07 E | 55 |
| Chicago, Ill., U.S. | 2,896,016 | 41 52 N | 87 37 W | 84 |
| Chico, Calif., U.S. | 59,954 | 39 43 N | 121 50 W | 82 |
| Chicoutimi, Qué., Can. | 60,008 | 48 25 N | 71 06 W | 85 |
| Chidley (cape), Newf., Can. | | 60 23 N | 64 26 W | 77 |
| Chihuahua, Mex. | 657,876 | 28 38 N | 106 05 W | 89 |
| **Chile** | **16,134,219** | **32 00 S** | **71 00 W** | **91** |
| Chilliwack, Br. Col., Can. | 62,927 | 49 10 N | 121 55 W | 80 |
| Chiloé (isl.), Chile | | 42 00 S | 74 00 W | 96 |
| Chimborazo (mt.), Ecuador | | 01 28 S | 78 48 W | 94 |
| **China** | **1,313,973,713** | **35 00 N** | **105 00 E** | **54** |
| Chişinău,* Moldova | 654,927 | 47 00 N | 28 50 E | 44 |
| Chittagong, Bangladesh | 2,095,846 | 22 15 N | 91 55 E | 53 |
| Chongqing, China | 9,691,901 | 29 34 N | 106 35 E | 54 |
| Chonos (arch.), Chile | | 45 00 S | 74 00 W | 96 |
| Christchurch, N.Z. | 316,224 | 43 32 S | 172 39 E | 59 |
| Christmas (isl.), Kiribati | | 10 30 S | 105 40 E | 13 |
| Chuckchi (pen.), Russia | | 66 00 N | 175 00 W | 47 |
| Churchill (river), Man., Can. | | 58 47 N | 94 11 W | 76 |
| Churchill, Man., Can. | 963 | 58 46 N | 94 10 W | 76 |
| Chuuk (isls.), Micronesia | 53,595 | 07 25 N | 151 45 E | 62 |
| Cimarron (river), U.S. | | 36 07 N | 96 30 W | 81 |
| Cincinnati, Ohio, U.S. | 331,285 | 39 06 N | 84 31 W | 84 |
| Ciudad Guayana, Ven. | 453,047 | 08 22 N | 62 40 W | 94 |
| Ciudad Juárez, Mex. | 1,187,275 | 31 44 N | 106 29 W | 89 |
| Clarksville, Tenn., U.S. | 103,455 | 36 31 N | 87 21 W | 84 |
| Clearwater, Fla., U.S. | 108,787 | 27 58 N | 82 48 W | 87 |
| Cleveland, Ohio, U.S. | 478,403 | 41 30 N | 81 41 W | 84 |
| Clipperton (isl.), Fr. | | 10 13 N | 109 10 W | 12 |
| Cluj-Napoca, Rom. | 317,953 | 46 45 N | 23 36 E | 44 |
| Coast Ranges (mts.), Br. Col.,Yukon Terr., Can. | | 42 00 N | 123 15 W | 76 |
| Cocos (isls.), Austl. | 630 | 12 30 S | 96 50 E | 48 |
| Cod (cape), Mass., U.S. | | 41 42 N | 70 04 W | 85 |
| Cologne, Germany | 962,507 | 51 00 N | 07 00 E | 42 |
| **Colombia** | **43,593,035** | **05 00 N** | **74 00 W** | **94** |
| Colombo,* Sri Lanka | 642,163 | 06 55 N | 79 50 E | 53 |
| Colorado (river), Arg. | | 39 51 S | 62 08 W | 96 |
| Colorado (river), Mexico,U.S. | | 31 49 N | 114 45 W | 82 |
| Colorado (river), Texas, U.S. | | 28 52 N | 96 02 W | 83 |
| Colorado (state), U.S. | 4,301,261 | 39 00 N | 105 30 W | 82 |
| Colorado Springs, Colo., U.S. | 360,890 | 38 50 N | 104 48 W | 83 |
| Columbia, Mo., U.S. | 84,531 | 38 57 N | 92 20 W | 86 |
| Columbia (plat.), U.S. | | 46 00 N | 118 00 W | 80 |
| Columbia (river), Ore.,Wash., U.S. | | 46 15 N | 123 40 W | 80 |
| Columbia,* S.C., U.S. | 116,278 | 34 00 N | 81 02 W | 87 |
| Columbus, Ga., U.S. | 186,291 | 32 27 N | 84 59 W | 87 |
| Columbus,* Ohio, U.S. | 711,470 | 39 57 N | 83 00 W | 84 |
| Comorin (cape), India | | 07 37 N | 77 28 E | 53 |
| **Comoros** | **690,948** | **12 00 S** | **44 00 E** | **65** |
| Conakry,* Guinea | 1,091,483 | 09 31 N | 13 42 W | 68 |
| Concepción, Chile | 326,784 | 36 50 S | 73 01 W | 96 |
| Concord, Calif., U.S. | 121,780 | 37 58 N | 122 01 W | 82 |
| Concord,* N.H., U.S. | 40,687 | 43 12 N | 71 32 W | 85 |
| Concord,* N.C., U.S. | 55,977 | 35 24 N | 80 34 W | 87 |
| Congo (basin), D.R. Congo | | 00 00 | 22 00 E | 69 |
| Congo (river), Congo,D.R. Congo | | 06 05 S | 12 20 E | 70 |
| **Congo, Dem. Rep. of the** | **62,660,551** | **02 00 S** | **24 00 E** | **65** |
| **Congo, Rep. of the** | **3,702,314** | **00 00** | **15 00 E** | **65** |
| Connecticut (state), U.S. | 3,405,565 | 41 38 N | 72 45 W | 85 |
| Constantine, Alg. | 449,602 | 36 23 N | 06 38 E | 68 |
| Cook (isls.), N.Z. | 19,103 | 20 00 S | 158 00 W | 63 |
| Cook (mt.), N.Z. | | 43 36 S | 170 08 E | 59 |
| Cook (strait), N.Z. | | 41 15 S | 174 30 E | 59 |
| Coppermine (river), N.W. Terrs., Nun., Can. | | 66 30 N | 115 00 W | 76 |
| Copenhagen,* Denmark | 499,148 | 55 40 N | 12 35 E | 43 |
| Coral (sea) | | 14 00 S | 156 00 E | 59 |
| Córdoba, Arg. | 1,267,521 | 31 25 S | 64 10 W | 96 |
| Córdoba, Spain | 308,072 | 37 54 N | 04 46 W | 42 |
| Corfu (isl.), Greece | 111,975 | 39 38 N | 19 56 E | 44 |
| Corinth (gulf), Greece | | 38 19 N | 22 04 E | 44 |
| Cork, Ireland | 123,338 | 51 55 N | 08 30 W | 42 |
| Corner Brook, Newf., Can. | 20,103 | 48 57 N | 57 57 W | 85 |
| Cornwall, Ont., Can. | 48,287 | 45 02 N | 74 44 W | 84 |
| Coromandel Coast, India | | 13 00 N | 80 15 E | 53 |
| Corpus Christi, Texas, U.S. | 277,454 | 27 47 N | 97 25 W | 86 |
| Corsica (isl.), Fr. | 260,196 | 42 00 N | 09 00 E | 42 |
| Corvallis, Ore., U.S. | 49,322 | 44 34 N | 123 16 W | 80 |
| **Costa Rica** | **4,075,261** | **10 00 N** | **84 00 W** | **88** |
| **Côte d'Ivoire** | **17,654,843** | **07 00 N** | **05 00 W** | **68** |
| Cotonou, Benin | 536,827 | 06 21 N | 02 26 E | 68 |
| Council Bluffs, Iowa, U.S. | 58,268 | 41 15 N | 95 51 W | 81 |
| Coventry, Eng., U.K. | 299,316 | 52 25 N | 01 33 W | 42 |
| Cranbrook, Br. Col., Can. | 18,476 | 49 30 N | 115 46 W | 80 |
| Crater Lake Nat'l Pk., Ore., U.S. | | 42 30 N | 122 30 W | 80 |
| Crete (isl.), Greece | 601,131 | 35 15 N | 25 00 E | 44 |
| Crimea (pen.), Ukraine | | 45 00 N | 34 00 E | 44 |
| **Croatia** | **4,494,749** | **45 30 N** | **16 00 E** | **44** |
| **Cuba** | **11,382,820** | **22 00 N** | **80 00 W** | **89** |
| Cumberland (pen.), Nun., Can. | | 66 00 N | 65 00 W | 77 |
| Cumberland (sound), Nun., Can. | | 64 00 N | 67 00 W | 77 |
| Curaçao (isl.), Neth. Ant. | 151,448 | 12 11 N | 69 00 W | 89 |
| Curitiba, Brazil | 1,587,315 | 25 25 S | 49 15 W | 96 |
| Cyclades (isls.), Greece | 112,615 | 37 00 N | 25 00 E | 44 |
| **Cyprus** | **784,301** | **35 00 N** | **33 00 E** | **52** |
| **Czech Republic** | **10,235,455** | **49 00 N** | **17 00 E** | **44** |
| Czectochowa, Poland | 251,436 | 50 49 N | 19 06 E | 44 |

| NAME | POPULATION | LATITUDE | LONGITUDE | PAGE |
|---|---|---|---|---|
| **D** | | | | |
| Da Hinggan (mts.), China | | 48°30′ N | 120°00′ E | 55 |
| Dakar,* Senegal | 1,641,358 | 14 40 N | 17 28 W | 68 |
| Dalian, China | 3,245,191 | 38 55 N | 121 39 E | 55 |
| Dallas, Texas, U.S. | 1,188,580 | 32 47 N | 96 47 W | 86 |
| Damascus,* Syria | 1,549,000 | 33 35 N | 36 28 E | 52 |
| Damavand (mt.), Iran | | 35 57 N | 52 08 E | 52 |
| Da Nang, Vietnam | 369,734 | 16 04 N | 108 13 E | 56 |
| Danube (river), Europe | | 45 20 N | 29 40 E | 44 |
| Dardanelles (strait), Turkey | | 40 07 N | 26 23 E | 44 |
| Dar es Salaam,* Tanzania | 1,360,850 | 06 48 S | 39 17 E | 70 |
| Darling (river), Austl. | | 32 00 S | 142 57 E | 59 |
| Dartmouth, N.S., Can. | 65,629 | 44 40 N | 63 34 W | 85 |
| Darwin, Austl. | 68,694 | 12 27 S | 130 50 E | 59 |
| Davao, Phil. | 1,006,840 | 07 18 N | 125 25 E | 57 |
| Davenport, Iowa, U.S. | 98,359 | 41 31 N | 90 35 W | 81 |
| Davis (strait), Can.,Greenland | | 66 30 N | 58 00 W | 77 |
| Davis, Calif., U.S. | 60,308 | 38 32 N | 121 44 W | 82 |
| Dawson, Yukon Terr., Can. | 1,251 | 64 04 N | 139 27 W | 76 |
| Dayton, Ohio, U.S. | 166,179 | 39 45 N | 84 11 W | 84 |
| Daytona Beach, Fla., U.S. | 64,112 | 29 12 N | 81 01 W | 87 |
| Dead (sea), Asia | | 31 30 N | 35 30 E | 52 |
| Dease (strait), Nun., Can. | | 68 00 N | 108 00 E | 76 |
| Death Valley Nat'l Park, Calif., U.S. | | 37 00 N | 117 07 W | 82 |
| Debrecen, Hungary | 212,335 | 47 32 N | 21 38 E | 44 |
| Decatur, Ala., U.S. | 53,929 | 34 36 N | 86 59 W | 87 |
| Decatur, Ill., U.S. | 81,860 | 39 50 N | 88 57 W | 81 |
| Deccan (plat.), India | | 17 00 N | 78 00 E | 53 |
| Delaware (river), U.S. | 783,600 | 39 00 N | 75 30 W | 84 |
| Delgado (cape), Moz. | | 10 41 S | 40 38 E | 70 |
| Delhi, India | 9,817,439 | 28 29 N | 77 15 E | 53 |
| **Denmark** | **5,450,661** | 56 00 N | 10 30 E | 43 |
| Denver,* Colo., U.S. | 554,636 | 39 44 N | 104 59 W | 83 |
| Des Moines,* Iowa, U.S. | 198,682 | 41 35 N | 93 37 W | 81 |
| Detroit, Mich., U.S. | 951,270 | 42 20 N | 83 02 W | 84 |
| Devon (isl.), Nun., Can. | | 75 00 N | 86 00 W | 77 |
| Dezhneva (cape), Russia | | 66 05 N | 169 40 W | 47 |
| Dhaka,* Bangladesh | 5,378,023 | 23 45 N | 90 25 E | 53 |
| Diefenbaker (lake), Sask., Can. | | 50 30 N | 107 00 W | 80 |
| Diego Garcia (isl.), U.K. | | 07 36 S | 72 28 E | 13 |
| Dili,* East Timor | 13,000 | 08 35 S | 125 35 E | 57 |
| Dinaric Alps (mts.), Bosnia and Herzegovina,Croatia | | 43 30 N | 17 00 E | 44 |
| District of Columbia, U.S. | 572,059 | 38 54 N | 77 01 W | 84 |
| Diyarbakir, Turkey | 551,046 | 37 55 N | 40 14 E | 44 |
| Dixon (strait), Can.,U.S. | | 54 00 N | 132 00 W | 76 |
| **Djibouti** | **486,530** | 12 00 N | 43 00 E | 69 |
| Djibouti,* Djibouti | 200,000 | 11 35 N | 43 09 E | 69 |
| Dnipropetrovs'k, Ukraine | 1,065,008 | 48 27 N | 35 01 E | 44 |
| Dnipro (river), Ukraine | | 46 30 N | 32 36 E | 44 |
| Dnister (river), Moldova,Ukraine | | 46 20 N | 30 18 E | 44 |
| Doğukaradeniz (mts.) Turkey | | 40 30 N | 39 00 E | 44 |
| Doha,* Qatar | 217,294 | 25 17 N | 51 32 E | 52 |
| Dolphin and Union (strait), Nun., Can. | | 69 00 N | 116 00 W | 76 |
| **Dominica** | **68,910** | 15 25 N | 61 20 W | 89 |
| **Dominican Republic** | **9,185,984** | 19 00 N | 70 00 W | 89 |
| Don (river), Russia | | 47 04 N | 39 18 E | 44 |
| Donets (river), Ukraine | | 47 36 N | 40 54 E | 44 |
| Donets'k, Ukraine | 1,016,194 | 48 00 N | 37 48 E | 44 |
| Dortmund, Germany | 590,213 | 51 30 N | 07 30 E | 42 |
| Dothan, Ala., U.S. | 57,737 | 31 13 N | 85 23 W | 87 |
| Douala, Cameroon | 1,029,731 | 04 03 N | 09 37 E | 68 |
| Douro (river), Port.,Spain | | 41 09 N | 08 39 W | 42 |
| Dover (strait), Europe | | 51 00 N | 01 30 E | 42 |
| Dover,* Del., U.S. | 32,135 | 39 10 N | 75 31 W | 84 |
| Drake (passage), Antarctica,S. America | | 60 00 S | 67 00 W | 96 |
| Dresden, Germany | 476,668 | 51 10 N | 13 45 E | 42 |
| Drummondville, Qué., Can. | 46,599 | 46 53 N | 72 29 W | 85 |
| Dubayy, United Arab Emirates | 669,181 | 25 15 N | 55 17 E | 44 |
| Dublin,* Ire. | 495,781 | 53 20 N | 06 10 W | 42 |
| Dubrovnik, Croatia | 30,436 | 42 38 N | 18 07 E | 44 |
| Dubuque, Iowa, U.S. | 57,686 | 42 30 N | 90 40 W | 81 |
| Duluth, Minn., U.S. | 86,918 | 46 47 N | 92 06 W | 81 |
| Dundee, Scot. | 151,010 | 56 30 N | 02 58 W | 42 |
| Durango, Mex. | 427,135 | 24 02 N | 104 40 W | 89 |
| Durango, Colo., U.S. | 13,922 | 37 16 N | 107 51 W | 82 |
| Durban, S. Afr. | 669,242 | 29 51 S | 31 00 E | 70 |
| Durham, N.C., U.S. | 187,035 | 35 59 N | 78 54 W | 87 |
| Dushanbe,* Tajik. | 602,000 | 38 33 N | 68 48 E | 46 |
| Düsseldorf, Germany | 568,855 | 51 20 N | 06 40 E | 42 |
| Dvina, Northern (river), Russia | | 64 32 N | 40 37 E | 46 |
| **E** | | | | |
| East China (sea), China, Japan | | 30°00′ N | 125°00′ E | 55 |
| Easter (isl.), Chile | 2,764 | 27 08 S | 109 25 W | 63 |
| Eastern Ghats (mts.), India | | 17 30 N | 83 00 E | 53 |
| East London, S. Afr. | 135,560 | 33 01 S | 27 55 E | 70 |
| Eastmain (river), Qué., Can. | | 53 00 N | 75 00 W | 77 |
| **East Timor** | **1,062,777** | 08 40 S | 126 00 E | 57 |
| Eau Claire (lake), Qué., Can. | | 56 00 N | 75 00 W | 77 |
| Eau Claire, Wis., U.S. | 61,704 | 44 48 N | 91 30 W | 81 |
| Ebro (river), Spain | | 40 43 N | 00 54 E | 42 |
| Ecatepec, Mex. | 1,621,827 | 19 35 N | 99 04 W | 88 |
| Eclipse (sound), Nun., Can. | | 72 00 N | 80 00 W | 77 |
| **Ecuador** | **13,547,510** | 01 00 S | 79 00 W | 94 |
| Edinburgh,* Scot. | 447,550 | 55 55 N | 03 10 W | 42 |
| Edmonton,* Alta., Can. | 666,104 | 53 33 N | 113 28 W | 80 |
| Edmundston, N.B., Can. | 17,373 | 47 22 N | 68 20 W | 85 |
| Edward (lake), D.R. Congo,Uganda | | 00 20 S | 29 36 E | 69 |
| Edwards (plat.), Texas, U.S. | | 30 30 N | 101 00 W | 83 |
| Efate (isl.), Vanuatu | | 17 40 S | 168 23 E | 62 |
| **Egypt** | **78,887,007** | 27 00 N | 30 00 E | 69 |
| Elbe (river), Ger. | | 53 30 N | 09 45 E | 42 |
| Elbert (mt.), Colo., U.S. | | 39 06 N | 106 27 W | 82 |
| El'brus (mt.), Georgia,Russia | | 43 21 N | 42 26 E | 45 |
| Elburz (mts.), Iran | | 36 00 N | 52 00 E | 52 |
| El Cajon, Calif., U.S. | 94,869 | 32 47 N | 116 57 W | 82 |
| Elgin, Ill., U.S. | 94,487 | 42 02 N | 88 17 W | 84 |
| Elkhart, Ind., U.S. | 51,874 | 41 41 N | 85 58 W | 84 |
| Ellesmere (isl.), Nun., Can. | | 79 00 N | 82 00 W | 77 |
| El Paso, Texas, U.S. | 563,662 | 31 45 N | 106 29 W | 82 |
| **El Salvador** | **6,822,378** | 13 30 N | 89 00 W | 88 |
| Enewetak (isl.), Marshall Isls. | | 11 11 N | 162 21 E | 62 |
| England, U.K. | 49,138,831 | 53 00 N | 01 00 W | 42 |
| English (chan.), Fr.,U.K. | | 50 00 N | 02 30 W | 42 |
| **Equatorial Guinea** | **540,109** | 01 30 N | 10 00 E | 68 |
| Erie (lake), Can.U.S. | | 42 20 N | 81 00 W | 84 |
| Erie, Pa., U.S. | 103,717 | 42 07 N | 80 05 W | 84 |
| **Eritrea** | **4,786,994** | 15 00 N | 40 00 E | 69 |
| Erzgebirge (mts.), Czech. Rep.,Ger. | | 50 30 N | 13 00 E | 42 |
| Esfahān, Iran | 1,266,072 | 32 40 N | 51 38 E | 52 |
| Espiritu Santo (isl.), Vanuatu | | 15 15 S | 166 55 E | 62 |
| Essen, Germany | 599,515 | 51 30 N | 07 00 E | 42 |
| **Estonia** | **1,324,333** | 59 00 N | 26 00 E | 43 |
| **Ethiopia** | **74,777,981** | 10 00 N | 40 00 E | 69 |
| Eugene, Ore., U.S. | 137,893 | 44 03 N | 123 05 W | 80 |
| Euphrates (river), Asia | | 38 00 N | 39 05 E | 52 |
| Europe (cont.) | 729,239,896 | | | 39 |
| Evans (strait), Nun., Can. | | 63 00 N | 81 00 W | 77 |
| Evans, mt.), Colo., U.S. | | 39 34 N | 105 38 W | 83 |
| Evansville, Ind., U.S. | 121,582 | 37 58 N | 87 33 W | 84 |
| Everest (mt.), China,Nepal | | 27 58 N | 87 05 E | 53 |
| Everett, Wash., U.S. | 91,488 | 47 58 N | 122 12 W | 80 |
| Everglades Nat'l Park, Fla., U.S. | | 25 15 N | 81 00 W | 87 |
| Eyre (lake), Austl. | | 28 30 S | 137 15 E | 59 |
| **F** | | | | |
| Fairbanks, Alaska, U.S. | 30,224 | 64°51′ N | 147°43′ W | 78 |
| Fairfield, Calif., U.S. | 96,178 | 38 15 N | 122 02 W | 82 |
| Fairweather (mt.), Br. Col., Can. | | 58 15 N | 137 29 W | 82 |
| Faisalabad, Pak. | 2,008,861 | 31 25 N | 73 05 E | 53 |
| Falkland (isls.), U.K. | 2,379 | 52 00 S | 59 00 W | 96 |
| Fall River, Mass., U.S. | 91,938 | 41 42 N | 71 09 W | 85 |
| Farīdābād, India | 1,054,981 | 28 26 N | 77 19 E | 53 |
| Fargo, N.D., U.S. | 90,599 | 46 52 N | 96 47 W | 81 |
| Faroe (isls.), Den. | 46,345 | 62 00 N | 07 00 W | 39 |
| Fayetteville, Ark., U.S. | 58,047 | 36 03 N | 94 09 W | 83 |
| Fayetteville, N.C., U.S. | 121,015 | 35 03 N | 78 52 W | 87 |
| Fear (cape), N.C., U.S. | | 33 50 N | 77 58 W | 87 |
| Ferrara, Italy | 131,713 | 44 50 N | 11 40 E | 42 |
| Fès, Morocco | 920,737 | 34 02 N | 04 59 E | 68 |
| Fezzan (region), Libya | | 27 00 N | 14 00 E | 68 |
| **Fiji** | **905,949** | 17 00 S | 179 00 E | 62 |
| Finisterre (cape), Spain | | 42 53 N | 09 16 W | 42 |
| **Finland** | **5,231,372** | 64 00 N | 26 00 E | 43 |
| Finland (gulf), Europe | | 60 00 N | 27 00 E | 43 |
| Fisher (strait), Nun., Can. | | 63 00 N | 83 00 W | 77 |
| Flagstaff, Ariz., U.S. | 52,894 | 35 12 N | 111 39 W | 82 |
| Flin Flon, Man.-Sask., Can. | 6,267 | 54 46 N | 101 53 W | 76 |
| Flint, Mich., U.S. | 124,943 | 43 00 N | 83 41 W | 84 |
| Florence, Italy | 374,501 | 43 46 N | 11 13 E | 42 |
| Flores (isl.), Indon. | | 08 30 S | 121 00 E | 57 |
| Flores (sea), Indon. | | 05 39 S | 119 54 E | 56 |
| Florida (keys), Fla., U.S. | | 24 44 N | 81 00 W | 87 |
| Florida (state), Cuba,U.S. | 15,982,378 | 28 00 N | 82 00 W | 87 |
| Florida (straits), Cuba,U.S. | | 24 00 N | 82 00 W | 88 |
| Forillon Nat'l Pk., Qué., Can. | | 49 00 N | 64 30 W | 85 |
| Fortaleza, Brazil | 2,141,402 | 03 41 S | 38 33 W | 95 |
| Fort Collins, Colo., U.S. | 118,652 | 40 35 N | 105 04 W | 83 |
| Fort-de-France,* Mart. | 94,152 | 14 36 N | 61 05 W | 89 |
| Fort Frances, Ont., Can. | 8,275 | 48 37 N | 93 25 W | 81 |
| Fort Lauderdale, Fla., U.S. | 152,397 | 26 07 N | 80 08 W | 87 |
| Fort McMurray, Alta., Can. | 41,466 | 56 44 N | 111 23 W | 76 |
| Fort Myers, Fla., U.S. | 48,208 | 26 38 N | 81 52 W | 87 |
| Fort Nelson, Br. Col., Can. | 4,188 | 58 49 N | 122 36 W | 76 |
| Fort Peck (lake), Mont., U.S. | | 47 31 N | 106 30 W | 80 |
| Fort Saint John, Br. Col., Can. | 16,034 | 56 15 N | 120 51 W | 76 |
| Fort Smith, Ark., U.S. | 80,268 | 35 23 N | 94 24 W | 86 |
| Fort Smith, N.W. Terrs., Can. | 2,185 | 60 00 N | 112 00 W | 76 |
| Fort Wayne, Ind., U.S. | 205,727 | 41 04 N | 85 08 W | 84 |
| Fort Worth, Texas, U.S. | 534,694 | 32 45 N | 97 19 W | 86 |
| Foxe (chan.), Nun., Can. | | 65 00 N | 81 00 W | 77 |
| Foxe (pen.), Nun., Can. | | 65 00 N | 76 00 W | 77 |
| Foxe Basin (bay), Nun., Can. | | 68 00 N | 78 00 W | 77 |
| **France** | **60,876,136** | 47 00 N | 02 00 E | 42 |
| Frankfort,* Ky., U.S. | 27,741 | 38 12 N | 84 52 W | 84 |
| Frankfurt, Germany | 643,821 | 50 10 N | 08 30 E | 42 |
| Franklin D. Roosevelt (lake), Wash., U.S. | | 49 00 N | 118 00 W | 80 |
| Franz Josef Land (isls.), Russia | | 81 00 N | 51 00 E | 46 |
| Fraser (river), Br. Col., Can. | | 49 08 N | 123 10 W | 80 |
| Frederick, Md., U.S. | 52,767 | 39 25 N | 77 24 W | 84 |
| Fredericton,* N.B., Can. | 47,560 | 45 58 N | 66 41 W | 85 |
| Freetown,* Sierra Leone | 469,776 | 08 29 N | 13 13 W | 68 |
| French Guiana, Fr. | 195,506 | 04 00 N | 53 00 W | 95 |
| French Polynesia, Fr. | 270,485 | 15 00 S | 140 00 W | 63 |
| Fresno, Calif., U.S. | 427,652 | 36 45 N | 119 46 W | 82 |
| Frobisher (bay), Nun., Can. | | 63 00 N | 66 00 W | 77 |
| Frozen (strait), Nun., Can. | | 65 00 N | 81 30 W | 77 |
| Fukuoka, Japan | 1,341,470 | 33 35 N | 130 24 E | 55 |
| Funafuti,* Tuvalu | 3,839 | 08 31 S | 179 08 E | 62 |
| Fundy (bay), Can.,U.S. | | 45 00 N | 66 00 W | 85 |
| Fundy Nat'l Pk., N.B., Can. | | 46 00 N | 65 00 W | 85 |
| Fury and Hecla (strait), Nun., Can. | | 70 00 N | 84 00 W | 77 |
| Fushun, China | 1,434,447 | 41 52 N | 123 53 E | 55 |
| Fuzhou, China | 2,124,435 | 26 05 N | 119 19 E | 55 |
| **G** | | | | |
| **Gabon** | **1,424,906** | 00°00′ | 12°00′ E | 68 |
| Gaborone,* Bots. | 186,007 | 24 40 S | 25 54 E | 70 |
| Gainesville, Fla., U.S. | 95,447 | 29 39 N | 82 19 W | 87 |
| Galápagos (isls.), Ecuador | 18,640 | 00 15 S | 90 00 W | 12 |
| Galați, Rom. | 298,861 | 45 26 N | 28 03 E | 44 |
| Galesburg, Ill., U.S. | 33,706 | 40 57 N | 90 22 W | 84 |
| Galveston, Texas, U.S. | 57,247 | 29 18 N | 94 48 W | 86 |
| **Gambia, The** | **1,641,564** | 13 30 N | 15 30 W | 68 |
| Gäncä, Azer. | 301,800 | 40 40 N | 46 22 E | 45 |
| Ganges (river), Bangladesh,India | | 26 00 N | 80 15 E | 53 |
| Garonne (river), Fr. | | 45 01 N | 00 36 W | 42 |
| Gary, Ind., U.S. | 102,746 | 41 35 N | 87 20 W | 84 |
| Gaspé, Qué., Can. | 14,932 | 48 50 N | 64 29 W | 85 |
| Gaspé (cape), Qué., Can. | | 48 50 N | 64 00 W | 85 |
| Gaspé (pen.), Qué., Can. | | 48 30 N | 65 00 W | 85 |
| Gastonia, N.C., U.S. | 66,277 | 35 15 N | 81 11 W | 87 |
| Gatineau, Qué., Can. | 217,609 | 45 29 N | 75 40 W | 84 |
| Gaza Strip | 1,376,289 | 31 30 N | 34 30 E | 52 |
| Gaziantep, Turkey | 862,033 | 37 05 N | 37 22 E | 44 |
| Gdańsk, Poland | 461,334 | 54 20 N | 18 30 E | 43 |
| Gdynia, Poland | 253,458 | 54 32 N | 18 33 E | 43 |
| Geneva (lake), Fr.,Switz. | | 46 25 N | 06 25 E | 42 |
| Geneva, Switz. | 177,964 | 46 12 N | 06 10 E | 42 |
| Genoa, Italy | 632,366 | 44 25 N | 08 55 E | 42 |
| Georgetown,* Guyana | 72,049 | 06 49 N | 58 10 W | 94 |
| George Town, Malaysia | 219,376 | 05 25 N | 100 19 E | 56 |
| **Georgia** | **4,661,473** | 42 00 N | 43 00 E | 45 |
| Georgia (state), U.S. | 8,186,453 | 32 30 N | 83 15 W | 87 |
| Georgian (bay), Ont., Can. | | 45 15 N | 80 45 W | 84 |
| **Germany** | **82,422,299** | 51 00 N | 10 00 E | 42 |
| **Ghana** | **22,409,572** | 07 00 N | 01 00 W | 68 |
| Ghent (Gent), Belgium | 230,246 | 51 10 N | 03 40 E | 42 |
| Gibraltar (strait), Morocco,Spain | | 35 55 N | 05 35 W | 42 |
| Gibraltar, U.K. | 28,074 | 36 08 N | 05 22 W | 42 |
| Gijón, Spain | 266,419 | 43 32 N | 05 40 W | 42 |
| Glace Bay, N.S., Can. | 21,187 | 46 12 N | 59 57 W | 85 |
| Glacier Nat'l Park, Br. Col., Can. | | 51 00 N | 118 00 W | 80 |
| Glacier Nat'l Park, Mont., U.S. | | 48 35 N | 114 00 W | 80 |
| Glasgow, Scot. | 618,430 | 55 50 N | 04 10 W | 42 |
| Gobi (desert), China,Mongolia | | 43 00 N | 110 00 E | 54 |
| Godavari (river), India | | 19 00 N | 79 00 E | 53 |
| Godwin Austen (K2) (mt.), China,Pak. | | 35 53 N | 76 30 E | 53 |
| Goiânia, Brazil | 1,093,007 | 16 40 S | 49 16 W | 95 |
| Good Hope (cape), S. Afr. | | 34 21 S | 18 29 E | 70 |
| Göteborg, Sweden | 433,020 | 57 43 N | 11 58 E | 43 |
| Gotland (isl.), Sweden | 57,313 | 57 45 N | 18 45 E | 43 |
| Gouin (res.), Qué., Can. | | 48 30 N | 75 30 W | 84 |
| Grampians (mts.), Scot.,U.K. | | 56 45 N | 04 30 W | 42 |
| Granada, Spain | 240,661 | 37 11 N | 03 36 W | 42 |
| Gran Chaco (region), Arg.,Para. | | 24 00 S | 62 00 W | 96 |
| Grand (lake), Newf., Can. | | 49 00 N | 58 00 W | 85 |
| Grand Canyon Nat'l Park, Ariz., U.S. | | 36 03 N | 112 08 W | 82 |
| Grande Prairie, Alta., Can. | 36,483 | 55 10 N | 118 48 W | 76 |
| Grand Falls, Newf., Can. | 5,858 | 48 56 N | 55 40 W | 85 |
| Grand Forks, N.D., U.S. | 49,321 | 47 55 N | 97 02 W | 81 |
| Grand Rapids, Mich., U.S. | 197,800 | 42 57 N | 85 40 W | 84 |
| Grand Teton (mt.), Wyo., U.S. | | 43 44 N | 110 48 W | 80 |
| Grand Teton Nat'l Park, Wyo., U.S. | | 43 45 N | 110 45 W | 80 |
| Graz, Austria | 237,810 | 47 00 N | 15 30 E | 42 |
| Great Australian Bight (bay), Austl. | | 33 00 S | 130 00 E | 59 |
| Great Barrier (reef), Austl. | | 16 00 S | 145 50 E | 59 |
| Great Bear (lake), N.W. Terrs., Can. | | 66 00 N | 121 00 W | 76 |
| Great Britain (isl.), U.K. | 58,789,194 | 54 00 N | 02 00 W | 42 |
| Great Dividing Range (mts.), Austl. | | 35 00 S | 149 35 E | 59 |
| Great Falls, Mont., U.S. | 56,690 | 47 30 N | 111 18 W | 80 |
| Great Indian (desert), India | | 28 00 N | 73 00 E | 53 |
| Great Plains (plain), Can.,U.S. | | 46 00 N | 102 00 W | 81 |
| Great Rift (valley), Tanz.,Zambia | | 09 00 N | 31 00 E | 69 |
| Great Salt (lake), Ut., U.S. | | 41 05 N | 112 30 W | 82 |
| Great Sandy (desert), Austl. | | 20 00 S | 124 00 E | 59 |
| Great Slave (lake), N.W. Terrs., Can. | | 61 00 N | 114 00 W | 76 |
| Great Victoria (desert), Austl. | | 27 00 S | 130 00 E | 59 |
| Greater Antilles (isls.), N. America | | 18 00 N | 74 00 W | 89 |
| **Greece** | **10,688,058** | 39 00 N | 23 00 E | 44 |
| Greeley, Colo., U.S. | 76,930 | 40 25 N | 104 42 W | 83 |
| Green Bay, Wis., U.S. | 102,313 | 44 30 N | 88 00 W | 84 |
| Greenland (isl.), Den. | 56,361 | 70 00 N | 40 00 W | 73 |
| Greenland (sea) | | 75 00 N | 15 00 W | 71 |
| Greensboro, N.C., U.S. | 223,891 | 36 04 N | 79 47 W | 87 |
| Greenville, N.C., U.S. | 60,476 | 35 36 N | 77 23 W | 87 |
| Greenville, S.C., U.S. | 56,002 | 34 51 N | 82 23 W | 87 |
| **Grenada** | **89,703** | 12 05 N | 61 40 W | 89 |
| Grenoble, Fr. | 156,203 | 45 10 N | 05 43 E | 42 |
| Gros Morne Nat'l Pk., Newf., Can. | | 49 30 N | 58 00 W | 85 |
| Guadalajara, Mex. | 1,646,183 | 20 40 N | 103 20 W | 88 |
| Guadalcanal (isl.), Sol. Is. | 60,275 | 09 40 S | 160 15 E | 62 |
| Guadalupe (isl.), Mex. | | 29 11 N | 118 17 W | 73 |
| Guadalupe (mt.), Texas, U.S. | | 31 53 N | 104 51 W | 83 |
| Guadarrama (mts.), Spain | | 41 00 N | 03 30 W | 42 |
| Guadeloupe (isl.), Fr. | 448,713 | 16 15 N | 61 35 W | 89 |
| Guajira (pen.), Col. | | 11 30 N | 72 45 W | 94 |
| Guam (isl.), U.S. | 154,805 | 13 30 N | 144 47 E | 62 |
| Guangzhou, China | 8,524,826 | 23 07 N | 113 15 E | 55 |
| **Guatemala** | **12,293,545** | 15 30 N | 90 15 W | 88 |
| Guatemala,* Guat. | 823,301 | 14 37 N | 90 31 W | 88 |
| Guayaquil, Ecuador | 1,985,379 | 02 12 S | 79 53 W | 94 |
| Guelph, Ont., Can. | 106,920 | 43 33 N | 80 15 W | 84 |
| Guiana Highlands (plat.), S. America | | 05 00 N | 60 00 W | 94 |
| **Guinea** | **9,690,222** | 10 00 N | 11 00 W | 68 |
| Guinea (gulf), Africa | | 03 00 N | 04 00 E | 68 |
| **Guinea-Bissau** | **1,442,029** | 11 50 N | 15 00 W | 68 |
| Guiyang, China | 2,985,105 | 26 35 N | 106 43 E | 54 |
| Gulfport, Miss., U.S. | 71,127 | 30 22 N | 89 05 W | 87 |
| Guwāhāti, India | 808,021 | 26 10 N | 91 45 E | 53 |
| **Guyana** | **767,245** | 05 00 N | 59 00 W | 94 |

# Index of the World


## H

| NAME | POPULATION | LATITUDE | LONGITUDE | PAGE |
|---|---|---|---|---|
| Hadhramaut (region), Yemen | | 16° 00′ N | 51° 00′ E | 52 |
| Hadley (bay), Nun., Can. | | 72 00 N | 109 00 W | 76 |
| Hagåtña,* Guam | 1,122 | 13 29 N | 144 47 E | 62 |
| Hague, The,* Netherlands | 445,287 | 52 05 N | 04 20 E | 42 |
| Haifa, Israel | 252,300 | 32 50 N | 35 00 E | 52 |
| Hainan (isl.), China | 7,870,000 | 19 00 N | 110 00 E | 55 |
| Haiphong, Vietnam | 449,747 | 20 52 N | 106 41 E | 55 |
| **Haiti** | **8,308,504** | **19 00 N** | **72 30 W** | **89** |
| Halifax,* N.S., Can. | 276,221 | 44 39 N | 63 36 W | 85 |
| Hall (pen.), Nun., Can. | | 62 00 N | 65 00 W | 77 |
| Halle, Germany | 254,380 | 51 30 N | 12 00 E | 42 |
| Halmahera (isl.), Indon. | | 01 30 N | 128 00 E | 57 |
| Hamburg, Germany | 1,704,735 | 53 30 N | 10 00 E | 42 |
| Hamilton, Ont., Can. | 490,268 | 43 15 N | 79 51 W | 84 |
| Hamilton, Ohio, U.S. | 60,690 | 39 24 N | 84 33 W | 84 |
| Hampton, Va., U.S. | 146,437 | 37 01 N | 76 21 W | 84 |
| Hangzhou, China | 2,451,319 | 30 17 N | 120 10 E | 55 |
| Hannover, Germany | 514,718 | 52 20 N | 09 30 E | 42 |
| Hanoi,* Vietnam | 1,089,760 | 21 02 N | 105 50 E | 54 |
| Happy Valley-Goose Bay, Newf., Can. | | 53 18 N | 60 23 W | 77 |
| Harare,* Zim. | 1,189,103 | 17 50 S | 31 03 E | 70 |
| Harbin, China | 3,481,504 | 45 42 N | 126 36 E | 55 |
| Harlingen, Texas, U.S. | 57,564 | 26 11 N | 97 41 W | 86 |
| Harney (mt.), S.D., U.S. | | 43 52 N | 103 31 W | 81 |
| Harrisburg,* Pa., U.S. | 48,950 | 40 16 N | 76 52 W | 84 |
| Hartford,* Conn., U.S. | 121,578 | 41 45 N | 72 41 W | 85 |
| Hatteras (cape), N.C., U.S. | | 35 13 N | 75 32 W | 87 |
| Havana,* Cuba | 2,175,888 | 23 08 N | 82 24 W | 88 |
| Haverhill, Mass., U.S. | 58,969 | 42 46 N | 71 04 W | 85 |
| Hawaii (isl.), Hawaii, U.S. | | 19 30 N | 155 30 W | 78 |
| Hawaii (state), U.S. | 1,211,537 | 21 00 N | 00 10 E | 78 |
| Hayes (mt.), Alaska, U.S. | | 63 00 N | 146 30 W | 76 |
| Hay River, N.W. Terrs., Can. | 3,510 | 60 51 N | 115 42 W | 76 |
| Heard (isl.), Austl. | | 53 07 S | 73 20 E | 71 |
| Hebrides (isls.), U.K. | | 57 20 N | 07 00 W | 42 |
| Hecate (strait), Br. Col., Can. | | 53 20 N | 131 00 W | 76 |
| Hefei, China | 1,659,075 | 31 51 N | 117 17 E | 55 |
| Helena,* Mont., U.S. | 25,780 | 46 35 N | 112 02 W | 80 |
| Helmand (river), Afghan. | | 31 00 N | 64 00 E | 52 |
| Helsingborg, Sweden | 109,273 | 56 07 N | 12 45 E | 43 |
| Helsinki,* Finland | 559,717 | 60 12 N | 25 00 E | 43 |
| Henderson, Nev., U.S. | 175,381 | 36 02 N | 114 59 W | 82 |
| Herāt, Afghan. | 177,300 | 34 20 N | 62 12 E | 52 |
| Hermosillo, Mex. | 545,928 | 29 04 N | 110 58 W | 89 |
| High Point, N.C., U.S. | 85,839 | 35 37 N | 80 00 W | 87 |
| Hijāz (region), S. Ar. | | 24 30 N | 39 00 E | 52 |
| Hilton Head Island, S.C., U.S. | 33,862 | 32 13 N | 80 45 W | 87 |
| Himalaya (mts.), Asia | | 28 00 N | 81 00 E | 53 |
| Hindu Kush (mts.), Asia | | 35 45 N | 70 30 E | 53 |
| Hiroshima, Japan | 1,126,239 | 34 24 N | 132 25 E | 55 |
| Hiva Oa (isl.), Fr. Polynesia | | 09 46 S | 139 00 W | 63 |
| Hobart, Austl. | 125,162 | 42 52 S | 147 18 E | 59 |
| Ho Chi Minh City, Vietnam | 2,899,753 | 10 47 N | 106 41 E | 56 |
| Hokkaido (isl.), Japan | 5,683,062 | 43 00 N | 143 00 E | 55 |
| Hollywood, Fla., U.S. | 139,357 | 26 00 N | 80 09 W | 87 |
| Homyel', Belarus | 503,000 | 52 25 N | 31 00 E | 43 |
| **Honduras** | **7,326,496** | **15 00 N** | **87 00 W** | **88** |
| Hong Kong, China | 6,940,432 | 22 15 N | 114 10 E | 55 |
| Honiara,* Sol. Is. | 49,107 | 09 25 S | 160 00 E | 62 |
| Honolulu,* Hawaii, U.S. | 371,657 | 21 18 N | 157 51 W | 78 |
| Honshu (isl.), Japan | 102,324,961 | 36 00 N | 137 00 E | 55 |
| Hood (mt.), Ore., U.S. | | 45 22 N | 121 42 W | 80 |
| Horn (cape), Chile | | 55 59 S | 67 16 W | 96 |
| Houston, Texas, U.S. | 1,953,631 | 29 45 N | 95 21 W | 86 |
| Howrah, India | 1,008,704 | 22 35 N | 82 20 E | 53 |
| Hrodna, Belarus | 295,400 | 53 41 N | 23 50 E | 44 |
| Huang (river), China | | 38 06 N | 118 24 E | 55 |
| Hudson (bay), Can. | | 59 00 N | 86 00 W | 77 |
| Hudson (strait), Nun.,Qué., Can. | | 61 30 N | 72 00 W | 77 |
| Hue, Vietnam | 211,718 | 16 29 N | 107 34 E | 56 |
| Hull, Eng., U.K. | 310,636 | 53 45 N | 00 20 W | 42 |
| Humphreys (mt.), Ariz., U.S. | | 35 21 N | 111 41 W | 82 |
| **Hungary** | **9,981,334** | **47 00 N** | **19 00 E** | **44** |
| Huntington, W. Va., U.S. | 51,475 | 38 24 N | 82 26 W | 84 |
| Huntsville, Ala., U.S. | 158,216 | 34 43 N | 86 35 W | 87 |
| Huron (lake), Can.,U.S. | | 44 30 N | 82 30 W | 84 |
| Hyderabad, India | 3,449,878 | 17 15 N | 78 30 E | 53 |
| Hyderabad, Pak. | 1,166,894 | 25 28 N | 68 35 E | 53 |

## I

| NAME | POPULATION | LATITUDE | LONGITUDE | PAGE |
|---|---|---|---|---|
| Ibadan, Nigeria | 1,295,000 | 07° 23′ N | 03° 54′ E | 68 |
| Ibiza (isl.), Spain | 88,076 | 39 00 N | 01 25 E | 42 |
| **Iceland** | **299,388** | **65 00 N** | **19 00 W** | **39** |
| Idaho (state), U.S. | 1,293,953 | 44 00 N | 114 00 W | 80 |
| Idaho Falls, Idaho, U.S. | 50,730 | 43 28 N | 112 02 W | 80 |
| Île-à-la-Crosse (lake), Sask., Can. | | 55 00 N | 107 30 W | 80 |
| Iliamna (lake), Alaska, U.S. | | 59 30 N | 155 00 W | 78 |
| Illinois (state), U.S. | 12,419,293 | 40 00 N | 89 15 W | 84 |
| Inch'on, S. Korea | 2,466,338 | 36 51 N | 127 26 E | 55 |
| **India** | **1,095,351,995** | **23 00 N** | **80 00 E** | **53** |
| Indiana (state), U.S. | 6,080,485 | 40 00 N | 86 00 W | 84 |
| Indianapolis,* Ind., U.S. | 791,926 | 39 46 N | 86 09 W | 84 |
| **Indonesia** | **245,452,739** | **05 00 S** | **120 00 E** | **56** |
| Indore, India | 1,597,441 | 22 40 N | 75 58 E | 53 |
| Indus (river), Pak. | | 33 00 N | 71 30 E | 53 |
| Inner Mongolia (region), China | | 42 00 N | 110 00 E | 55 |
| Inuvik, N.W. Terrs., Can. | 2,894 | 68 21 N | 133 43 W | 76 |
| Ionian (sea), Greece, Italy | | 38 00 N | 19 00 E | 44 |
| Iowa (state), U.S. | 2,926,324 | 42 00 N | 93 30 W | 81 |
| Iowa City, Iowa, U.S. | 62,220 | 41 39 N | 91 32 W | 83 |
| Iqaluit,* Nun., Can. | 5,236 | 63 45 N | 68 31 W | 77 |
| **Iran** | **68,688,433** | **33 00 N** | **55 00 E** | **52** |
| **Iraq** | **26,783,383** | **33 00 N** | **44 00 E** | **52** |
| **Ireland** | **4,062,235** | **53 00 N** | **08 00 W** | **42** |
| Irish (sea), Ireland,U.K. | | 53 40 N | 04 30 W | 42 |
| Irkutsk, Russia | 591,047 | 52 16 N | 104 20 E | 47 |
| Irtysh (river), Russia | | 61 02 N | 68 47 E | 46 |
| Irving, Texas, U.S. | 191,615 | 32 49 N | 96 57 W | 86 |
| Ishevsk, Russia | 653,691 | 56 51 N | 53 14 E | 45 |
| Islamabad,* Pakistan | 529,180 | 33 42 N | 73 10 E | 53 |
| Isle Royale Nat'l Pk., Mich., U.S. | | 48 00 N | 89 00 W | 81 |
| **Israel** | **6,352,117** | **32 00 N** | **35 00 E** | **52** |
| Istanbul, Turkey | 8,831,805 | 41 10 N | 29 00 E | 44 |
| Itaipu (res.), Brazil,Para. | | 25 00 S | 54 30 W | 96 |
| **Italy** | **58,133,509** | **42 00 N** | **13 00 E** | **39** |
| Ivanovo, Russia | 458,531 | 57 00 N | 40 59 E | 43 |
| Iwo Jima (isl.), Japan | | 24 47 N | 141 20 E | 62 |
| Izmir, Turkey | 2,250,149 | 38 25 N | 27 10 E | 44 |

## J

| NAME | POPULATION | LATITUDE | LONGITUDE | PAGE |
|---|---|---|---|---|
| Jabalpur, India | 951,469 | 23° 10′ N | 79° 57′ E | 53 |
| Jackson,* Miss., U.S. | 184,256 | 32 18 N | 90 11 W | 87 |
| Jackson, Tenn., U.S. | 59,643 | 35 37 N | 88 49 W | 87 |
| Jacksonville, Fla., U.S. | 735,617 | 30 20 N | 81 39 W | 87 |
| Jaipur, India | 2,324,319 | 26 55 N | 75 49 E | 53 |
| Jakarta,* Indon. | 8,389,443 | 06 10 S | 106 50 E | 56 |
| **Jamaica** | **2,758,124** | **18 15 N** | **77 30 W** | **89** |
| James (bay), Ont.,Qué., Can. | | 53 00 N | 80 30 W | 77 |
| James Ross (strait), Nun., Can. | | 69 00 N | 97 00 W | 76 |
| Janesville, Wis., U.S. | 59,498 | 42 41 N | 89 01 W | 84 |
| Jan Mayen (isl.), Norway | | 71 00 N | 08 30 W | 39 |
| **Japan** | **127,463,611** | **38 00 N** | **138 00 E** | **55** |
| Japan (sea), Asia | | 40 00 N | 135 00 E | 55 |
| Jasper Nat'l Pk., Alta., Can. | | 53 00 N | 118 00 W | 80 |
| Java (isl.), Indon. | 124,503,770 | 07 00 S | 110 00 E | 56 |
| Java (sea), Indon. | | 05 00 S | 110 00 E | 56 |
| Jayapura, Indon. | 166,201 | 02 32 S | 140 42 E | 57 |
| Jefferson City,* Mo., U.S. | 39,636 | 38 34 N | 92 10 W | 83 |
| Jerusalem,* Israel | 591,426 | 31 46 N | 35 14 E | 52 |
| Jidda, S. Ar. | 2,021,095 | 21 29 N | 39 12 E | 52 |
| Jilin, China | 1,953,134 | 43 51 N | 126 33 E | 55 |
| Jinan, China | 2,999,934 | 36 40 N | 117 00 E | 55 |
| Johannesburg, S. Afr. | 752,349 | 26 12 S | 28 03 E | 70 |
| Johnson City, Tenn., U.S. | 55,469 | 36 19 N | 82 21 W | 87 |
| Johnston Atoll (isl.), U.S. | 800 | 16 44 N | 169 31 W | 63 |
| Joliet, Ill., U.S. | 106,221 | 41 31 N | 88 05 W | 84 |
| Jonesboro, Ark., U.S. | 55,515 | 35 50 N | 90 42 W | 87 |
| Jonquière, Qué., Can. | 54,802 | 48 24 N | 71 15 W | 85 |
| **Jordan** | **5,906,760** | **31 00 N** | **37 00 E** | **52** |
| Joshua Tree Nat'l Park, Calif., U.S. | | 33 55 N | 115 56 W | 82 |
| Juan de Fuca (strait), Can.,U.S. | | 49 15 N | 123 30 W | 80 |
| Juan Fernández (isls.), Chile | | 33 36 S | 78 55 W | 12 |
| Juneau,* Alaska, U.S. | 30,711 | 58 18 N | 134 25 W | 78 |
| Jura (mts.), Fr.,Switz. | | 47 10 N | 07 00 E | 42 |
| Jutland (pen.), Den. | | 56 00 N | 09 00 E | 43 |
| Juventud (isl.), Cuba | | 21 40 N | 82 50 W | 88 |

## K

| NAME | POPULATION | LATITUDE | LONGITUDE | PAGE |
|---|---|---|---|---|
| Kabul,* Afghan. | 1,424,400 | 34° 31′ N | 69° 00′E | 52 |
| Kahoolawe (isl.), Hawaii, U.S. | | 20 33 N | 156 37 W | 78 |
| Kaifeng, China | 796,171 | 34 48 N | 114 21 E | 55 |
| Kalaallit Nunaat (Greenland) (isl.), Den. | 56,384 | 70 00 N | 40 00 W | 73 |
| Kalahari (desert), Bots.,Namb. | | 23 00 S | 22 00 E | 70 |
| Kalamazoo, Mich., U.S. | 77,145 | 42 17 N | 85 35 W | 84 |
| Kalimantan (region), Indon. | | 01 00 S | 113 00 E | 56 |
| Kalyān, India | 1,193,266 | 19 15 N | 73 09 E | 53 |
| Kama (river), Russia | | 55 10 N | 49 20 E | 45 |
| Kamchatka (pen.), Russia | | 56 00 N | 160 00 E | 47 |
| Kamloops, Br. Col., Can. | 77,281 | 50 40 N | 120 19 W | 80 |
| Kampala,* Uganda | 1,208,544 | 00 19 N | 32 35 E | 69 |
| Kananga, D.R. Congo | 371,800 | 05 54 S | 22 25 E | 70 |
| Kanazawa, Japan | 456,438 | 36 34 N | 136 39 E | 55 |
| Kandahār, Afghan. | 225,500 | 31 32 N | 65 30 E | 52 |
| Kanin (pen.), Russia | | 67 30 N | 45 00 E | 43 |
| Kano, Nigeria | 700,000 | 12 00 N | 08 31 E | 68 |
| Kanpur, India | 2,532,138 | 26 28 N | 80 21 E | 53 |
| Kansas (state), U.S. | 2,688,418 | 38 30 N | 98 30 W | 83 |
| Kansas City, Kans., U.S. | 146,866 | 39 07 N | 94 37 W | 83 |
| Kansas City, Mo., U.S. | 441,545 | 39 06 N | 94 34 W | 83 |
| Kaohsiung, Taiwan, China | 1,423,821 | 22 38 N | 120 17 E | 55 |
| Kara (sea), Russia | | 72 00 N | 62 00 E | 46 |
| Karāchi, Pak. | 9,339,023 | 24 55 N | 67 00 E | 53 |
| Karaj, Iran | 940,968 | 35 48 N | 50 59 E | 52 |
| Karakoram (mts.), China | | 36 00 N | 77 00 E | 53 |
| Karakumy (desert), Trkm. | | 41 30 N | 58 00 E | 45 |
| Karlsruhe, Germany | 277,204 | 49 00 N | 08 28 E | 42 |
| Kasai (river), D.R. Congo | | 03 10 S | 16 11 E | 70 |
| Kassel, Germany | 196,201 | 51 20 N | 09 15 E | 42 |
| Katahdin (mt.), Maine, U.S. | | 45 54 N | 68 55 W | 85 |
| Katmandu,* Nepal | 671,846 | 27 45 N | 85 25 E | 53 |
| Katowice, Poland | 327,222 | 50 16 N | 19 00 E | 44 |
| Kattegat (strait), Den.,Sweden | | 57 00 N | 11 30 E | 43 |
| Kauai (isl.), Hawaii, U.S. | | 22 05 N | 159 30 W | 78 |
| Kaunas, Lithuania | 378,943 | 54 54 N | 23 54 E | 43 |
| Kavir, Dasht-e (desert), Iran | | 35 00 N | 55 00 E | 52 |
| Kawasaki, Japan | 1,249,905 | 35 30 N | 139 47 E | 55 |
| **Kazakhstan** | **15,233,244** | **48 00 N** | **67 00 E** | **46** |
| Kazan', Russia | 1,091,656 | 55 45 N | 49 08 E | 45 |
| Keele (mt.), Yukon Terr., Can. | | 63 00 N | 130 19 W | 76 |
| Kelowna, Br. Col., Can. | 96,288 | 49 53 N | 119 29 W | 80 |
| Kemerovo, Russia | 492,240 | 55 20 N | 86 05 E | 47 |
| Kenora, Ont., Can. | 11,806 | 49 46 N | 94 28 W | 81 |
| Kenosha, Wis., U.S. | 90,352 | 42 35 N | 87 49 W | 84 |
| Kentucky (lake), Ky.,Tenn., U.S. | | 37 00 N | 88 16 W | 87 |
| Kentucky (state), U.S. | 4,041,769 | 37 30 N | 85 00 W | 87 |
| **Kenya** | **34,707,817** | **00 00** | **38 00 E** | **69** |
| Kenya (mt.), Kenya | | 00 08 S | 37 18 E | 69 |
| Kerguélen (isls.), Fr. | | 49 00 S | 69 00 E | 13 |
| Kermān, Iran | 384,991 | 30 17 N | 57 05 E | 52 |
| Keweenaw (mt.), Mich., U.S. | | 47 24 N | 87 42 W | 84 |
| Key West, Fla., U.S. | 25,478 | 24 33 N | 81 47 W | 87 |
| Khabarovsk, Russia | 608,853 | 48 30 N | 135 06 E | 55 |
| Kharkiv, Ukraine | 1,470,902 | 50 00 N | 36 15 E | 44 |
| Khartoum,* Sudan | 924,505 | 15 35 N | 32 33 E | 69 |
| Khulna, Bangladesh | 773,216 | 22 48 N | 89 33 E | 53 |
| Kiel, Germany | 233,795 | 54 20 N | 10 10 E | 42 |
| Kiev,* Ukraine | 2,611,327 | 50 27 N | 30 32 E | 44 |
| Kigali,* Rwanda | 232,770 | 01 57 S | 30 04 E | 70 |
| Kilimanjaro (mt.), Tanz. | | 03 04 S | 37 21 E | 70 |
| Killeen, Texas, U.S. | 86,911 | 31 07 N | 97 43 W | 83 |
| Kimberley, S. Afr. | 62,526 | 28 43 S | 24 46 E | 70 |
| Kimberley (plat.), Austl. | | 16 00 S | 127 00 E | 59 |
| King George (isls.), Nun., Can. | | 56 30 N | 79 00 W | 77 |
| Kings (mt.), Utah., U.S. | | 40 46 N | 110 22 W | 82 |
| Kingston,* Jamaica | 103,771 | 18 00 N | 76 48 W | 89 |
| Kingston, Ont., Can. | 108,158 | 44 14 N | 76 30 W | 84 |
| Kingstown,* St. Vincent and the Grenadines | 15,466 | 13 09 N | 61 13 W | 89 |
| Kinshasa,* D.R. Congo | 3,800,000 | 04 19 S | 15 23 E | 70 |
| Kirgiz Steppe (grassland), Kazak. | | 49 30 N | 57 00 E | 45 |
| **Kiribati** | **105,432** | **00 00** | **175 00 E** | **62** |
| Kirov, Russia | 465,628 | 58 33 N | 49 42 E | 45 |
| Kitakyushu, Japan | 1,011,471 | 33 53 N | 130 50 E | 55 |
| Kitchener, Ont., Can. | 190,399 | 43 27 N | 80 29 W | 84 |
| Kjölen (mts.), Norway,Sweden | | 65 00 N | 15 00 E | 43 |
| Kluane Nat'l Pk., Yukon Terr., Can. | | 61 00 N | 140 00 W | 76 |
| Knoxville, Tenn., U.S. | 173,890 | 35 57 N | 83 55 W | 87 |
| Kobe, Japan | 1,493,398 | 34 41 N | 135 10 E | 55 |
| Kodiak (isl.), Alaska, U.S. | | 57 30 N | 153 30 W | 78 |
| Kola (pen.), Russia | | 67 20 N | 37 00 E | 43 |
| Kolguyev (isl.), Russia | | 68 30 N | 49 00 E | 43 |
| Kolkata (Calcutta), India | 4,580,544 | 22 30 N | 88 30 E | 53 |
| Kolyma (mts.), Russia | | 63 00 N | 160 00 E | 47 |
| Kolyma (river), Russia | | 69 30 N | 161 12 E | 47 |
| Komandorskiye (isls.), Russia | | 55 00 N | 167 00 E | 47 |
| Konya, Turkey | 761,145 | 37 52 N | 32 31 E | 44 |
| Kootenay Nat'l Pk., Br. Col., Can. | | 50 30 N | 116 30 W | 80 |
| **Korea, North** | **23,113,019** | **40 00 N** | **127 00 E** | **55** |
| **Korea, South** | **48,846,823** | **37 30 N** | **128 00 E** | **55** |
| Koror,* Palau | 10,600 | 07 20 N | 134 28 E | 62 |
| Kosciusko (mt.), Austl. | | 36 28 S | 148 16 E | 59 |
| Kota Kinabalu, Malaysia | 75,787 | 05 59 N | 116 04 E | 56 |
| Kouchibouguac Nat'l Pk., N.B., Can. | | 46 30 N | 65 00 W | 85 |
| Kraków, Poland | 758,544 | 50 05 N | 19 55 E | 44 |
| Krasnodar, Russia | 639,917 | 45 02 N | 39 00 E | 44 |
| Krasnoyarsk, Russia | 876,418 | 56 02 N | 92 48 E | 46 |
| Krishna (river), India | | 15 57 N | 80 59 E | 53 |
| Krung Thep (Bangkok),* Thailand | 5,876,000 | 13 45 N | 100 30 E | 56 |
| Kryvyy Rih, Ukraine | 668,900 | 47 55 N | 33 21 E | 44 |
| Kuala Lumpur,* Malaysia | 1,145,075 | 03 09 N | 101 42 E | 56 |
| Kuching, Malaysia | 147,729 | 01 34 N | 111 22 E | 56 |
| Kugluktuk, Nun., Can. | 1,212 | 67 50 N | 115 05 W | 77 |
| Kumamoto, Japan | 662,012 | 32 48 N | 130 43 E | 55 |
| Kumasi, Ghana | 399,300 | 06 41 N | 01 37 W | 68 |
| Kunming, China | 3,035,406 | 25 04 N | 102 41 E | 54 |
| Kunlun (mts.), China | | 36 00 N | 85 00 E | 54 |
| Kura (river), Azer. | | 39 24 N | 49 19 E | 45 |
| Kuril (isls.), Russia | | 45 00 N | 150 00 E | 47 |
| Kutch (Kachchh), Rann of (salt lake), India | | 24 00 N | 70 00 E | 53 |
| **Kuwait** | **2,418,393** | **29 30 N** | **47 45 E** | **52** |
| Kuwait,* Kuwait | 31,241 | 29 20 N | 48 02 E | 52 |
| Kwajalein (isl.), Marshall Isls. | 10,902 | 08 43 N | 167 44 E | 62 |
| Kwangju, Korea | 1,350,948 | 35 09 N | 126 55 E | 55 |
| Kyoto, Japan | 1,467,785 | 34 58 N | 135 45 E | 55 |
| **Kyrgyzstan** | **5,213,898** | **41 00 N** | **75 00 E** | **46** |
| Kyushu (isl.), Japan | 13,445,561 | 33 00 N | 131 00 E | 55 |

## L

| NAME | POPULATION | LATITUDE | LONGITUDE | PAGE |
|---|---|---|---|---|
| Labrador (region), Newf., Can. | | 54° 00′ N | 60° 00′ W | 77 |
| Labrador, (sea), Newf., Can. | | 56 00 N | 55 00 W | 77 |
| Laccadive, (sea), India | | 11 00 N | 73 00 E | 53 |
| La Crosse, Wis., U.S. | 51,818 | 43 48 N | 91 14 W | 84 |
| Ladoga (lake), Russia | | 61 00 N | 31 00 E | 43 |
| Lafayette, Ind., U.S. | 56,397 | 40 25 N | 86 53 W | 84 |
| Lafayette, La., U.S. | 110,257 | 30 13 N | 92 01 W | 86 |
| Lagos, Nigeria | 1,347,000 | 06 27 N | 03 25 E | 68 |
| Lahore, Pak. | 5,143,495 | 31 37 N | 74 18 E | 53 |
| Lake Charles, La., U.S. | 71,757 | 30 13 N | 93 13 W | 86 |
| Lakeland, Fla., U.S. | 78,452 | 28 02 N | 81 56 W | 87 |
| Lake of the Woods (lake), Can.,U.S. | | 49 30 N | 94 30 W | 81 |
| La Martre (lake), N.W. Terrs., Can. | | 62 30 N | 119 00 W | 76 |
| Lancaster (sound), Nun., Can. | | 74 15 N | 84 00 W | 77 |
| Lancaster, Pa., U.S. | 56,348 | 40 02 N | 76 18 W | 84 |
| Land's End (prom.), Eng., U.K. | | 50 05 N | 05 30 W | 42 |
| Languedoc (region), Fr. | | 43 00 N | 03 00 E | 42 |
| Lansing,* Mich., U.S. | 119,128 | 42 44 N | 84 34 W | 84 |
| Lanzhou, China | 2,087,759 | 36 03 N | 103 41 E | 54 |
| **Laos** | **6,368,481** | **19 00 N** | **103 00 E** | **49** |
| La Paz,* Bolivia | 1,487,248 | 16 29 S | 68 09 W | 94 |
| La Pérouse (strait), Japan,Russia | | 45 45 N | 142 00 E | 55 |
| La Plata (river), Arg.,Uruguay | | 36 00 S | 55 00 W | 96 |
| Lapland (region), Europe | | 68 00 N | 23 00 E | 43 |
| Laptev (sea), Russia | | 76 00 N | 126 00 E | 47 |
| Laramie, Wyo., U.S. | 27,204 | 41 19 N | 105 35 W | 83 |
| Laramie (mt.), Wyo., U.S. | | 42 16 N | 105 27 W | 81 |
| Laredo, Texas, U.S. | 176,576 | 27 30 N | 99 30 W | 86 |
| La Ronge (lake), Sask., Can. | | 55 00 N | 105 00 W | 76 |
| Larsen (sound), Nun., Can. | | 71 00 N | 99 30 W | 76 |
| Las Cruces, N.M., U.S. | 74,267 | 32 18 N | 106 46 W | 82 |
| Las Palmas, Canary Is., Spain | 354,853 | 28 06 N | 15 24 W | 65 |
| Las Vegas, Nev., U.S. | 478,434 | 36 10 N | 115 08 W | 82 |
| Lassen (mt.), Calif., U.S. | | 40 29 N | 121 29 W | 80 |
| Lassen Volcanic Nat'l Pk., Calif., U.S. | | 40 30 N | 121 30 W | 80 |
| **Latvia** | **2,274,735** | **57 00 N** | **24 00 E** | **43** |
| Laurentian (plat.), Can. | | 54 00 N | 90 00 W | 76 |
| Lausanne, Switz. | 124,914 | 46 31 N | 06 37 E | 42 |

| NAME | POPULATION | LATITUDE | LONGITUDE | PAGE |
|---|---|---|---|---|
| Laval, Qué., Can. | 343,005 | 45 35 N | 73 45 W | 85 |
| Lawrence, Mass., U.S. | 72,043 | 42 42 N | 71 09 W | 85 |
| Lawton, Okla., U.S. | 92,757 | 34 36 N | 98 23 W | 83 |
| **Lebanon** | **3,874,050** | **33 45 N** | **35 45 E** | **52** |
| Leeds, Eng., U.K. | 424,194 | 53 50 N | 01 25 W | 42 |
| Leeward, (isls.), N. America | | 18 00 N | 61 00 W | 89 |
| Le Havre, Fr. | 193,259 | 49 25 N | 00 10 E | 42 |
| Leipzig, Germany | 489,532 | 51 20 N | 12 20 E | 42 |
| Lena (river), Russia | | 72 00 N | 127 00 E | 47 |
| León, Mex. | 1,020,818 | 21 07 N | 101 40 W | 88 |
| **Lesotho** | **2,022,331** | **29 15 S** | **28 15 E** | **70** |
| Lesser Antilles, (isls.), N. America | | 12 00 N | 67 00 W | 89 |
| Lésvos (Lesbos) (isl.), Greece | 109,118 | 39 20 N | 26 15 E | 44 |
| Lethbridge, Alta., Can. | 67,374 | 49 42 N | 112 49 W | 80 |
| Lévis, Qué., Can. | 40,926 | 46 48 N | 71 11 W | 85 |
| Lexington, Ky., U.S. | 260,512 | 38 03 N | 84 30 W | 87 |
| Leyte (isl.), Phil. | | 10 50 N | 125 00 E | 57 |
| Lhasa, China | 223,001 | 29 39 N | 91 06 E | 54 |
| Liard (river), Br. Col.,Yukon Terr., Can. | | 61 50 N | 121 19 W | 76 |
| **Liberia** | **3,042,004** | **06 00 N** | **09 00 W** | **68** |
| Libreville,* Gabon | 362,386 | 00 24 N | 09 27 E | 68 |
| **Libya** | **5,900,754** | **27 00 N** | **17 30 E** | **69** |
| Libyan (desert), Africa | | 28 00 N | 25 00 E | 69 |
| **Liechtenstein** | **33,987** | **47 10 N** | **09 32 E** | **42** |
| Liège, Belgium | 194,596 | 50 40 N | 05 35 E | 42 |
| Ligurian (sea), Fr.,Italy | | 43 00 N | 09 00 E | 42 |
| Lille, Fr. | 191,164 | 50 40 N | 03 00 E | 42 |
| Lilongwe,* Malawi | 440,471 | 13 59 S | 33 47 E | 70 |
| Lima, Ohio, U.S. | 40,081 | 40 44 N | 84 06 W | 84 |
| Lima,* Peru | 375,957 | 12 03 S | 77 03 W | 94 |
| Limpopo (river), Africa | | 25 12 S | 33 31 E | 70 |
| Lincoln,* Neb., U.S. | 225,581 | 40 48 N | 96 38 W | 83 |
| Line (isls.), Kiribati | | 04 00 S | 155 00 W | 63 |
| Linz, Austria | 203,044 | 48 18 N | 14 15 E | 42 |
| Lion (gulf), Fr. | | 43 00 N | 03 45 E | 42 |
| Lisbon,* Port. | 564,657 | 38 43 N | 09 10 W | 42 |
| **Lithuania** | **3,585,906** | **55 00 N** | **24 00 E** | **43** |
| Little Rock,* Ark., U.S. | 183,133 | 34 44 N | 92 17 W | 86 |
| Liverpool, Eng., U.K. | 481,786 | 53 28 N | 02 55 W | 42 |
| Liverpool (bay), N.W. Terrs., Can. | | 70 30 N | 130 00 W | 76 |
| Liverpool (cape), Nun., Can. | | 74 00 N | 78 04 W | 77 |
| Livorno, Italy | 161,288 | 43 33 N | 10 19 E | 42 |
| Ljubljana,* Slovenia | 258,873 | 46 03 N | 14 31 E | 44 |
| Llanos (plain), Col.,Ven. | | 05 00 N | 70 00 W | 94 |
| Lloydminster, Alta.,Sask.,Can. | 20,988 | 53 17 N | 109 59 W | 80 |
| Łódź, Poland | 789,318 | 51 46 N | 19 25 E | 44 |
| Logan, Utah, U.S. | 42,670 | 41 44 N | 111 50 W | 82 |
| Loire (river), Fr. | | 47 20 N | 02 00 E | 42 |
| Lolo (mt.), Mont., U.S. | | 46 40 N | 114 14 W | 80 |
| Lomas de Zamora, Arg. | 591,345 | 34 46 S | 58 24 W | 96 |
| Lombok (isl.), Indon. | | 08 48 S | 115 52 E | 56 |
| Lomé,* Togo | 450,000 | 06 07 N | 01 14 E | 68 |
| London,* Eng., U.K. | 6,679,699 | 51 30 N | 00 07 W | 42 |
| London, Ont., Can. | 337,318 | 42 59 N | 81 14 W | 84 |
| Long (isl.) N.Y., U.S. | | 40 45 N | 73 00 W | 85 |
| Long Beach, Calif., U.S. | 461,522 | 33 46 N | 118 11 W | 82 |
| Longview, Texas, U.S. | 73,344 | 32 30 N | 94 44 W | 86 |
| Lookout (cape), N.C., U.S. | | 34 35 N | 76 32 W | 87 |
| Lopatka (cape), Russia | | 50 52 N | 156 40 E | 47 |
| Lorraine (region), Fr. | | 49 00 N | 06 00 E | 42 |
| Los Angeles, Calif., U.S. | 3,694,820 | 34 03 N | 118 14 W | 82 |
| Louisiana (state), U.S. | 4,468,976 | 31 00 N | 92 30 W | 86 |
| Louisville, Ky., U.S. | 256,231 | 38 14 N | 85 45 W | 87 |
| Lowell, Mass., U.S. | 105,167 | 42 38 N | 71 19 W | 85 |
| Loyalty (isls.), New Cal. | 20,877 | 21 00 S | 168 00 E | 62 |
| Luanda,* Angola | 1,530,000 | 08 49 S | 13 14 E | 70 |
| Lubbock, Texas, U.S. | 199,564 | 33 34 N | 101 51 W | 83 |
| Lübeck, Germany | 213,326 | 53 50 N | 10 40 E | 42 |
| Lubumbashi, D.R. Congo | 739,000 | 11 40 S | 27 28 E | 70 |
| Lucknow, India | 2,207,340 | 26 46 N | 80 59 E | 53 |
| Ludhiāna, India | 1,395,053 | 30 54 N | 75 51 E | 53 |
| Lusaka,* Zambia | 982,362 | 15 25 S | 28 18 E | 70 |
| **Luxembourg** | **474,413** | **49 45 N** | **06 10 E** | **42** |
| Luxembourg,* Lux. | 78,329 | 49 35 N | 06 12 E | 42 |
| Luzon (isl.), Phil. | | 15 00 N | 121 00 E | 57 |
| L'viv, Ukraine | 732,818 | 49 51 N | 24 02 E | 44 |
| Lynchburg, Va., U.S. | 65,269 | 37 24 N | 79 08 W | 87 |
| Lyon, Fr. | 453,187 | 45 40 N | 04 40 E | 42 |

## M

| NAME | POPULATION | LATITUDE | LONGITUDE | PAGE |
|---|---|---|---|---|
| Maanselkä (mts.), Finland,Russia | | 66° 30′ N | 29° 00′ E | 43 |
| Macau, China | 439,162 | 22 12 N | 113 33 E | 55 |
| **Macedonia, Former Yugoslav Republic of** | **2,050,554** | **42 00 N** | **21 26 E** | **44** |
| Maceió, Brazil | 797,759 | 09 40 S | 35 44 W | 95 |
| Mackenzie (bay), N.W. Terrs., Yukon Terr., Can. | | 69 30 N | 138 00 W | 76 |
| Mackenzie (mts.), N.W. Terrs., Can. | | 64 00 N | 130 00 W | 76 |
| Mackenzie (river), N.W. Terrs., Can. | | 68 00 N | 134 00 W | 76 |
| Macon, Ga., U.S. | 97,255 | 32 50 N | 83 38 W | 87 |
| **Madagascar** | **18,595,469** | **18 00 S** | **47 00 E** | **70** |
| Madeira (isl.), Port. | 245,011 | 32 45 N | 17 00 W | 68 |
| Madeira (river), Brazil | | 03 23 S | 58 45 W | 94 |
| Madeleine (isl.), Qué., Can. | | 47 26 N | 61 44 W | 85 |
| Madison,* Wis., U.S. | 208,054 | 43 04 N | 89 24 W | 84 |
| Madrid,* Spain | 2,938,723 | 40 25 N | 03 42 W | 42 |
| Madura (isl.), Indon. | | 07 00 S | 113 00 E | 56 |
| Madurai, India | 922,913 | 09 55 N | 78 15 E | 53 |
| Magdalena (river), Col. | | 11 06 N | 75 00 W | 94 |
| Magdeburg, Germany | 235,073 | 52 10 N | 11 00 E | 42 |
| Magellan (strait), Arg.,Chile | | 54 00 S | 71 00 W | 96 |
| Magnitogorsk, Russia | 426,866 | 53 28 N | 59 00 E | 46 |
| Maine (gulf), U.S. | | 43 00 N | 69 00 W | 85 |
| Maine (state), U.S. | 1,274,923 | 45 30 N | 69 00 W | 85 |
| Majorca (isl.), Spain | 676,516 | 39 35 N | 03 00 E | 42 |


| NAME | POPULATION | LATITUDE | LONGITUDE | PAGE |
|---|---|---|---|---|
| Majuro,* Marshall Is. | 23,676 | 07 04 N | 171 12 E | 62 |
| Makassar (strait), Indon. | | 03 57 S | 119 32 E | 56 |
| Malabar Coast, India | | 12 50 N | 75 00 E | 53 |
| Malabo,* Eq. Guin. | 30,418 | 03 45 N | 08 46 E | 68 |
| Malacca (strait), Indon.,Malaysia | | 03 10 N | 100 45 E | 56 |
| Málaga, Spain | 524,414 | 36 43 N | 04 25 W | 42 |
| Malang, Indonesia | 757,383 | 07 59 S | 112 37 E | 56 |
| Malatya, Turkey | 381,081 | 38 21 N | 38 19 E | 44 |
| **Malawi** | **13,013,926** | **13 30 S** | **34 30 E** | **70** |
| Malay (pen.), Malaysia,Thai. | | 05 00 N | 102 00 E | 56 |
| Malaya (reg.), Malaysia | 17,047,400 | 03 00 N | 103 00 E | 56 |
| **Malaysia** | **24,385,858** | **04 00 N** | **102 00 E** | **56** |
| Male,* Maldives | 74,069 | 04 10 N | 73 30 E | 49 |
| **Maldives** | **359,008** | **04 00 N** | **73 00 E** | **49** |
| **Mali** | **11,716,829** | **17 30 N** | **04 00 W** | **68** |
| Malmö, Sweden | 233,870 | 55 35 N | 13 00 E | 43 |
| **Malta** | **400,214** | **35 55 N** | **14 23 E** | **44** |
| Mammoth Cave Nat'l Pk., Ky., U.S. | | 37 11 N | 86 08 W | 87 |
| Man, Isle of (isl.), U.K. | 76,315 | 54 15 N | 04 30 W | 42 |
| Managua,* Nic. | 882,945 | 12 08 N | 86 18 W | 88 |
| Manama,* Bahrain | 140,401 | 26 14 N | 50 35 W | 52 |
| Manaus, Brazil | 1,405,835 | 03 08 S | 60 01 W | 94 |
| Manchester, Eng., U.K. | 402,889 | 53 30 N | 02 13 W | 42 |
| Manchester, N.H., U.S. | 107,006 | 42 60 N | 71 28 W | 85 |
| Mandab, Bab al (strait), Africa,Asia. | | 12 39 N | 43 26 E | 52 |
| Mandalay, Myanmar. | 532,949 | 21 59 N | 96 05 E | 53 |
| Manicouagan (res.), Qué., Can. | | 51 24 N | 68 44 W | 85 |
| Manicouagan (river), Qué., Can. | | 50 00 N | 68 45 W | 85 |
| Manila,* Phil. | 1,654,761 | 14 36 N | 120 59 E | 57 |
| Manitoba (lake), Man., Can. | | 50 30 N | 98 20 W | 81 |
| Manitoba (prov.), Can. | 1,119,585 | 55 00 N | 97 00 W | 76 |
| Manitoulin (isl.), Ont., Can. | | 45 50 N | 82 25 W | 84 |
| Mannar (gulf), India,Sri Lanka | | 08 00 N | 79 00 E | 53 |
| Mannheim, Germany | 307,730 | 49 30 N | 08 28 E | 42 |
| Maputo,* Moz. | 966,837 | 25 58 S | 32 35 E | 70 |
| Maracaibo (lake), Ven. | | 09 20 N | 71 30 W | 94 |
| Maracaibo, Ven. | 1,249,670 | 10 38 N | 71 38 W | 94 |
| Marajó (isl.), Brazil | | 01 00 S | 50 00 W | 95 |
| Marañón (river), Peru | | 04 30 S | 73 26 W | 94 |
| Marcy (mt.), N.Y., U.S. | | 44 06 N | 73 55 W | 84 |
| Margarita (isl.), Ven. | | 11 00 N | 64 00 W | 94 |
| Marie Byrd Land (region), Antarctica | | 80 00 S | 120 00 W | 71 |
| Marietta, Ga., U.S. | 58,748 | 33 57 N | 84 33 W | 87 |
| Mariupol', Ukraine | 492,176 | 47 05 N | 37 36 E | 44 |
| Markham, Ont., Can. | 208,815 | 43 52 N | 79 16 W | 84 |
| Marmara (sea), Turkey | | 40 42 N | 28 12 E | 44 |
| Marquesas (isls.), Fr. Polynesia | 8,064 | 09 00 S | 139 30 W | 63 |
| Marquette, Mich., U.S. | 19,661 | 46 32 N | 87 23 W | 84 |
| Marrakech, Morocco | 823,154 | 31 38 N | 08 00 W | 68 |
| Marsala, Italy | 80,818 | 37 48 N | 12 26 E | 42 |
| Marseille, Fr. | 807,071 | 43 18 N | 05 23 E | 42 |
| **Marshall Islands** | **60,422** | **09 00 N** | **168 00 E** | **62** |
| Martinique (isl.), Fr. | 432,900 | 14 40 N | 61 00 W | 89 |
| Maryland (state), U.S. | 5,296,486 | 39 00 N | 76 30 W | 84 |
| Maseru,* Lesotho | 109,382 | 29 19 S | 27 29 E | 70 |
| Mashhad, Iran | 1,887,405 | 36 18 N | 59 36 E | 52 |
| Massachusetts (state), U.S. | 6,349,097 | 42 20 N | 72 00 W | 85 |
| Massif Central (plat.), Fr. | | 45 00 N | 08 00 E | 42 |
| Mato Grosso (plat.), Brazil | | 14 30 S | 54 00 W | 95 |
| Maui (isl.), Hawaii, U.S. | | 20 48 N | 156 20 W | 78 |
| Mauna Loa (mt.), Hawaii, U.S. | | 19 29 N | 155 36 W | 78 |
| Mauricie Nat'l Pk., Qué., Can. | | 46 30 N | 73 00 W | 85 |
| **Mauritania** | **3,177,388** | **20 00 N** | **11 00 W** | **68** |
| **Mauritius** | **1,240,827** | **20 15 S** | **57 30 E** | **13** |
| May (cape), N.J., U.S. | | 39 01 N | 74 53 W | 84 |
| Mayotte (isl.), Fr. | 193,633 | 13 00 S | 45 00 E | 65 |
| Mazār-e Sharif, Afghan. | 130,600 | 36 42 N | 67 06 E | 52 |
| McAllen, Texas, U.S. | 106,414 | 26 12 N | 98 13 W | 86 |
| M'Clintock (chan.), Nun., Can. | | 71 30 N | 103 00 W | 76 |
| McKinley (mt.), Alaska, U.S. | | 63 04 N | 151 00 W | 78 |
| Mecca, S. Ar. | 952,429 | 21 29 N | 39 45 E | 52 |
| Medan, Indon. | 1,911,997 | 03 35 N | 98 40 E | 56 |
| Medellín, Col. | 1,484,757 | 06 15 N | 75 34 W | 94 |
| Medford, Ore., U.S. | 63,154 | 42 19 N | 122 52 W | 80 |
| Medicine Hat, Alta., Can. | 51,249 | 50 03 N | 110 40 W | 80 |
| Mediterranean (sea) | | 40 00 N | 10 00 E | 42 |
| Mekong (river), Cambodia, Vietnam | | 16 00 N | 105 00 E | 56 |
| Melanesia (isls.) | | 10 00 S | 160 00 E | 62 |
| Melbourne, Fla., U.S. | 71,382 | 28 04 N | 80 36 W | 87 |
| Melbourne, Austl. | 3,132,900 | 37 50 S | 145 00 E | 59 |
| Melville (isl.), N.W. Terrs.,Nun., Can. | | 75 30 N | 112 00 W | 77 |
| Melville (lake), Newf., Can. | | 53 00 N | 59 30 W | 77 |
| Melville (pen.), Nun., Can. | | 67 00 N | 84 00 W | 77 |
| Memphis, Tenn., U.S. | 650,100 | 35 09 N | 90 03 W | 87 |
| Mendocino (cape), Calif., U.S. | | 40 27 N | 124 26 W | 78 |
| Mendoza, Arg. | 110,993 | 32 53 S | 68 49 W | 96 |
| Merced, Calif., U.S. | 63,893 | 37 18 N | 120 29 W | 82 |
| Mérida, Mex. | 662,530 | 20 58 N | 89 37 W | 88 |
| Mesa, Ariz., U.S. | 396,375 | 33 25 N | 111 50 W | 82 |
| Mesopotamia (region), Iraq | | 34 00 N | 44 00 E | 52 |
| Meta Incognita (pen.), Nun., Can. | | 62 00 N | 68 00 W | 77 |
| Meuse (river), Fr. | | 51 49 N | 05 01 E | 42 |
| Mexicali, Mex. | 662,530 | 32 38 N | 115 29 W | 89 |
| **Mexico** | **107,449,525** | **22 00 N** | **102 00 W** | **88** |
| Mexico (gulf), N. America | | 25 00 N | 90 00 W | 88 |
| Mexico,* Mex. | 8,605,239 | 19 26 N | 99 01 W | 88 |
| Miami, Fla., U.S. | 362,470 | 25 46 N | 80 11 W | 87 |
| Miami Beach, Fla., U.S. | 87,922 | 25 47 N | 80 07 W | 87 |
| Michigan (lake), Mich.,Wis., U.S. | | 44 00 N | 87 00 W | 84 |
| Michigan (state), U.S. | 9,938,444 | 44 00 N | 85 00 W | 84 |
| Micronesia (reg.) | | 10 00 N | 154 00 E | 62 |
| **Micronesia, Fed. States of** | **108,004** | **08 00 N** | **150 00 E** | **62** |
| Midland, Texas, U.S. | 94,996 | 32 00 N | 102 04 W | 86 |


| NAME | POPULATION | LATITUDE | LONGITUDE | PAGE |
|---|---|---|---|---|
| Midway (isls.), U.S. | | 28 15 N | 177 20 W | 62 |
| Milan, Italy | 1,301,551 | 45 30 N | 09 10 E | 42 |
| Milwaukee, Wis., U.S. | 596,974 | 43 02 N | 87 54 W | 84 |
| Minami-Tori-Shima (isl.), Japan | | 24 20 N | 154 00 E | 62 |
| Mindanao (isl.), Phil. | | 08 00 N | 125 00 E | 57 |
| Mindoro (isl.), Phil. | | 12 50 N | 121 10 E | 57 |
| Minneapolis, Minn., U.S. | 382,618 | 44 58 N | 93 15 W | 81 |
| Minnesota (state), U.S. | 4,919,479 | 46 30 N | 94 30 W | 81 |
| Minorca (isl.), Spain | 71,524 | 40 00 N | 04 00 E | 42 |
| Minsk,* Belarus | 1,654,800 | 53 50 N | 27 35 E | 44 |
| Miramichi, N.B., Can. | 18,508 | 47 01 N | 65 29 W | 85 |
| Miskolc, Hungary | 196,442 | 48 10 N | 20 50 E | 44 |
| Mississippi (river), U.S. | | 29 10 N | 89 16 W | 79 |
| Mississippi (state), U.S. | 2,844,658 | 33 00 N | 89 45 W | 87 |
| Missoula, Mont., U.S. | 57,043 | 46 52 N | 113 59 W | 80 |
| Missouri (river), U.S. | | 38 50 N | 90 10 W | 79 |
| Missouri (state), U.S. | 5,595,211 | 38 30 N | 92 30 W | 83 |
| Mistassini (lake), Qué., Can. | | 50 50 N | 74 00 W | 84 |
| Mitchell (mt.), N.C., U.S. | | 35 45 N | 82 15 W | 87 |
| Mobile, Ala., U.S. | 198,915 | 30 41 N | 88 02 W | 87 |
| Modesto, Calif., U.S. | 188,856 | 37 38 N | 120 59 W | 82 |
| Mogadishu,* Somalia | 600,000 | 02 03 N | 45 20 E | 69 |
| Mojave (desert), Calif., U.S. | | 35 00 N | 117 00 W | 82 |
| **Moldova** | **4,466,706** | **47 00 N** | **29 00 E** | **44** |
| Molokai (isl.), Hawaii, U.S. | | 21 08 N | 157 00 W | 78 |
| Moluccas (isls.), Indon. | | 02 30 S | 129 00 E | 57 |
| Mona (passage), N. America | | 18 15 N | 68 00 W | 89 |
| **Monaco** | **32,543** | **43 44 N** | **07 25 E** | **42** |
| Moncton, N.B., Can. | 61,046 | 46 06 N | 64 47 W | 85 |
| **Mongolia** | **2,832,224** | **47 00 N** | **102 00 E** | **54** |
| Monroe, La., U.S. | 53,107 | 32 30 N | 92 07 W | 86 |
| Monrovia,* Liberia | 421,058 | 06 19 N | 10 48 W | 68 |
| Montana (state), U.S. | 902,195 | 47 00 N | 110 00 W | 80 |
| **Montenegro** | **620,150** | **42 30 N** | **19 15 E** | **44** |
| Monterey, Calif., U.S. | 29,674 | 36 36 N | 121 53 W | 82 |
| Monterrey, Mex. | 1,110,909 | 25 45 N | 100 20 W | 88 |
| Montevideo,* Uruguay | 1,344,839 | 34 53 S | 56 10 W | 96 |
| Montgomery,* Ala., U.S. | 210,568 | 32 22 N | 86 17 W | 87 |
| Montpelier,* Vt., U.S. | 8,035 | 44 15 N | 72 34 W | 85 |
| Montréal, Qué., Can. | 1,783,027 | 45 30 N | 73 36 W | 84 |
| Montserrat (isl.), Fr. | 9,341 | 16 44 N | 62 10 W | 89 |
| Moose Jaw, Sask., Can. | 32,131 | 50 24 N | 105 32 W | 81 |
| Morelia, Mex. | 549,996 | 19 42 N | 101 07 W | 88 |
| Morena (mts.), Spain | | 38 30 N | 05 00 W | 42 |
| **Morocco** | **33,241,259** | **33 00 N** | **07 00 W** | **68** |
| Morón, Arg. | 309,380 | 34 39 S | 58 37 W | 96 |
| Moroni,* Comoros | 30,000 | 11 41 S | 43 16 E | 65 |
| Moscow (Moskva),* Russia | 8,297,056 | 55 45 N | 37 35 E | 43 |
| Moscow (upland), Russia | | 55 00 N | 33 00 E | 43 |
| Mosquitos (coast), Nic. | | 13 00 N | 88 00 W | 88 |
| Mosul, Iraq | 664,221 | 36 20 N | 43 08 E | 52 |
| Mount Rainier Nat'l Pk., Wash., U.S. | | 46 30 N | 122 00 W | 80 |
| Mount Revelstoke Nat'l Pk., Br. Col., Can. | | 51 00 N | 118 00 W | 80 |
| **Mozambique** | **19,686,505** | **18 00 S** | **35 00 E** | **70** |
| Mozambique (channel), Africa | | 22 00 S | 38 00 E | 70 |
| Multān, Pakistan | 1,197,384 | 30 11 N | 71 29 E | 53 |
| Mumbai (Bombay), India | 11,914,398 | 19 00 N | 72 48 E | 53 |
| Muncie, Ind., U.S. | 67,430 | 40 11 N | 85 23 W | 84 |
| Munich (München), Germany | 1,194,560 | 48 10 N | 11 30 E | 42 |
| Murcia, Spain | 370,745 | 37 43 N | 01 08 W | 42 |
| Murmansk, Russia | 378,552 | 68 58 N | 33 05 E | 43 |
| Murray (river), Austl. | | 35 33 S | 144 00 E | 59 |
| Muscat,* Oman | 67,000 | 23 37 N | 58 35 E | 52 |
| Muskegon, Mich., U.S. | 40,105 | 43 14 N | 86 15 W | 84 |
| **Myanmar (Burma)** | **47,382,633** | **20 00 N** | **96 00 E** | **49** |
| Mykolayiv, Ukraine | 514,136 | 46 58 N | 32 00 E | 44 |
| Myrtle Beach, S.C., U.S. | 22,759 | 33 41 N | 78 53 W | 87 |

## N

| NAME | POPULATION | LATITUDE | LONGITUDE | PAGE |
|---|---|---|---|---|
| Naberezhnye Chelny, Russia | 521,282 | 55° 42′ N | 52°19′ E | 45 |
| Nafūd (desert), S. Ar. | | 28 00 N | 41 00 E | 52 |
| Nagoya, Japan | 2,171,557 | 35 10 N | 137 55 E | 55 |
| Nagpur, India | 2,051,320 | 21 15 N | 79 12 E | 53 |
| Nairobi,* Kenya | 2,143,254 | 01 17 S | 36 49 E | 69 |
| Najd (region), S. Ar. | | 25 00 N | 43 00 E | 52 |
| Namib (desert), Namibia | | 23 00 S | 14 00 E | 70 |
| **Namibia** | **2,044,147** | **23 00 S** | **17 00 E** | **70** |
| Nanaimo, Br. Col., Can. | 73,000 | 49 09 N | 123 57 W | 80 |
| Nanchang, China | 1,844,253 | 28 40 N | 115 53 E | 55 |
| Nancy, Fr. | 105,830 | 48 40 N | 06 10 E | 42 |
| Nanjing, China | 3,624,234 | 32 03 N | 118 48 E | 55 |
| Nantes, Fr. | 277,728 | 47 15 N | 01 30 W | 42 |
| Nantucket (isl.), Mass., U.S. | | 41 16 N | 70 05 W | 85 |
| Napa, Calif., U.S. | 72,585 | 38 18 N | 122 17 W | 82 |
| Naples, Italy | 1,000,470 | 40 51 N | 14 15 E | 42 |
| Nāshik, India | 1,076,967 | 19 59 N | 73 48 E | 53 |
| Nashville,* Tenn., U.S. | 569,891 | 36 10 N | 86 47 W | 87 |
| Nashua, N.H., U.S. | 86,605 | 42 45 N | 71 28 W | 85 |
| Nassau,* Bahamas | 212,432 | 25 05 N | 77 21 W | 89 |
| Nasser (lake), Egypt | | 24 00 N | 32 50 E | 69 |
| Naucalpan, Mex. | 853,053 | 19 28 N | 99 14 W | 88 |
| **Nauru** | **13,287** | **00 32 S** | **166 56 E** | **62** |
| N'Djamena,* Chad | 529,555 | 12 07 N | 15 04 E | 68 |
| Nebraska (state), U.S. | 1,711,263 | 41 30 N | 100 00 W | 83 |
| Negrais (cape), Myanmar | | 16 02 N | 94 12 E | 56 |
| Negro (river), Arg. | | 41 02 S | 62 47 W | 96 |
| Negro (river), Brazil | | 03 10 S | 59 55 W | 94 |
| Negros (isl.), Phil. | | 10 00 N | 123 00 E | 57 |
| Nelson (river), Man., Can. | | 57 00 N | 92 38 W | 76 |
| **Nepal** | **28,287,147** | **28 00 N** | **84 00 E** | **53** |
| **Netherlands** | **16,491,461** | **52 00 N** | **05 30 E** | **42** |
| Netherlands Antilles | 219,958 | 12 10 N | 69 00 W | 89 |
| Nevada (state), U.S. | 1,000,667 | 39 00 N | 117 00 W | 82 |
| Nevis (isl.), St. Kitts and Nevis | 11,181 | 17 10 N | 62 38 W | 89 |
| Newark, N.J., U.S. | 273,546 | 40 44 N | 74 10 W | 84 |
| New Bedford, Mass., U.S. | 93,768 | 41 38 N | 70 56 W | 85 |
| New Britain (isl.), P.N.G. | 404,641 | 05 55 S | 150 20 E | 62 |
| New Britain, Conn., U.S. | 71,538 | 41 40 N | 72 47 W | 85 |
| New Brunswick (prov.), Can. | 729,500 | 46 30 N | 66 45 W | 85 |

# Index of the World

# Index of the World